LE BOOGIE WOOGIE

THE COSMOPOLITAN LIFE

THE COSMOPOLITAN LIFE

Teenage Suicide Notes: An Ethnography of Self-Harm, Terry Williams

LE BOOGIE WOOGIE

INSIDE AN AFTER-HOURS CLUB

TERRY WILLIAMS

Columbia University Press *New York*

Columbia University Press
Publishers Since 1893
New York Chichester, West Sussex
cup.columbia.edu

Library of Congress Cataloging-in-Publication Data
Names: Williams, Terry M. (Terry Moses), 1948– author.
Title: Le Boogie Woogie : inside an after-hours club / Terry Williams.
Other titles: Boogie Woogie
Description: New York : Columbia University Press, [2020] | Series: The cosmopolitan life | Includes bibliographical references and index.
Identifiers: LCCN 2019023885 (print) | LCCN 2019023886 (ebook) | ISBN 9780231177887 (cloth) | ISBN 9780231177894 (paperback) | ISBN 9780231549387 (ebook)
Subjects: LCSH: Le Boogie Woogie (Nightclub)—History. | Nightlife—New York (State)—New York—History—20th century. | Harlem (New York, N.Y.)—Social life and customs—20th century. | New York (N.Y.)—Social life and customs—20th century. | African Americans—New York (State)—New York—Social life and customs—20th century. | Cocaine abuse—New York (State)—New York—History—20th century.
Classification: LCC TX950.57.N7 W55 2020 (print) | LCC TX950.57.N7 (ebook) | DDC 647.95747/1—dc23
LC record available at https://lccn.loc.gov/2019023885
LC ebook record available at https://lccn.loc.gov/2019023886

Columbia University Press books are printed on permanent and durable acid-free paper.
Printed in the United States of America

Cover design: Julia Kushnirsky
Cover photograph: Bryan Steenhuis / EyeEm / Getty Images

Dedicated to Elijah Anderson

CONTENTS

PREFACE

Several decades ago, after completing a year of graduate study in sociology at the City University of New York, I accepted a teaching position at John Jay College. One of my first teaching assignments was in a satellite program established by the college, commuting from the main campus to the Rikers Island correctional facility. After a year in this special program, I had become friendly with inmates serving relatively light sentences. Upon their release, three contacted me and offered to take me out on the town, introducing me to small, intimate clubs known as after-hours spots. In these haunts, I met a bewildering variety of people, all of whom were there to share in a lifestyle based around the enjoyment of cocaine. I mentioned this experience to a professor at the university, who encouraged me to "nose around," see what I could find out, and perhaps do a study of cocaine use in after-hours clubs. No study had been done on cocaine users in their natural setting or to describe users as they lived. I decided that such a study would pose several questions:

(1) How do people represent to themselves and to others their reasons for using cocaine in after-hours clubs?

(2) What relationship does the dealer have to the club?
(3) What role does the after-hours club play in the dealer's life?

Before working at Rikers, I had heard mention of after-hours clubs in my early student days because a relative managed one. Though I was told never to go to "those kinds of places" by my older sisters, I was curious, and I wanted to write about that world. They told me it was not a good idea, but my job as a researcher is to see if I can gain the trust and acceptance of people other than my kinfolk. I used my connections to find several places to visit. Once there, people had no idea I was doing a study. I kept notes on overheard conversations and bar talk—and since people on cocaine like to talk, it was easy to eavesdrop on conversations or engage with patrons.

The transient population of after-hours patrons is not at all like the population of regulars at a bar who show up for a drink after work every day. Those considered regulars who saw me there on multiple occasions eventually assumed I was an employee of the owner. The fact that I never snorted was not questioned. I was viewed like the doorman or the bouncer or the manager, who were also not seen using the drug. I did casual, unstructured interviews, for instance, with several barmaids and house "girls," as they were called, who worked at the bar serving drinks. They became prize contacts. I have always felt comfortable talking to women in my fieldwork; they are often engaging, easy to talk to, and open. But generally, people like to tell me about themselves. I'm told I have a "mealy face," which is a face people feel comfortable talking with.

Some barmaids were not the best at their jobs, though that didn't matter to me. This was all grist for my ethnographic mill. Hang-ups, problems on the floor, slip-ups, embarrassing moments—all these situations congeal around conversations, and conversations are the heart and soul of my practice. I spent most of my time speaking to and gathering information from the regulars. I quickly came to appreciate the problems I had in trying to reconstruct the language, indirect talk, and nuances of the events I witnessed, which made my account not as strong as it could be. But this is just one of the unavoidable difficulties of the job: "ethnographic research has always been about collecting transient data—practices, beliefs, artifacts, languages as they are embodied and expressed in everyday life—with, somewhat, the idea to record and preserve them."[1] Only on a few occasions did I use a tape recorder or openly take notes. I relied on memory for the most part, even though I was concerned that reconstructing conversations was problematic and porous and would affect my narrative. But I developed strategies for jotting down words and jokes. I'd frequently run to the bathroom to record some juicy phrase or ribald punch line. I made so many trips one night a fellow said to me, "You don't have to go back there to sniff, man; it's OK to do it here."

I got the sense that many people experimented with cocaine at the after-hours clubs specifically because of the allure generated by micro- and mass-media stories, musical lyrics spiced with drug themes, and other accounts of drug users' social lives. People also were intrigued by the gossip and rumors surrounding such places, which stirred up curiosity about this particular slice of edge-urban mythology. Interest is generated, newcomers buy paraphernalia, and more members are recruited into a drug-centric social world. I heard several patrons talk about how they liked to be in the city because the city's density and anonymity helped them hide from prying eyes, and being able to remain at least in part a stranger is a prerequisite for people who seek to live alternative lifestyles. The after-hours club is an urban social institution offering a sense of security in the pursuit of an illegal lifestyle.

After a year of tagging along with my Rikers friends, I mentioned to a few patrons at the club I here call Le Boogie Woogie that I was writing about the club, and they began to tell me stories. This strategy is what is called the "tag along, go along" approach, and I used it here as part of my ethnographic toolkit.[2] The only formal interviews I did were with people who requested them. A few occurred after two years of being out in the field. One of my first key informants was Conchita, a young woman who definitely knew her way around town. She worked part-time at various bars and was the kind of person every ethnographer is grateful to know. She took me around her circle of crew members and shared with me a journal of her exploits, excerpts of which I include in this text.

Another key informant was Frenchy. I recall his striking and intimidating physical and verbal presence. He stood over six feet tall, weighed about 240 pounds, and was both articulate and a no-nonsense type of tough guy. He was a sharp dresser in the club but not flashy; he always wore a pair of overalls, which provided him with the many pockets he needed to carry his product and cash. This was especially true when he dealt drugs in the street. At the club he had a favorite piece of jewelry: a scorpion-shaped, diamond-studded pinky ring. He had several gold watches, and though getting information about his life was like pulling teeth, he eventually, reluctantly, began to tell me about the thug's life he'd led, which would prove invaluable to this study.

His information came in dribs and drabs. I thought if I could get him into a more formal meeting he might divulge more, but he always backed out at the last minute. He would on occasion tolerate my questions and probes. I was patient and got as close as I could, but it was slow going. Not everyone wants to tell their secrets, but I was lucky. Not only did he eventually tell me about "the life," but he also talked about the police, women, politicians, and society in general with such thoroughness and thoughtfulness that I would later think of him and people like him as constituting a kind of intelligentsia of the underworld. This was a thug's world of artists, poets, doyennes, and philosophers whose truths were only heard on street corners or within their own self-styled hoodsville coteries. Luckily for me, Le Boogie Woogie was one of those special places. It was only later that I found out that Frenchy co-owned the place. He gave me the go-ahead to observe and record what was essentially the nightly business of the Le Boogie Woogie operation.

At the time—the late 1980s and 1990s—social clubs were plentiful, and every neighborhood had them. After-hours clubs were impossible to ignore and naturally the place for me to continue the sociological work on drug-dealing operations I analyzed in my books *Cocaine Kids* (1989) and *Crackhouse* (1992). This was ethnographer's luck. My earlier experiences made it possible for me to sit around in these kinds of places and observe, ask questions, and gather information. I could visit whenever I wanted, and that was fine as long as it lasted—which wasn't long. After about four months, Frenchy became unreliable, to say the least. His so-called ownership was suspect. He'd been a front man until he got arrested three times in as many years. The time I spent with him was fraught with disappointment. He missed many appointments and canceled as many others. He blew off an uncountable number of our meeting dates.

I tried to go to other places without a connection, but because clubs change hands, hire new workers, and frequently replace doormen, if you were not a regular customer, you would be denied entry. I ended up trying to start all over again, making contacts and attempting to get into places the best I could. Sometimes the tricks I used worked, but most of the time they didn't. Other problems cropped up, and ethical issues still hound me, even though this fieldwork was completed decades ago. I had no delusions about the danger involved in researching drug users. I was then, as I am now, concerned about possible legal consequences for me or my informants that might arise as a result of this work. If there is one consolation, however, it is that people have been going to after-hours clubs and doing what they do in them since the days of Storyville in New Orleans, and I knew my study would not affect their continued existence at all.

LE BOOGIE WOOGIE

INTRODUCTION

Sniffing cocaine is the *thing to do in the club life. Everyone has a small silver or gold spoon disguised as a pendant around their necks, one long pinky fingernail, and a small origami-like paper or foil packet filled with the powdery substance. Baggies can even be seen littering the edges of tables. This is a cocaine world of padded shoulders, balloon pants, spiked hair, higher heels—and runny noses. No one goes to the bathroom to sneak a sniff these days. No need to. Although the drug is illegal, it is considered legal currency in clubs and bars all over the city. This loft space is large with a mélange of types, from hippie-looking white boys to grunge-girl Latina types. Cocaine flows like water, and money on the floor is not picked up but kicked around like trash. The action is frenetic; loud music and vociferous talk animate the scene as much as "dirty dancing," kissing, touching—all part of what the drug provokes. This is a cocaine world of free spirits and abounding joy. The night seems to have no end.*

—Soho, New York City, 1982

This book is primarily a journey inside an after-hours cocaine club. These clubs were often profit-making businesses that were moderately commodious and reasonably safe for illegal drug taking and liminal erotics. I had connections to many after hours clubs over the years, but by the end of the 1990s I had lost contact with them all. It was not until 2016, while preparing this book for publication, that I found myself inside one of these clubs again. I wanted to know if they still functioned as an institution that established a sense of structure and stability for social cocaine users in a natural setting.

The after-hours club called Le Boogie Woogie, the main setting of this book, and Murphy's Bar, the club I visited twenty years later, are two special locales I discovered in the after-hours cocaine scene. After-hours clubs occupy a marginal place with regard to their physical locale, hours of operation, and extralegal status. Access is limited and exclusive, the social structure is complex, social controls are informal but ritualized, and the setting is amenable to a wide range of drug use. Eroticization and other kinds of sex play are overt and visible. Though this book draws on fieldwork and notes taken in the past at Le Boogie Woogie, when reentering the similar space of Murphy's Bar more recently, I was reminded that every social world employs its own argot, which serves as a means of understanding its operational nature. This is the case among subcultures as diverse as jazz musicians, skateboarders, hip-hoppers, teen rockers, and the criminal underworld. It is a verbal rationalization of the acts undertaken in that social sphere.

Profanity, for instance, of a sexual nature was as commonplace with the hipsters, beatniks, and hippies of yesterday as it is for the cocaine-clubbing set today. Slang developed because new situations had arisen, and people needed names for them. They had to "man up" or "size things up" or "get down."[1] Snorters have a vocabulary of hundreds of verbs, adjectives, and nouns to punctuate their experiences. There are few neutral words in the argot; it is spirited and direct. Either you "my nig-gah" or are not; you are expected to "get widdit" or "dig that," "check it out," "get hip," "cool out," or "kill me." The language gives extremely frank descriptions. A "cat" who had problems hearing was called "Deaf"; an excessive talker, "Motor Mouth"; and a woman with a penchant for wigs, "Wiggy." A patron having a good time was "getting their jollies off."

The patron's argot placed everything into the floating plane of a new-age, space-age, information-age, hallucinogenic, mind-expanding space that butted up against the geometrically "solid," "square," or "octagon-headed." Those regulars that were "high" on cocaine are getting "lit" or are "way out there," "gone," "spaced," "wigged out," "tripped out," "far out," "zooted," or "decked out." The earthbound regular is into the "real deal," "the struggle," "surviving," or "tightening up." One regular, speaking to another, put it succinctly when she was asked, "How you doing, baby?" "I ain't doing," was the reply, with a sly, wry frown on her face. When the regular leaves the club she "books," "splits," "spaces," or "hits the bricks." "Motherfucker," "blow," "coca cola," "get yo' shit together," "the joint," and "player" are only a fraction of the words frequently heard on the lips of these nocturnal "night trippers."

The wee hours of the morning are a feast for the senses, "something to get down behind." To "get down" is pleasurable, and the past is in the past and of no consequence. The patrons in their search for hedonistic delights used sexual innuendo as a crucial part of their vernacular. Unsurprisingly, nouns for genitalia or other sexually related matters were a constant and included such colorful terms as boy pussy, cat, cunt, jaws, prick, dick, peter, gimme some, meat rack, tea room, rough trade, TV, transie, baby pro, chicken, box, fuck, screw, jam, go down, head, AC/DC, blow, booty bandit, cream, head hunter, stuff, joint, wiener, jelly roll, and thang. This language was comical, satirical, and truthful. An unknown in the spot were "thots" or "those hoe over there." To be "crazy" was an exclamation of approval. To "grease" was to eat food. The use of this special nocturnal language was not just ghetto thuggishness developed into snobbishness but a parody of daytime culture. In the company of a "lame," the regular knew he was scoring a point on the outsider because suddenly the "lame" was caught in a social web of night creatures speaking a strange tongue. The daytime outsider was now the nighttime insider. To be "down" in the after-hours club was not always possible for the "lame" because the "lame" was inevitably "un-down" and not "on the up and up." Times changed, and after-hours clubs came and went. But what remains is that people on the margins of society will find others like them so they can have a place where they feel they belong.

In this after-hours world, cocaine was an essential element in the quest to stay "cool." The after-hours world also regulated its use. Even though my research is descriptive and might best be described as a microethnography based on personal observation, I make analytical sense of this social world as it existed within the ecological and cultural networks of the city. This narrative is a theory of how a particular human group makes sense of their world. I continually ask, "What does it all mean?" By providing descriptions of what's going on in the club, I seek to uncover the importance and meaning of relations and how those relations are framed and maintained by unwritten rules of established order within the club. Le Boogie Woogie is an example of what it means to be part of a subculture—a subculture that no longer exists as it once did. In Le Boogie Woogie, the cocaine club's primary group bond was the intimacy among patrons. It was a sharing, touching, nose-to-nose relationship where everyone was breaking the law together.

I summon in this narrative a retrospective approach and a cursory but important history about cocaine use within the Black and Latino communities and, by proxy, the white community. Back in the 1990s, for example, when the sociologist Mitch Duneier was doing the research that would become his book *Sidewalk*, it was clear that at least a significant part of that work would become historical—that is, the phenomena he was describing were changing or disappearing. It was thus critically important for his study to *describe* the physical setting as best as possible. In *Sidewalk*, the setting (stage) was the place along Sixth Avenue where a complex social history of the selling of written matter (magazines, books) intersected with other broad issues, including homelessness, informal social work, intellectual life, panhandling, interracial and interclass interactions, and so forth. The attention to detail in Duneier's *Sidewalk* project is important because the setting on Sixth Avenue has now changed. The stores and people he witnessed firsthand during the 1990s are now gone. Here I look back on the after-hours club scene to see how people of that community adapted to enduring social problems in one particular historical moment, in order to understand cultural adaptations, contradictions, and contemporary issues.

I seek to discover cultural patterns that may prove useful in shaping a more fair, equal, and humane social world in the city today and in the future. Howard Becker writes: "The degree to which other people will respond to a given act as deviant varies greatly."[2] Several kinds of variation seem worth noting. First and foremost is variation over time. A person believed to have committed a given "deviant" act may at one point in time be treated more leniently than at some other time. At various times enforcement officials may decide to make an all-out attack on a behavior they see as deviant, such as gambling, drug addiction, or homosexuality. It is obvious that it is much more dangerous to engage in one of these activities when such a drive is on than at other times. My work articulates the humanity of a community by acknowledging that drug use is an aspect of cosmopolitan life in general and a part of life in the Black community specifically. There is a history to cocaine use that has profoundly shaped the Black community via the criminal-justice system.

The idea of drug enforcement being a "smokescreen" for racial injustice is a truism, and, in fact, it becomes evident that prosecuting drug use in our society is a form of racism that has reshaped communities—especially poor communities of color—and has deeply influenced ethnography in ways that the discipline has yet to acknowledge. Various chemicals were outlawed not only because of their pharmacology but because of their connotations with certain minority groups and social classes that the larger society perceived as dangerous, maladjusted, and threatening. Since Americans are never going to live in a "drug-free" society, it is crucial to understand how a chemo-centric society works and how it shapes our social interactions and communities. What kind of social choice is made when people decide to use cocaine? What choices do people make when they join the subculture of cocaine users?

The overlap of many social worlds makes clear the challenge of ethnographic representation in urban sociology. It forces me to think about the complexity of the city generally, urban social life more specifically, and, by extension, neighborhoods and communities as layers of human expression and existence. In this way we can think about how the city is not just about good or bad, rich or poor, Black or Latino or white, but is a mélange of people and their experiences. For example, the ethnographic depiction of African Americans, often in poor communities, is often as ex-convicts, drug addicts, gang members, or welfare mothers with children from assorted fathers. Such depictions are elevated to a kind of ethnographic genre. It is a social red-light district in the sense that much can take place within poor and low-income Black and Latino areas so long as they do not contaminate other, more privileged areas; that is to say, communities of color are seen as zones where vice of all kinds can take place with little or no policing. As long as the drugs, prostitution, crime, and other social maladies do not overflow these geographic boundaries, they can continue.

Marcella, a loquacious, outspoken, rather brilliant public character in Harlem, drew my attention to drug use in ignored, minority neighborhoods. "When we had dope fiends all over this neighborhood, nobody gave a damn until white folks started getting addicted, and then all of sudden there is a 'dope crisis.' Where was this 'crisis'"—she uses both hands to indicate quotation marks—"when all them black folks were dying from overdoses? I wonder."

Bars and taverns are ubiquitous in the city and are good places to study human behavior, but they are over-researched. The after-hours cocaine club, by contrast, has been largely ignored by social scientists, for a number of reasons: (1) They are not open to the general public. (2) They have only existed for a relatively short period of time, compared to bars and regular nightclubs. (3) They were and are patently illegal and difficult to access. Although cocaine use has changed from sniffing (intranasal) and shooting (intravenous) to smoking (inhalation), it has been part of U.S. drug-taking culture for over a hundred years, and the bar, the saloon, or nightclub associated with cocaine also has a long history.

Illegal substances and illegal spaces are made for each other. After-hours clubs are semisecret, drug-using institutions where cocaine, marijuana, alcohol, and sex are exchanged, bought, sold, bartered, and used after regular bars have closed. They exist almost anywhere there are sex workers, musicians, bartenders, and other off-hour workers whose occupations involve the late-night hours and who want a leisure place of their own after official closing times. One thing I explore in this book is how the after-hours club functions in its neighborhood as an institution and how that institution establishes various social controls over cocaine users and nonusers in a natural setting.

Cassandra sat on the sofa, twitched her fingers, and folded her legs underneath her. When standing, she's tall and has a slim body. Her eyes twinkle, and she wets her lips when the word coke or cocaine is uttered. "Cocaine was my drug," she says in a low tone. "Although I come from a family of addicts, since my mother was an alcoholic, and my father too. But I went to college, and my sister is an accomplished bureaucrat. So you might say I have a family history of good people and bad addicted people." She never drank. "I never liked anything that reminded me of my mother or my father. I'd rather take my coke and that's it." I could argue the cocaine she's using is nothing more than a substitute for the alcohol her parents were taking, but it is not my business to psychoanalyze. Cassandra was stigmatized for her drug of choice because it is illegal.

The ethnographic method is interpretive. Mario Small states this point succinctly:

> The view that such ethnographers are merely "reporting the facts" require one (a) to believe that a single trait, violence, can capture either the essence of a neighborhood or the character of a population and (b) to presume that writing does not involve choice. Even in the nation's most violent neighborhood, many residents do not sell drugs or rob people. And even a full-time drug dealer thinks about other things—faith, politics, loneliness, film, etc.

> Focusing on violence is only unavoidable if one's view of a place or its people is itself narrow. All writing is a choice.[3]

While Small only mentions violence in his example, his point is well taken with respect to other behaviors in the community, including religion, politics, and other aspects of middle-class life. I make the case for an ethnography that my colleague Sarah Daynes calls "of the middle." She argues for

> a multiplicity of ethnographic styles, in between the two extreme poles of self-absorption on one hand and the negation of subjectivity on the other hand. . . . If this middle position seems tedious, so be it. It reflects reality, but it is also a meaningful cause for us precisely because of its lack of sensationalism. And perhaps this very lack of sensationalism makes it somewhat scandalous! Either way, we promote an ethnography without excuses as much as without orthodoxy. Ethnographic research is characterized by its uniqueness in time and space; it happens in a moment. It cannot be repeated, and no data ever collected through participant observation could exist, or be collected, again. In fact, ethnographic research has always been about collecting transient data—practices, beliefs, artifacts, languages as they are embodied and expressed in everyday life—with, somewhat, the idea to record and preserve them.[4]

This point was important to the anthropologists working at the turn of the century, particularly those working with human (and nonhuman) populations whose lifeways were challenged or even threatened with extinction. Eduardo Kohn, in his book *How Forests Think*, called on ethnographers to

> develop a method for crafting new conceptual tools out of the unexpected properties of the world beyond the human that we

> discover ethnographically. And in so doing [this method] seeks to liberate us from our own mental enclosures. As we learn to attend ethnographically to that which lies beyond the human, certain strange phenomena suddenly come to the fore, and these strange phenomena amplify, and in the process come to exemplify, some of the general properties of the world in which we live.[5]

We could make the same argument about most ethnographic work today, in both rural and urban settings. In the 1980s I already saw that the drug culture I was witnessing in my neighborhood was quickly changing, and this realization spurred my fieldwork with drug dealers and users. As I write this narrative, looking at the various notebooks and journal entries I've accumulated over the past few decades, I realize that much of what I was recording in those notes was about communities that are rapidly disappearing. The Harlem Worlds, the 125th Street vendors, jazz clubs and bars like the Lenox Lounge, the Shalimar, and the Cozy Bar, which are the field for many of my notes, have become radically different—if they are not gone altogether. They are now commodified and hypergentrified, safe and squeaky-clean versions of what I knew as a neighborhood resident for decades. There is only a smidgen of the past there today.

One of the people who lived through the period and remembers Harlem World is Tania, a fifty-year-old Harlem resident:

> Well, I worked at Harlem World and knew a bookkeeper, and I basically lived there. It was all-out drugs back then and more drugs, and people knew it was the spot to be at. Harlem was rocking then since crack had not come into its own yet, but cocaine, the sniffing variety was all over the place. You also had places in the city like Studio 54, the Electric Circus, downtown where the

> rich snorted coke just like it was water up front; and places like Disco Fever, uptown, on 35th [135th]; and the Cozy Bar, though it wasn't an after-hours spot on a regular, it was a gambling spot and would open up around nine o'clock and all these places were where there was hustlers, hustling, dealing of one kind or another. People sniffed coke in all these places. But you know, honey, that was Harlem World, both the place and the spot was right smack dab in the middle of the action.

Though discussing a very different place and time, Tania's account of Harlem World is reminiscent of what Phil Brown did in his book *Catskill Culture*, an exciting exploration of a local history that involves ethnography, personal memory, and family mementoes, which he used as a guide to his engaging descriptive, nostalgic, reflective storytelling approach.[6] "This art of documenting should not be constrained and weighted down by moralizing stances and orthodoxies of any kind, scholarly or not. We have purposely used many notes and case studies in this book that describe practices, beliefs, and worlds some might find objectionable. But human life is not sanitized, so why should ethnographic accounts be?"[7]

The after-hours club and cocaine use were not fads in the eighties and nineties in Harlem, like they may have been downtown. They had been around a long time and changed little over the years. The illegal black market, sex work, hustlers, gangsters, and thugs persisted. The after-hours club was an enduring phenomenon that began with the jazz life. Cocaine was always the primary reason people went to them. Commercialized vice in the city has a long history in African American communities as a result of residential segregation. As Blacks moved into previous immigrant neighborhoods, they inherited gambling joints, sex strolls, houses of prostitution, and various vice resorts, after-hours clubs among them. Music plays a role in these happenings, with songs like "Come Back Pussy," "Let Me Funk with You," and "Nasty Blues Singers" and the rhythm and blues of Stax Records and the Motown sound. Add to that the sexual freedom permitted in such places, and the after-hours club offers an intriguing array of entertainment options.

Music and raunchy behavior have been part of Black culture for a long time. Drugs simply pushed those elements closer to the edge. As Ralph Ellison once reminded us, Black folk have had rhythmic freedom in place of social liberty, linguistic freedom in place of monetary wealth.[8] This linguistic richness is not just a meeting of the minds. In the club, bodies meet while dancing, and dancing becomes more sexual after a sniff of cocaine, which also converts an evening out into an all-night affair. But what ultimately is at stake in seeking these personal pleasures?

The nightclub's predecessors (speakeasies, for example) and drugs such as cocaine, heroin, and marijuana all were answers to people's need for new and bold behavior. The issue of commercialized vice in all its manifestations within lower socioeconomic Black enclaves raises much deeper questions about how these communities operate as social red-light districts. Visible retail drug dealing (at the street level) and other forms of vice take place in Black communities more than in white communities, where they are less conspicuous and where there are far more stringent controls put in place by the police. This means people across all social strata can be found in Black communities seeking drugs, sex, and vice. That whites come to these areas to participate in vice is well known. It could even be argued that run-down slum sections of Black neighborhoods make it easy—or even possible—for white vice to prosper.

Here I portray the after-hours club as a result of a history of spaces and places where people go to indulge in behavior they found pleasurable but forbidden. That desire is and has been and will be unstoppable. People will always find ways to do the things that give them pleasure. It might be in the dingiest, most dangerous, most ridiculous, most horrific location in the world, but people will find a way to get there and do what they do, no matter what. The after-hours club is one of those types of places—dark, smoky, dingy, funky, and raunchy, spawned like the speakeasies of the 1920s—an underground phenomenon that saw vice pushed into poor immigrant and later poor minority ghetto communities, where it thrived when slumming was in vogue.

1

THE SETTING

I cannot say I have forgotten the city, but I let the memory of it sleep. Of course, it was always there, as it always will be, hanging in the mind like the mirage which travelers so often see.

— Lawrence Durrell, *Balthazar*

THE AFTER-HOURS CLUB: A HISTORICAL VIEW

The after-hours clubs' predecessors included the saloon, beer garden, shebeen, speakeasy, bar, nightclub, and lounge, and each era brought a new intoxicant to be devoured on their premises. One year it's beer, another year it's tincture of laudanum (an opium derivative), at other times heroin, whiskey, or cocaine. Illegal substances are nothing more than a historical accident. At one point certain drugs are legal, and in another period they are not. The purpose of the after-hours clubs is to extend nightlife's possibilities by offering various forms of recreational drug use, sexual adventure, and gambling, all in a somewhat safe social setting. Society is often given the impression that drug users and others who participate in the drug business are only there to get high. In fact, the clubs play a much larger role of facilitating a way of "talking back," a way of controlling the rage and anger many in this country feel.

In her brilliant account *Spectacular Wickedness: Sex, Race, and Memory in Storyville, New Orleans*, Emily Epstein Landau points out the roles that sex, race, and memory play in that city. Musicians, prostitutes, pimps, madams, and drug takers have all been part of the scene over the generations and across the city. She writes how the beer gardens, saloons, honky-tonks, and other early jook joints, including the late-night locales found in Storyville, were places that offered a respite for recreational drug use, dance, music, and sexual promiscuity. The sociologist Richard Ocejo's sterling book *Upscaling Downtown: From Bowery Saloons to Cocktail Bars in New York City* (2014) highlights nightlife on the Lower East Side of Manhattan. It complements Landau's study and my own in that it shows how bars and places like Le Boogie Woogie in the 1980s and in Murphy's in the 2010s have evolved.

After-hours clubs and their relationship to a life of music and drugs have historical roots dating back to the late 1880s. Cocaine use in these places are part of a tradition reaching back to New Orleans, where proto–jazz musicians, sailors, prostitutes, businessmen, and assorted others partied all night in a place called Storyville. It was a scene that defied authority and resisted the moral and social order of the day. Ragtime, the predecessor to jazz, started in the 1800s in a New Orleans brothel. The town had a great number of ragtime musicians who found that the brothels and other jook joints were the few places they could play their music and be accepted. These were also some of the few places they could earn a steady income for their artistry because racial discrimination at the time prevented many "colored" musicians from working in the white clubs, taverns, and other establishments where a decent wage was offered.

In 1897, Sidney Story, a New Orleans politician, made history by complying with the wishes of a large portion of the population in creating a legitimate red-light district. Through this legislative action, "Storyville" was born. Ten blocks long, it contained thirty-five brothels and 2,200 prostitutes. The houses included a potpourri of crib joints, gambling parlors, cabarets, cafés, opium dens, honky-tonks, and dance schools. Storyville's main source of entertainment was sex and music. Brothel owners, some of whom paid thousands of dollars to own a house within its boundaries, hired musicians when they came into the city. In exchange for performing, many could live at the brothels, get free liquor and food, and earn a few dollars. The musicians, in turn, had to play for hours on end. They could play any tune they wished, as long as they did not stop. They could also improvise as much as they pleased. They often played "double": during the day they would play six to eight hours, then play in brothels at night until early morning. The musicians would often chew calabash to help keep them going during these long musical stretches; cocaine was then sold in pill boxes by bootblacks on street corners and could be legally purchased. Piano players were the most sought-after musicians for this kind of work because the piano could be played quietly during the early morning hours, although other instruments were also used. It has been said that jazz music and its originators, including Buddy Bolden, Louis Armstrong, King Oliver, Freddie Keppard, and hundreds of other musicians, started in Storyville.

The red-light district became synonymous with ragtime. "Rag" derives from playing "ragged," that is, music in which the beats are syncopated, not played exactly in 4/4 lockstep. Ragtime and, later, jazz became part of a "street" lifestyle, and "street," in those days, meant to be lowlife and was associated with whores, pimps, con men, and other drifters. New Orleans became the haven for these itinerant types, which included steamboat workers, gamblers, hustlers, and a mixture of Italians, French, Germans, Spanish, Indians, and Blacks, all of whom made New Orleans a choice place for diverse ethnicities. Musicians found in the brothel a home for their music. A rapport developed between the musicians, who used the brothel as a place to improvise and create new works, and the audience, who respected the musicians' skill. The brothels employed musicians to enliven and cheer the patrons, and so the marriage was consummated.

For more than a thousand years, the leaves of *Erythroxylon coca* have been eaten, chewed, and smoked by the various Indian peoples of Peru, Bolivia, Chile, Colombia, and other South American countries. Coca has had many functions, including increasing the workrate of laborers and as a consumable in ceremonies and for recreation. The evergreen plant supports the general physical and psychological well-being of its users. When various European adventurers brought the coca plant back to Europe to demonstrate its euphoric and "magical" effects, it proved useless. The plant's properties had diminished during the long voyage back. But successive trips to South American countries by other Europeans (Tschudi, Markham, Poeppig) led to a successful isolation of the active principles in coca.

Albert Neimann, a German scientist, isolated cocaine in 1860, and Europeans became genuinely interested in its medicinal properties. Sigmund Freud was one of the first to describe the effects of the drug on humans. His early writings and assumptions about cocaine as a cure for morphine addiction were condemned by many colleagues. Albrecht Erlenmeyer accused Freud of advocating a dangerous habit-forming drug. It is likely that the use of cocaine by North Americans began after their interest was stirred by Europeans.

A medical doctor writing in the *Detroit Therapeutic Gazette* recommended coca to patients as a cure for opium addiction.

Cocaine is a derivative of coca and therefore not the same. Cocaine is only one of thirteen different alkaloids present in the coca leaf, and to extract cocaine from that leaf several precursor chemicals are required, including benzene, potassium permanganate, and ethyl ketone. Although its use as a treatment for opioid addiction failed, by 1887 commercial products containing coca or cocaine mixtures proliferated. In 1886, John Pembleton, an Atlanta pharmacist, developed a beverage made of kola nut extract and cocaine he called "Coca-Cola." The popularity of Coca-Cola and other such mixtures grew enormously after 1892, when Asa Griggs Candler purchased the patent rights for the cocaine cola drink and sold it in drug stores. In addition to Coca-Cola, sixty-nine other cocaine-cola drinks were being manufactured at that time. Some of the other cola-cocaine beverages were "Koca Nola," "Kola-ade," "Kos-nola," and "Wise-ola." Before 1914, cocaine was legally prescribed by doctors and sold in alcohol, cigarettes, elixirs, medicines, tonics, cordials, and tablets.

As early as 1898, writers and medical doctors began associating cocaine use with Blacks. W. Scheppegrell's article on the "Abuse and Dangers of Cocaine" in 1898 casually mentioned how bootblacks and newsboys were selling cocaine for ten cents a sniff and larger amounts for twenty-five cents, which amounted to a full day's supply of cocaine. The larger amounts were sold in paper pill boxes. Although cocaine was used by most everybody at that time, at the turn of the century racial myths circulated about "cocainized Blacks" who were part of a crime wave that included a high number of rapes of white women. One article mentioned how Blacks who ingested cocaine could not be harmed if shot by small-caliber bullets. As a result, local law-enforcement agencies were equipped with larger-caliber guns. These myths understandably generated a strong reaction against cocaine use and became yet another element of the general race prejudice against Blacks. The patent-medicine industry suffered as a result of the widespread but misleading evidence about cocaine because it was the producer of many of the drug's products—not to mention the promoter of cocaine's wonder-drug status.

The 1914 Harrison Act restricted the distribution of cocaine, and forty-six states initiated some form of legislation restricting its use. After these legal restrictions forced cocaine underground, only those who were privileged could order it legally through their doctors. The Harrison Act was the first federal law to prohibit the dispensation of cocaine and other dangerous substances by persons without a license and/or a demonstrated medical reason. A two-thousand-dollar fine and five-year prison sentence were handed out to those convicted. The Harrison Act was amended in 1919 to make for more stringent control of both opium and cocaine. By 1922, cocaine was classified as a narcotic drug, though it technically is a stimulant. The ban on the importation of cocaine and coca leaves was imposed under an amended, stricter version of the Narcotic Drugs Importation Act, which was also passed in 1914.

These legislative restrictions made cocaine an expensive yet much-desired drug, and in the underground honky-tonks, speakeasies, after-hours joints, and cafés, it became associated and defined as a status "high" mainly because of its illegality and the myths surrounding it. The wealthy upper classes and the low-paid artists, musicians, and experimental poet/writers of the 1920s all found cocaine available, delightful, and a symbol of their lifestyles. The Depression quieted cocaine use somewhat, but in the late 1940s and 1950s the spirit and enthusiasm for cocaine reemerged. Once again, some of the first places cocaine was seen were the speakeasies and after-hours clubs.

The tradition where musicians could freely exchange musical ideas evolved into what became known as the "jam session," or after-hours "cutting session," which in turn became an institution where musicians gathered after work to continue to play after every other club had closed. These sessions, called "spooks' breakfasts," provided opportunities for young musicians to learn from the old masters, and in this way the after-hours club became the institution for a musical apprenticeship in jazz.

A New Orleans cabaret owned by Peter Lala, the owner of the infamous Café Lala, may be one of the first after-hours clubs. In Buerkle and Barker's *Bourbon Street Black*, the setting is described: It was principally at Lala's that musicians gathered after work to socialize and discuss musical ideas. It was here that jazz came alive, branching off from its immediate predecessors and becoming a distinct musical form and identity. It need not have received that final catalytic boost in these after-hours surroundings. But it did. But while Storyville nurtured jazz and its players, it also contributed to an image that was to brand the music and the men performing it as deviant.[1]

Later, during the 1920s and 1930s in New York, Baltimore, Kansas City, Chicago, and other cities, speakeasies and after-hours clubs flourished. Musicians of every distinction and category frequented these dives, often competing to outplay one another in sessions that lasted into the morning. Albert Murray's *Stomping the Blues* describes how the emergence of Saturday-night functions, honky-tonks, and jook joints became one of the secular alternatives to church and gospel music, which in turn had been seen as counteragents to or exorcists of the music called "the blues." The New Orleans after-hours clubs were legitimate, but by the 1930s unlicensed after-hours clubs, which generally opened at 4 a.m., were increasingly viewed by the law as illegal.

Some of these clubs stayed open even after 1933, when Prohibition was repealed and the sale of alcoholic beverages became legal again. If it was chartered after January 1, 1926, cabaret licensing was required for any social club selling food or drink and/or providing dancing or other entertainment. Another history places the origin of the after-hours clubs in San Francisco, in the Barbary Coast Hall, or '49 Hall, the taxi-dance hall with the ten-cents-a-lesson dance-ticket system and music and musicians who would play at "spooks' breakfasts."

After-hours clubs proliferated before World War I, dropped off after World War II, reemerged during the 1960s, and continued well into the 1980s. Le Boogie Woogie turned the patron into the performer: cutting and taking cocaine became an ostentatious performance of the thuggish lifestyle. Outcasts, Beckerian "outsiders," and fugitive contrarian refuseniks had finally found a home they could escape to.

Both Le Boogie Woogie and the cocaine available there offer the patron a carefree zone that has the same function as does a trance in the Peruvian highlands. As I watched and listened, it was clear many of those patrons still had hopes of taking part in—in rejoining—the world outside, but they needed time and space to reflect on this decision. They needed to think about how they could functionally and socially fit into a world that only wanted conformity and standardization, because they conceived of themselves as lively individualists, spontaneously alive with more than one possibility.

LE BOOGIE WOOGIE: THE SETTING

The place reeked of scent and harlotry. Le Boogie Woogie was not open to the general public. It had been established for transgressive purposes, including gambling, private sex parties, drug selling, policy-number operations, topless dancing, and as a meeting place for people who wanted to be out without being seen. When and if the average "joe" showed up at the club, he was turned away unless someone inside vouched for him. In this chapter, I frame the various kinds of activities at Le Boogie Woogie, but, more specifically, I outline the reasons for cocaine use at the club, how it is used, and the various techniques of that use. The club furnished the social atmosphere in which cocaine was used, sold, and sniffed, and it had been designed with various accouterments in mind—drinking, dancing, gambling, smoking—for the pleasure of its members, guests, close friends, strangers, and acquaintances. I always felt the interactions in the club to be more formal than a regular bar's and more reminiscent of a large private party. Formality meant that dress and the manner of interaction was more tailored than in a regular bar, and clothing was more of a status symbol.

Cocaine is generally sniffed through the nose, smoked in cigarettes called bazucos, or mixed with heroin to form a "speedball," which is taken intravenously. This was not done in the club, at least not where people could see.[2] Smoking powdered cocaine occurred in the open and was accomplished by sprinkling a small amount of the drug in a "joint" of marijuana, by sprinkling it into the cigarette filter, or by simply rolling cocaine into the tobacco and smoking it. This form of use was rare. Some people ate the drug, called "taking a freeze," in which the user applies cocaine to the back of the hand or spoon, so it can be licked off by the tongue or rubbed into the gums. Or a small dose was simply thrown into the back of the throat. The result is a freezing or numbing effect inside the mouth, lips, and gums. A "freeze" is not taken to achieve an instant "high" but rather to get the sensation of a "drop," which is a feeling in the back of the throat. Users will often say one sure sign of good cocaine is this "drop" effect or feeling.[3] Cocaine users take a "freeze" sometimes to rest their noses.

When snorted, the cocaine residue rests on the mucous lining of the nose and is quickly absorbed into the bloodstream. Dopamine levels in the brain rise, and the reward system of the brain is engaged. The more one takes of the drug over time, the more is needed to reach the same high. Neurotransmitters in the amygdala and striatum are activated during the rush, making the user feel good, but snorting too much cocaine can cause runny or bloody noses, nasal congestion, excessive sneezing, sores in the nose, and other problems. The most serious damage to the nose is the perforation of the septum and ulceration of the nasal cavity, all of which people risk to get high and stay high on the scene.

Cocaine was the preferred stimulant by most drug takers in Le Boogie Woogie, and only those few patrons experiencing negative effects rejected it. The drug gives users a feeling of well-being, happiness, euphoria, and relief from anxiety. These reactions are often accompanied by garrulousness, thirst, and a desire for social and physical contact, such as dancing and sex. Cocaine is a social drug, and patrons frequently find themselves engaged without inhibition. The drug is not believed to be "dangerous" by most casual users, mainly because they may have only experienced small amounts. At Le Boogie Woogie, patrons talked about the downside of cocaine use and its undesirable effects. They were aware that too much was not good. They also knew that it could kill, depending on a few factors. One is dosage, how much of the drug is ingested; two, purity level, how strong the drug is; and three, the route of administration, whether it's snorted, which most users in the club preferred, injected, or smoked. The effects of the drug differ according to the situations under which it is taken, and this means that the "scene," "place," or "set," that is, the physical surroundings in which cocaine is used, makes a great deal of difference to the overall experience.

I was sitting with two friends. Several people were passing cocaine around in a semicircle. One man talking with the others continued to refuse the cocaine offered. After the third time refusing, after about a half-hour of time had elapsed, he finally offered an explanation: "I'm trying to cool my head out," at which point the others accepted his explanation and continued to sniff. This is another way of saying that the sniffer has had enough cocaine, and no other words need be spoken. Often a simple wave of the hand or shake of the head will do as well. There are several reasons why a person may refuse cocaine in a group setting:

1. The sniffer may refuse because of nasal problems.
2. The person has taken cocaine to the point where abuse may be detrimental to health. Occasionally, patrons, having sniffed cocaine for several days, will refuse any more of the drug, to let their heads clear out.
3. The cocaine sniffer may simply be tired of cocaine and refuse it on what they call "GP," or general principle.
4. The person offering has a reputation for having poor-quality cocaine.

The opposite of "cooling one's head out" was "going on a binge." The binge was a state of heightened awareness, tenseness, depression, anxiety, and euphoria, all different phases of the cocaine high. The first phase begins with a few sniffs of the drug and then proceeds toward heavier use. The first and last stages are significant in that they are almost opposites. During the first phase of sniffing, a user usually reaches a calm sense of well-being, albeit with elements of euphoria, gregariousness, heightened movement, and sharpness of intellect. At the end stage, the user reaches a period of introspection and depression as the high ends. A form of dysphoria, reflection on past problems, and sexual aggressiveness is often mixed with wistfulness and sex-related daydreams.

GETTING IN

A small Pentecostal church sat adjacent to Le Boogie Woogie in a run-down section of upper Manhattan. Two candy stores and several burned-out tenements, two of which were in the process of renovation, filled the rest of the block. Few people are seen walking in this area of the city, where garbage-filled alleyways follow the sidewalk to the Eighth Avenue subway. For regulars, the venue was simply called "the spot," and it generally opened at 4 a.m. The outer part of the club had a green, red, and blue canopy protecting entering patrons from inclement weather, but there was no marquee to suggest the kind of place it was. The words "Le Boogie Woogie" hung on a sign beside the door.

When I rang the bell, a young Black male in a hat and gray turtleneck answered, peered through a peephole in the door, and escorted me to a small foyer. A fat neon light blinked above the door, indicating action behind it; beyond this point was another steel door, and after the second door closed, I was led into a narrow passageway. This area served as a middle space between the entrance and the club proper, where patrons were searched by an armed, unfriendly, unsmiling, muscular bouncer, patting down men and checking women's purses.

When the door closed, a boundary was created between the inside and outside world, and once in, a "house manager," the person responsible for making people feel comfortable, greeted the new arrivals.[4] The manager might offer patrons drinks or cocaine as a form of social etiquette; he was generally responsible for keeping a close watch on things as he patrolled the club, making sure customers had no complaints and that everything was running smoothly. He informed patrons of any special events taking place. "Gambling in the back, drinks at the bar, topless dancing in an hour."

I saw a large sign above the jukebox, which read "Come to our anniversary party, Sunday, February 1. We start early. Don't miss it." Once further inside, the dimensions of the space came into focus. Fifty feet in length and thirty feet in width, cheap tables, perhaps twenty or so, composed the room. The best placement of a circulation path through a small room is usually straight through, a few feet from one wall, but here an inefficient circulation was best because people wanted to mingle and be seen. Bumping into others was the desired effect. In this small room patrons split the room in two, and the circulation path ran diagonally through it. A gaudy Wurlitzer jukebox in front of a multicolored shade decorated a corner near the bar. When customers complained about a tune paid for but not playing, the waitress would walk over, kick and bang the sides of the box, and it would play more tunes than you paid for. The cigarette machine, displaying the major brands common to Black smokers—Kools, Newport, True, Now, Winston—spat out the wrong ones, like it had been drinking too much. The machine rested directly in front of the entrances to the two washrooms. The women's room was inscribed with "Mates" and the men's with "Captains," though the second *a* in "Capt–ins" was falling off. The bar sat twenty people. Mirrors lined the bar's rear, which was stocked with a wide assortment of alcoholic beverages. Some bottles had been watered down. These were served, I was told by a hostess, when a customer asked for ice in their drink. Drinking glasses hung overhead on racks within easy reach, and a small refrigerator sat underneath at the far-left counter.

There was no cash register. All money collected by the barmaid from patrons was put in a box. When the box was full, it was handed to the house manager. Five tables were positioned directly opposite the bar, with seating for two and four people. All the tables had Kleenex boxes on them and were strategically placed at intervals along the bar.

Patrons gave value to the space by calling it "my place," giving priority to appropriation over form. "My place" refers to property regardless of the type of space, atmosphere, or ambiance it has and is a way to define space as a "place."[5] The vibe of the club was about finding one's own place in this lifeworld specifically and in the underworld generally. The club was about affirmation, and the clientele on any given night was of a hustler variety. Cheap-looking men and frowzy women sniffed cocaine through dollar bills or foil, drank and drowned their sorrows with twist-off wine and the promise of sex. I was told that the barmaids who worked the place that night and the night waitresses (who appeared to be underage) kept the patrons drinking and snorting. There was always house coke for sale if a patron ran out of his or her own. Young women alternated every week or so and were rumored to be pushed by gradual steps into self-degradation; others argued they were hardly pushed at all but eagerly delved into drug dealing, drug misuse, sex work, or all three.

Angela was medium height, agitated in her movements. She spoke using a proper tone even while describing improper behavior.

> Listen, I will admit this, and I know it was not unusual to do some tricking in the bathroom at some spots, but I had my preferences; you see I wasn't into those super ghetto clubs, but I did go to the Sam's and Grants spots, and the Disco Lounge on

> 45th [145th] and Jason's spot on Eighth Avenue, they were the spots I went to just so I could do trickin'. I can't lie I did that too. I would do men in the bathroom, hand jobs, blow jobs for fifty, hundred dollars. Even when I did that, I never saw myself as a prostitute. But I like mixed clubs the best, with black and whites, not them spots that was too ghetto.[6]

I found this "never saw myself as prostitute" comment fascinating because I hear the word "sex worker" used these days, designating a more socially acceptable identity than prostitute. Even though the term "sex worker" originated in the late 1980s, it hadn't made it to Le Boogie Woogie yet.

It is important to keep in mind that the "spot" was relatively small. It had only one door in and out (that most customers knew about) and enjoyed a reputation for being the scene of action—in the Elizabethan sense. Whenever an actor entered or left the stage, it constituted a scene. To arrive at Le Boogie Woogie, one passed dilapidated buildings, elegant brownstones, and fully occupied tenements. The place opened in the early hours of the morning, frequented by maybe fifty people (on a good night), most of whom arrived either by cab or private car. It was difficult not to see the club as a community institution for those in the know, a haven for all sorts of illegal and hidden activities. Gambling, snorting, smoking, and sex all made their way in. It kept the squares out and admitted the hip, fresh, and cool crowds, and as such the club had special significance not only for regulars and purveyors but also for the police and other law-enforcement agencies, such as the New York State Liquor Authority and the Drug Enforcement Agency, to name only two.

New York City had and has many such clubs in different parts of the city, not just in zones in transition like the South Bronx or Harlem but in exclusive neighborhoods, though less conspicuously so in the latter and often hidden under terms like "social clubs." While these clubs are not as numerous as they once were, they are as notorious, raunchy, and private as ever. They open as early as midnight (on special occasions) and as late as 4 a.m., and they stay open until the last customer leaves. There is an entrance fee, and drinks cost anywhere from a few dollars to hundreds of dollars, depending on the club and the clientele. The security guards screen patrons for weapons and admit only those who are known to them or have been recommended. Although dealers sometimes go to these spots to sell drugs, most act as if they are there for recreation and take time out from selling cocaine to mix with cocaine-using friends and share stories with other dealers. Club friendship, also referred to as "coke friends," is fleeting and not meant to last more than the night.

Generally, cocaine dealers come to after-hours clubs with "CC" or "calling-card" cocaine to give out in part to initiate coke associations. This is a way to enhance status, help make friends for the night, and, most of all, attract new clients, both men and women. If patrons ask to buy, dealers typically reserve their highest-quality cocaine for first-time sales. In many clubs, dealers—regulars themselves—deplete their own supply over the course of the evening and will often purchase "house coke" from the in-house dealers. Most patrons snort some cocaine before coming to the club and are in a state of heightened excitability, ready to participate in the scene. They may be required to engage in conversation with anyone, be gamed on, listen to arguments, drink alcohol, use illegal drugs, and get involved in other taboo acts, whether they want to or not.[7]

Patrons came to Le Boogie Woogie around 4:30 a.m., after regular bars closed, and if they were alone, they usually sat or stood at the bar until others arrived. There were forty to fifty people on a busy night and more like twenty-five to thirty on a regular night. The dancer showed up around 4:45. The second wave of patrons to arrive would be told about her by the doorman and the house manager. "We got a dynamite dancer tonight! Go up, check her out." Le Boogie Woogie catered to those with an interest in risk taking and a penchant for danger, but it also was regulated by a specific code of behavior all its own. Manners and etiquette were taken seriously; antisocial behavior detracted from the atmosphere and was in bad taste. A third wave of patrons would come around 6 a.m. or later, and a fourth phase arrived between 10 a.m. and noon. The weekday patrons were mostly musicians, barmaids, sex workers, gamblers, dealers, bartenders, and a few working people. The patrons were largely Black. Some Latinos arrived in groups and conversed in Spanish part of the time. The occasional white male or two could be seen either in the pimping or drug game.

The action centered around cocaine. Angela spoke candidly to me about what was going on at Le Boogie Woogie. "Yeah, there was a lot of coke around, and people were more or less pleasant, but I do what everybody else did, or maybe a little more." She smiles. "But I was naïve too. I never really felt like I fit in some of those [after-hours] spots. Because a lot of the people I met there wanted to talk about dumb shit. Talking about their Benzes and shit. I didn't wanna talk about dumb shit. And a lot of them wanted to talk about dumb shit. That was not for me." Whether dumb shit or not, conversation was the mainstay at the clubs, which offered a time of self-discovery and self-love among Black people in a semiprivate space. And the rules that regulated its conduct and the conduct of the various drug users there made the whole private and illegal underground scene what it was: cool.[8]

At Le Boogie Woogie on weekends, patrons were more evenly mixed, racially and occupationally, with working people, secretaries, lawyers, photographers, and artists joining the scene. The members of this latter group were not considered regulars but referred to by the employees as "weekend warriors" or "weekend junkies." They were the "lames" or "squares" who like to get intoxicated with cocaine and other drugs and mingle in an exotic mixed crowd for a night. In general, patrons came and went as they liked. There was a core group of regulars, mixed with transients who would show up occasionally, with money to spend. Some came for a quick drink or sniff and then left; others remained for hours. Most of the money was made on drinks, entrance fees, house cocaine sales, and marijuana sales. At after-hours clubs in the present day, overpriced champagne and bottle liquor is also the key to the house's profits (see figures 1.1 and 1.2). An imperial-size Dom Pérignon Rosé (six liters) at Murphy's is $29,995. Some regulars hopped from one club to another, visiting three or more clubs each night. The fact that the clubs were expensive, costing at least two dollars for a watered-down drink in addition to the cocaine, did not deter patrons. Cokeheads feel that being high on anything but cocaine is "unhip," and they are not concerned about how much it costs to be in the club. That is incidental. What drove patrons to go from one "spot" to another was the variety, the conviviality, the intimacy, and the social networking, which varied from club to club.

Most older patrons were African American and, in later years, Latin American, as Dominicans, Colombians, and Puerto Ricans moved into the community.[9] These newer arrivals made up 24 percent of the neighborhood, and they tried to emulate the old-timers in some ways. The club was one of the first places they could mingle with their neighbors in an illegal fashion. Some old-timers were envious because some of these newcomers were connected and had access to the Latin American drug world. A mixture of languages was spoken, and the jukebox played Latin, soul, blues, and jazz music with equal frequency. The occasional

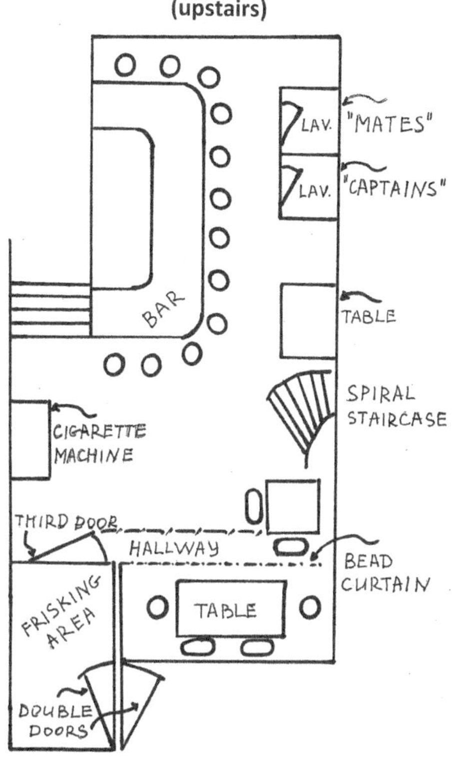

FIGURE 1.1 Murphy's champagne menu, listed with a 15 percent gratuity, 5 percent operation fee, and 8.875 percent NYC sales tax added to all checks.

tourists were the odd lot out, as were the rich folk from downtown who often slummed uptown or the adventurous teenager or two who would show on Saturday night. I heard one club employee call them "guttersnipes," meaning an uneducated person, uncouth, lower class. The idea of teenagers being allowed to enter the club is interesting because neighborhood teens at the time were emerging as crew leaders and money-making

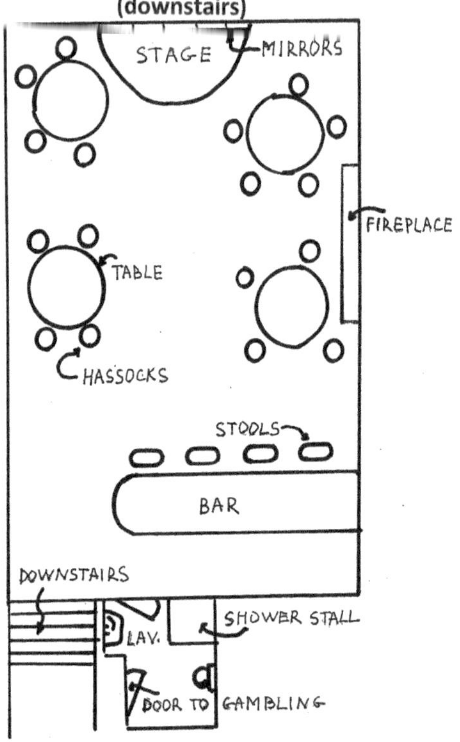

FIGURE 1.2 Bottle service menu, listed with a 15 percent gratuity, 5 percent operation fee, and 8.875 percent NYC sales tax added to all checks.

runners in the drug trade. In addition, they brought in cash and younger women, and this was attractive to management. How old were these teenagers? I believe most of the young women were at least eighteen years of age, though some looked younger. No one was carded, and when asked, they all said they were either nineteen or twenty-something, as if rehearsed. The barmaid who called them "guttersnipes" was insulted by their sneakers and the general disrespectful attitude of some of the kids.

When it was pointed out that the sneakers cost hundreds of dollars and were made by big-time designers, she shrugged and remained unimpressed.[10] "A sneaker is a sneaker no matter how you wear it," she said. I believe she was referring to one particular person she did not like, not casting aspersions on all the teens who came to the place.

Both the regulars and the weekenders sought the club's special ambience, its curious mixture of excitement, glitter, and menace. Teenage patrons looked for something out of the ordinary, be it the direct stimulation of cocaine or the atmosphere of illicit pleasure. I would say the same was true for the older patrons, too, because part of that pleasure comes from the ease of human contact that cocaine encourages. "Cocaine loosens the tongue, lowers inhibitions and draws the user into a setting where intense, open communication is not only possible but required. One expects, and is expected, to be sociable: strangers are obliged to become friends."[11]

UPSTAIRS

When the upstairs part of the club was active, it was all red velvet curtains. The curtains overwhelmed you. They were heavy, mysterious, funky, and loud. I knew nothing about the place, but I knew those curtains were more than mere decoration. They were there to send a message. In Le Boogie Woogie, different uses of space were marked by the floor, and if you paid close attention to its floor plan, you found single lines. In a regular apartment floor plan, there are double lines: the walls that separate the rooms. A club is an open space that requires informal and socially defined separations of space—single lines. Le Boogie Woogie didn't really have walls. The boundaries were defined by materials—a dance floor, a carpeted area for tables and chairs, a hard floor for the bar area. The red velvet curtains were for separation.[12]

At Le Boogie Woogie, the easy movement between spaces, the change from one body position to another and one location to another, emphasized that the position of the patron was not fixed; once inside, you could shift over to be someone else or live another life. "Your position in the real world doesn't matter; you are in a club," said Mavis, one of the player women who showed up whenever a new dancer was introduced. "There is a science-fiction feeling in Le Boogie Woogie, and by that, I mean not just escapism but an effort to provide an image to another kind of life." I asked her to repeat what she said because I didn't quite get her meaning, and I'm still not entirely sure what she meant, but I agree that Le Boogie Woogie presented as a physical environment with few limits. Limitation came in a social form.

While I did not try to analyze every gesture, I did try to make sense of what those gestures I did catch meant—what those glances suggested—both from the point of view of those expressing the gestures and those receiving them. When I saw something happening, whether a wink or a pose, I asked, "what did that mean? What did she say? What exactly did she mean by that smile, curse, joke, or movement?" The movement and detail of various actions or details of a specific act were important to understanding what was going on because so much took place at the level of innuendo. There was a rich symbolic language in Le Boogie Woogie, and it incorporated nonverbal components, such as clothing or body position. For instance, players would often hold their hands by their sides, fingers pointing backward and straight down. This posture was indicative of a certain lifestyle. I was able to make sense of the different levels of meaning simply by asking people questions.

I noted the sharp contrast in people's behavior and attitude between the time they knew I was at the club to do research and before. Before they knew, people were less self-conscious; they talked less for me and more for themselves. Once they knew I was interested in them, they embellished their stories yet were more cautious in what they said and how they said it. This was neither unusual nor unexpected and is referred to as the Hawthorne Effect. People change their behavior when being watched or observed. I explained to my research subjects that I was doing research, but on occasion I worked more covertly and only mentioned my project after our conversation was underway. People generally reacted accordingly, cautious initially, then reverting to form after a while. Those I continued to see, such as Conchita, Dana, Sam, Vital, Julio, and a few others, eventually all felt relaxed with me and went back to their old ways.[13] I did not tell every person who came into the club I was doing research, but sometimes the barmaids would say "He's a writer" or "He want to tell your story" or something to that effect. I would continue doing what I was doing without saying anything. The club acted as a translator of Black slang, Newyorican or Puerto Rican language, bourgeois primness and "proper" English, and other lexiconic pretensions, because for the club to function properly, these languages and registers all had to be accommodated. As I have noted in a previous ethnography I undertook in the same neighborhood:

> The language of the street is also used as the language of the business. Just as one must know the language of banking in order to talk to one's counterparts and make deals in banking, so it is with the language of drugs. It is commonplace to hear stories of young white males from the suburbs who are taken advantage of because they do not speak or understand the proper slang (or Spanish).

> Within this theater, where sexual activity is often a medium of exchange, certain behaviors and roles are also denoted with special words.[14]

At Le Boogie Woogie, patrons tended to explain their slang without my asking.

Nonverbal sounds were all part of the dynamic. Added to the symbolic importance of the physical space were the elements of human physicality: body odor, cheap fragrances, cologne, sweat, beer, expensive perfumes, and whiskey, mingling with cigarette smoke and the ethanol in the air. Baudelaire once wrote that every city and every country has its smells. New York has its seasonal aromas. Summer is fermented, heated garbage. Fall is denim. Winter is burning chestnuts. Spring is the flora and fauna of Central Park. The club was a physical space of social action. People looked at one another and made a move to talk, touch, or imbibe. A person would not say a word but lift a piece of tinfoil or a folded dollar bill, touch their nose or tilt their head in a lip pout: "Do you want some?" "Would you like to indulge with me?" These gestures, though wordless, had strong meaning, and I found myself reveling in this nonverbal scene, captured by the smells as much as by the action: smoky cigarette tobacco and marijuana, mixed body funk and harlotry, touches of jasmine and the faint, medicinal smell of cocaine. They all carried a certain aromatic intensity, blending with whiskey, spice, and everything nice. The nonverbal created images in your head, and I caught the scent of something, which overwhelmed a reality that was socially constructed in the half-light ambiance of Le Boogie Woogie. Cocaine makes you lose your inhibitions, and touch, smell, taste, and sound take over your sensorium like a Casanova adventurer in full attack.

As dance partners rose to dance, jackets, furs, coats, and money were sometimes left on the bar. Seldom was cocaine left unattended, but if it was, regulars respected the right of the snorter enough to leave it untouched until claimed. Snorters could take cocaine with them; however, if they went to the bathroom or moved from one area to another for any length of time, they were likely to lose their seats. The door to the bathroom was left slightly ajar; even in the main room you could hear the commode flushing. Sometimes it continued to run and was obviously stuck. Once I went inside and saw foil descending in a swirling avalanche of water. A man stood holding another piece of foil, sniffing with a silver spoon. He sniffed, winked, and grunted. Then he pissed. It was unclear what the maximum amount of time a snorter could leave cocaine unclaimed or unguarded before it became the property of the barmaid. Dana, for instance, a barmaid at the Le Boogie Woogie, one night said in a loud voice so all could hear: "Who's sitting here?" pointing to a spot where someone had left some cocaine. "Is this anybody's? If this ain't nobody's, I'm gonna take it," at which point a few patrons laughed. Leaving cocaine was analogous to patrons leaving change or bills on the counter in a regular bar. The bartender waited the appropriate time before considering the money "fare" game. The barmaid would try to find the owner of the cocaine, but she might not look very hard. To leave cocaine, money, or drinks at the table was both an act of trust and an indication that the space was occupied. One of the curious features about taking another's cocaine was the lack of concern about whether it was sanitary. Few people will eat or drink a stranger's leftovers. If a person were to leave a drink at the bar, the barmaid would throw it away. Yet strangers would sniff cocaine from a stranger's package without a second thought.

Though they might refuse cocaine if the offer was from someone they didn't particularly care to interact with, this refusal was not out of concern about the quality or safety of the cocaine.[15]

THE BAR

The bar was an elongated wooden sling curved at both ends; it was where single and solitary sniffers could be seen and heard producing an active social get-together. Men and women drank, smoked reefer, cursed, kissed, and did a variety of other things at the bar. The contour of the bar was not conducive to passing cocaine to many people. It was easier for a party of four or more to go to a table or upstairs if they wished to engage in the ritualized passing of the drug. Think of a living room. One can sit on a sofa, lie down on a couch, or read in a chair. A living room is the more public area of a house, and the bar is like that. If the bar area is like the living room of the club, Le Boogie Woogie is like a living room in the city; a request for a call for public life. The first place that single patrons headed to when they entered was the bar; couples usually looked for a table. The bar was a place for being alone or for watching people come and go, but it was also a place for actively looking for someone or something. The bar was a place from which to sit and attract. It was a place to get drunk, a place to dance, to share talk, to sniff cocaine. It was a place to go deep inside yourself and be transformed while being in public.

The bar was a place for drinking, smoking, chatting, and arguing. And ordering—and since the stools were limited in number, that was what most people did. One was free to choose different alternative seating arrangements in the club, but each activity had a body position attached and an element that forced this position. Patrons, both men and women, liked to show off by standing at the bar. Whether they had either a glimmer or a glare in the way they carried themselves, the bar was where you would find them. They stood at the bar because they were looking to "catch," meaning to pick up a man or a woman. To be seated suggested a less conspicuous but no less active social engaging. In all these various situations there were positions in the club from which to watch and from which to look for action.

Many patrons who showed up at Le Boogie Woogie on any given night were not from the neighborhood, and this was why the club could not be called a "home territory tavern," as Sherri Cavan[16] would describe it, where the bar is used as though it were a private place similar to one's residence.[17] Le Boogie Woogie was not necessarily a male-dominated space, and the gender dynamics were complex because on any given night both women and men sought "play."[18] Men looked for "play" from women, in search of a true "freak" (a woman with especially loose morals). Women came to the spot to find men for sport, in search of a "sugar daddy," for play, or for the man who has money or drugs or is a bad hustler. Many women believed they could handle any man they met, hustler, con man, pimp, whatever, and this belief was especially true of "player" women, a category not often mentioned in street-culture lore.[19] This concept of play was one kind of behavior expected at the club, especially at the bar, in the sense that you look for or "give" play. This expression meant to solicit and receive certain positive responses from a member of the opposite sex through talk or gestures. A smile or a raised eyebrow could be considered "play." This business of "play" was gender neutral. Men and women engaged in this act equally.

Many patrons were from downtown, out of state, out of the country, coming from work, from parties. They could be further broken down into those who were weekday patrons (Tuesday to Friday; the club was closed on Monday) and weekend patrons (Friday to Sunday). These visitation patterns may have had to do with disposable cash; a hustling class would certainly have had more money to spend, while the everyday patron would more likely spend less. Payday was a busy night. This raises a question: Do those with less patronage use less cocaine, or is the need to engage with others so profound a habit that they must come together regardless of cocaine usage? This fits into Van Gennep's "rites of incorporation" theory: "The rites of eating and drinking together is clearly a rite of incorporation, of physical union, and has been called a sacrament of communion. A union by this means may be permanent, but more often it lasts only during the period of digestion. Captain Lyons has noted that the Eskimo considers a man their guest only for twenty-four hours."[20] Arnold Van Gennep was the first anthropologist to refer to the systematic importance of the rituals connected to the transitional stages of man's life, and he coined the term "rites of passage," which is now part of the lexicon of both sociology and anthropology. Is Le Boogie Woogie part of a rite of passage? And if so, what kind of rite is it? One might say it is a social rite, where sobriety is expunged from the social graces of the culture. For example, a man was snorting cocaine, a woman seated nearby. He offered her cocaine, in a customary way, and she accepted it. This is "play." It is an affirmative gesture to begin a conversation.

Single men sat at the bar to check on single women as they entered. If a woman came in alone and did not stop at the bar but went upstairs instead, men at the bar would follow. This maneuver was accomplished within five or ten minutes, most of the time. The men wanted to be certain the women were seated before they went upstairs. It can be an embarrassing situation for the man if he attempted to go up before the women were settled. One night Tall Sam was seated at the bar when two young women came in. They looked over at the bar and then proceeded up the stairs. A few minutes later, Sam picked up his drink and foil cocaine packet and started to go up. When he got to the steps, the women were already coming back down. The stairway was narrow and allowed only one patron to go up or down at one time. To save face, he said, "Hey, baby, I was just coming up to give y'all some of this good blow." They smiled and left. When Sam got back to the bar, the cat next to him said,

CHAMPAGNE

Regular 750ml

Perrier Jouet Fleur	695
Perrier Jouet Fleur Rose	1295
Perrier Jouet Blanc de Blanc	1395
Cristal	995
Cristal Rose	1595
Ace of Spades	1095
Ace of Spades Rose	1595
Dom Perignon	825
Dom Perignon Rose	1095
Dom Perignon Luminous	995
Dom Perignon Luminous Rose	1250
Krug	1195
Krug Rose	1695
Moet Imperial	450
Moet Imperial Rose	495
Beau Joie Brut	750
Beau Joie Rose	850

Magnum 1.5l

Perrier Jouet Fleur	1295
Perrier Jouet Fleur Rose Fleur	2195
Krug	1895
Krug 1995	1995
Cristal (Based on Availability)	2495
Cristal Rose	3495
Ace of Spades	2495
Ace of Spades Rose	3295
Dom Perignon	1695
Dom Perignon Rose	2695
Dom Perignon Luminous	1895
Dom Perignon Luminous Rose	2995
Moet Imperial	695
Moet Imperial Rose	795

Large Format

Moet Imperial 3L	1950
Perrier Jouet Fleur 3L	2495
Perrier Jouet Fleur Rose 3L	4895
Cristal 3L	9995
Krug 3L	5495
Ace of Spades 3L	7995
Ace of Spades 6L	24,995
Dom Perignon 3L	5095
Dom Perignon Rose 3L	8495
Dom Perignon Rose 6L	29,995
Moet Imperial 6L	3695
Moet Imperial 9L	5995
Moet Imperial 12L	7995
Moet Imperial 15L	11995

Cognac

Hennessey Black	450
Hennessy VSOP	495
Hennessy XO	695
Remy VSOP	495
Remy Louis XIII	5995

Other

Fiji	8
Red Bull Sugar Free	8
Red Bull	8

15% Gratuity, 5% Operation Fee and 8.875% NY Tax is added to all checks

05/02

FIGURE 1.3 Upstairs at Le Boogie Woogie.

BOTTLE SERVICE

Vodka

Absolut / Flavors	425
Belvedere	475
Belvedere Intense	475
Belvedere Magnum	925
Ciroc	475
Grey Goose/ Flavors	500
Grey Goose / Magnum	1000
Stoli Elit	600
Stoli Elit Magnum	1100
Ultimat Vodka	550

Gin

Plymouth	450
Bombay Sapphire	450
Tanqueray	450
Hendricks	500

Scotch

Chivas 12 yr	450
Dewars 12 yr	425
JW Black	475
JW Blue	1000
Macallan 12 yr	525
Macallan 25 yr	1000
Oban	450

Tequila

DeLeon Silver	750
DeLeon Repasado	800
DeLeon Anejo	850
Patron Silver Magnum	1000
Patron Gran Platinum	1100
Patron Gran Platinum Mag	2300
Don Julio 1942	1000
Don Julio Silver	500
Don Julio Anejo	550
Don Julio REAL	1200
Corzo Silver	450
Corzo Anejo	500
Cuervo La Familia	800
Milagro Select Barrel Silver	475
Casa Dragones	2000

Bourbon

Woodford Reserve	500
Jack Daniels	450
Knob Creek	450
Makers Mark	450
Crown Royal	450
Jameson	475

Rum

10 Cane	475
Bacardi 8 yr	450
Malibu	450
Captain Morgan	450

15% Gratuity, 5% Operation Fee and 8.875% NY Tax is added to all checks

5/2

FIGURE 1.4 Downstairs at Le Boogie Woogie.

"Hey Sam, them chicks peeped yo' hole card, didn't they?" And they both laughed.[21]

At Le Boogie Woogie near the bar area, passing cocaine was restricted to a few close patrons near the person offering, usually no more than two or three, unless they were positioned slightly away from other people. It was difficult to pass cocaine to more than one person or two people at the bar because one did not want it spilled or sniffed by unauthorized noses. As the bar got crowded, fewer people around the counter were offered the drug. I know from conversing with patrons consuming wine, whiskey, and cocaine, however, that doing the drug itself was not the sole purpose of their coming out to the club, since most had a home and other places to go. They preferred to hang out with other people and indulge at Le Boogie Woogie. Some needed female companionship, but only this place offered this kind of action, since the women were seen as "loose" and available. Many men believed the cocaine acted as a sexual stimulant, more so than alcohol, and thus had more of a chance at a sexual encounter. By the same token, women saw men at the club as potential suckers, "good-time Charlies" to milk money or drugs from. In the plainest terms, most came for companionship, male or female companionship. Still others, or all, I should say, needed sex or someone to chat with, to get the latest information on the scene.

PICKING AND BLOWING THE NOSE

> *Some years ago, people made an art of blowing the nose. One imitated the sound of the trumpet, another, the screech of the cat. Perfection lay in making neither too much noise nor too little.*
>
> —Norbert Elias, *The Civilizing Process*

Norbert Elias wrote in *The Civilizing Process* of the need to hide certain behaviors from prying eyes. He mentioned sex as one taboo act people wish to shield from the public. Taking drugs such as cocaine is another prohibited tradition. A word about the nose, since so much of what goes on here involves the olfactory and the use of the nostril. And because the setting is a late-night place and therefore the behavior is not only unserious but "cool" and uninhibited, certain behavior that ordinarily might be considered indecent or shocking is allowed. One illustration of what this means relates to nose picking, blowing the nose, or pulling, pinching, or holding the nose. As kids we are taught not to pick our nose in public. In the daytime culture, to pick one's nose is a gross violation of tact, civility, and "good manners." On most occasions where this behavior is noticed, the people watching or catching such an act are often embarrassed to the point where they will look away rather than at the person.

In the cocaine night culture, regulars not only pick, pull, and blow but instruct others on how to pick their nose and when they should clean them, and this is all accomplished in a manner that is anything but embarrassing. What the regular is doing when she or he remarks to another as they are leaving—"hey, clean your nose" or "excuse me, but you got a little blow up there" or "you should wipe your nose"—is warning the snorter that they may face possible trouble. Sometimes a gesture of touching one's own nose indicates the person is "showing" white residue. This is a way of protecting the sniffer from detection by both everyday people "you don't want to know your business" and by law-enforcement agents, who may see the residue as an opportunity to stop, question, and frisk.

When blowing the nose, snorters do not turn away, as is customary in more "genteel" settings. If a conversation is in progress, the snorters will blow while looking up at the talker. It is here more important to maintain eye contact than to lose it and appear disinterested, even though it only takes a few seconds to blow your nose. If Kleenex is not available, snorters may ask their friends for a single tissue or the waitress for a box. People who blow their nose in an emergency with their hands will at least wipe the "snot" with the back of the hand; they do not ask for another's handkerchief. The forefinger is used if there is only a small amount of mucous, but if it is more than that, the back of the hand is used. A move to the bathroom for toilet tissue is a last resort.[22] Snorters do not like to use toilet paper for this function. When regulars are not actually blowing their noses, they may pick into the nostrils with their fingers. Whereas picking is acceptable, it is considered gross to look at the results of this action, yet looking at what is removed from the nose is done primarily to detect blood, which is an indication that too much cocaine has been consumed and that the person should stop snorting. This is not to say that in such circumstances one stops consuming the drug altogether. Some users resort to eating the cocaine if they cannot sniff anymore. Looking around the cocaine club, one saw the various environmental arrangements that signified something about the culture. For example, Kleenex boxes were conveniently placed on the tables so snorters, after excessive sniffing, could clear their noses. Cocaine users also needed Kleenex before sniffing to clear the nasal passages in preparation for the sniff. If tissues were not available, they could use personal handkerchiefs.

A final component of the scene—the jukebox—gave meaning to the after-hours club experience. The jukebox at Le Boogie Woogie was the Wurlitzer Seeburg, or Bullet Nose 1100 Bomber, multicolored green, pink, red. Wurlitzer is based in New York and first manufactured jukeboxes in the United States as the Rudolf Wurlitzer Company. They made some of the best-looking boxes around, so said the customers, especially Sam, who said he'd worked for the company at one time. The jukebox could play one hundred records, front and back, for a total of two hundred recordings. In the late 1970s, Wurlitzer introduced a new record-changer mechanism. It was extremely unreliable, and records often got stuck, but tonight people were dancing, and the jukebox was not skipping but playing the tunes smoothly.[23]

OVERHEARD AT THE BAR

The city is constantly changing, but it is always a spectacle,[24] especially when people are absorbed by a stimulant drug. Two early-to-arrive patrons were standing at the bar. One said to the other, "And I came here, right here looking for two fine asses, two mochas chizzles, two bia-tches getting down to rizzle my nizzle." I didn't quite understand what they meant, but it reminded me of the pig Latin my sisters used to use to confuse my parents. When I caught up to Mavis near the bar, she was talking about white girls being medicalized differently than black women; I interrupted to ask what "rizzle my nizzle" was. She said, "When a man gets his dick sucked." I was embarrassed when I was told this: I felt I should have known, but she just smiled and returned to her account of the white girls. "White girls [women] are medicalized because they get treatment, but Black women of color get criminalized when they get their drugs. White women can get all the prescription drugs they need and get help when they overdo it, but the only thing Black women get is *dis*-stress." And though nothing more was said about this, I thought to myself how the addicted rich were ensconced in treatment hideaways like the Hazelden Betty Ford Clinic, Passages Malibu Center, and other anonymous facilities far from the public eye. While the media loves the cliché "if it bleeds it leads," portraying addiction as a "white thing" goes against another, more tacit code. It might bleed, but more importantly, you do not portray negativity or reveal the weaknesses of the dominant class. I also noted that Mavis used the word "white girl" when referring to white women but said "black women," not "black girl." I felt this to be an interesting distinction.

Loquacity is one of the intriguing elements attached to the use of stimulant drugs, and exaggerated talk is often a feature. Here is some crosstalk to give a sense of what was typical to overhear at the bar when everyone was disinhibited.

MARGO: I'm leaving my husband, that's why I'm out tonight. I'm leaving for a lotta reason but not only because he's dull as a motherfucker but because he's the cause of dullness in the neighborhood.

JEAN: The doctor say she had a crack baby, I say the little bitch was a dealer who owed somebody money.

JESSICA: I looked over at her and she was so thin I could see both sides of her with one glance.

BAR TALK: But that bitch could suck some dick. I heard she could suck a golf ball through a water hose.

BAR TALK: I'm going to whip her ass so bad she'll either go all the way crazy or come back sane.

UNKNOWN MALE: I like to choke a bitch and stick my dick so far down her throat she gags.

UNKNOWN MALE: My daddy gave me a big dick.

BARMAID: I was raped, and after that I started stripping. I had hit rock bottom.

BARMAID: I tell a motherfucker you might get what you want out there but lose what you had. Be careful. Be very careful. I knew he wasn't gonna do nothing until somebody laced up his shoes.

MAVIS: When her baby was born, he was already on parole. Those little hellions get into more trouble than the devil.

PATRON: I was sitting at the bar, the dancer bent over, and our eyes met, and I gave her a dollar for the look.

PATRON: How much is coke these days, let's say an ounce going for right now?

VISITOR: About $700: I got a Dominican connection that will let me have it half for that.

PATRON: When you gonna see him again?

PATRON: "Bawd"? Don't you know what that mean? It means she's the madam. She's the one who keeps a house of prostitution.

VISITOR: Tomorrow. I was going to see him tonight, but I was going to go out to Camden and take something out there to Jersey, but it's about a forty-five-minute drive, and this was about eight before I could have left, and I'd have to leave at about 6:30, but then I said the hell with it, you know. Though it would have been money. But I was saying earlier that we would have a pretty good idea of what's going on, price wise, you know.

PATRON: Are people still buying coke like they used to? I mean in the street?

VISITOR: Yeah of course. Oh yeah. In some places they paying like $40 a gram [in Manhattan]. But across the bridge [Brooklyn] like it's $70, $80, and in Jersey it's like $100. But what you can't see, or by that I mean what you can't feel, is the risk. Do you know what I mean? I mean that feeling that at any moment a man can tap you on your shoulder and take you away from seeing birds, hearing traffic, children crying, the smell of home-cook food, the arguments, even those kinds of things you don't like to hear, you will miss once you're put away. That's the risk I'm talking about. You can't feel that because all you're doing [now speaking to me] is recording what's going down, and you leave here and at the end of the night and go back and play with your school friends and your little books and boys' and girls' play time. I gotta deal with cops and guns and killings and shootouts, all those kinds of things that makes you a man. That's the risk I'm talking about.

THE DANCER

Frenchy mentioned how certain owners were known to use cocaine and marijuana to barter in exchange for services rendered by the dancer, but Margo, who had worked both as a dancer at topless legal clubs and after-hours clubs said, "I don't play that," meaning dancing for trade. She talked about Sugar, another dancer who was paid by one owner she knew with cocaine.

> She [Sugar] dances for coke. It's not that she don't want the money, it's just that she prefers cocaine. She's got her spoon around her neck and shit. We both danced at the Bango Club uptown. First, he [the owner] ask if I wanted some reefer then coke instead of my $50, and I told him I wanted my money. But Sugar, she wanted coke. They "pay" in coke if you want it. All of them chicks be snorting, especially the ones who be doing doubles and shit [working double shifts—dancing from 1:00 a.m. to 4:00 a.m. in a regular club, then 4:30 a.m. to 8:00 a.m. in an after-hours club]. That's why I won't be no house girl, because you get no respect. If you a house girl, you gotta take the coke or whatever else they offer you. But you see, I ain't gonna do that, because I wanna get hooked up with respect, win, lose, or draw.

The nude dancer as entertainer in the club was a natural offshoot of the go-go-girl craze of the 1960s, when after-hours club owners found it profitable to have naked or topless female entertainment. Patrons stayed longer, purchased more drinks, and bought more cocaine and marijuana when a nude dancer performed. But the origin of the dance club and the nightclub began a long time ago, with the taxi-dance hall.[25] Illegality always operated in a context of legality. It was as if legality created room or space for illegality. The dancer was one of the main attractions in the club and was considered a "prize" if you were able to "pull" or get her as your friend. She was important to management in regard to the amount of time and money regulars would spend while she was there; her performance was a direct extension of the business's performance. The dancer was the one employee whose breach of the sniffing norm (overindulgence) was tolerated.

The dancer got short (twenty-minute) breaks during the night, and she would, during her breaks, sit and sniff cocaine with a patron of her choice. Patrons sitting next to the dance stage offered her cocaine during her performance, and when she finished for a break, she would sit down to sniff more cocaine. This encounter may have led to a further engagement by the patron with the dancer; sometimes sexual favors outside the club were granted, sometimes not.[26]

The after-hours club invented the grinding, doggy-style, front-piggy-backing, skirt-hiking, and hands-on-floor-train dance moves because these were forms of dancing perhaps improvised there on the floor because they were too risqué for polite company. When a woman hiked her skirt, bent over, stroked her ass against her partner's crotch, all to the syncopated sounds of Dicky Williams's "Come Back Pussy," it was a simulation of a sex act as close as I could imagine to the real thing. The dancing was part of the scene. The movement of bodies captivated the eye; women in protruding tight slacks and tight-fitting dresses undulated to rhythm and blues, raising their skirts. One couple did the swing, another slow danced to the same song, another bent down with hands on the floor, ass rubbing against men gyrating behind them; yet another couple was on the floor, the man pulling the woman's head closer to crotch level. Ironically, it was not freak houses that spawned freak dancing but after-hours clubs and juke joints.

My father owned such a place in Baertown, Mississippi, called the Joy Land Café, a disorderly, spectacularly wicked, razor-cutting, sawdust-floor pleasure house. It was a bawdy house where Black folk danced, drank illegal corn whiskey, and gambled. The folklorist Zora Neale Hurston defined the juke joint as an indigenous Black cultural formation. It is incongruous behavior, of course, found in such spots, but who cares. These melodic moments brought smiles all around, grins on the lips of patrons as they sniffed and snorted, laughed and hollered out loud, "the place is swinging!" The drug brought out the sensual in everyone. The music's urgent phrasing held everyone in its sway, and no one dropped, spilled, or wasted a grain. The gliding movement of hips, the tender tapping of toes choreographs a beat—a sing-song syncopation sweet to the sound and the echo of pleasurable motion. You could literally feel the floor tremble.[27]

GAMBLING

In Le Boogie Woogie a patron joined the game only if invited, but since this was late-night gambling, it did not matter whether you were known to any of the other members. Special games were set up where the stakes were so high a newcomers may have to be warned in advance that the game was not a "chump's game" (petty, with low stakes). At this warning a person would stay away unless they had "deep pockets," which meant they could put up the five-hundred-dollar stake needed to play.

Snow fell in tiny speckles across the green awning and down the interstices of tiny white cobblestone bricks as big cars pulled up and others pulled away. The warmly dressed patrons dusted off their hats and coats as they entered. The front part of the building had a buildup of snow; women stepped in gingerly holding up their skirts and dresses, stamping their feet to knock the wetness from the soles of their boots.

Frenchy had six employees: a barmaid, a waitress, a doorman, a guard, a manager, and a man to cut the crap game. On special-event nights he had an extra door guard (frisker), and as owner he usually oversaw the gambling game, which was in a private part of the club, especially if high rollers were in town.

Long before there was a hip-hop aesthetic, Harlem street "niggahs" knew the distinction between being on stage and being off stage. They knew that to be in an after-hours club was to be on stage in an off-stage kind of spot.[28] "Just give me a punk grand and take it all." Frenchy would say this about the pile of coke on the table. Implying, you might say, that this was so little money, I'll take it with no more questions asked. Of course, this was a scam, a con, a hoodwinking flim-flam approach to test the street mettle and manhood of the person standing in front of him. Other dudes were standing around or sitting around watching, and a challenge was afoot. This was a challenge to the man's out-of-pocket cash, a test of his manhood. If he didn't go for it, he was a punk, and a cheap punk at that. If he went for it, he was all man and muscle and had what it took to play in the big time.

This was the place where you had nowhere else to go. When you were here, there was nowhere else. It's four in the morning, the scene was here, the women were here, the action was here. You couldn't go anywhere, so you had to put up or be a punk and shut up. Since money was no object, and since money was everywhere, the cash was placed on the table. Gambling usually took place among fellow hustlers and their friends, although the owner would allow any person with enough money to play.

A patron, one of the few women who gambled with the men, explained the game to me. "The game in the back is CeeLo." She said, her face carefully made up with red lipstick, dark eyeshadow, and false eyelashes. "CeeLo is played with three dice. The house gets 10 percent usually, a 10 percent share of the money just about in every game won. I think when you think about it the object of the game is just like any other regular dice game, you know what I mean?" A man standing near us interrupted to say the house could get more than 10 percent if the players agreed to it. The woman I was talking to looked at the guy and said, "Excuse me, but this is my motherfucking story, so let me tell it. He's talking to me and when I'm finished you can tell him what you wanna say." She turned her head, looked up at the ceiling, and with "nigger please," continued. "Well, there may be some exception, when I think about it, because of course that third dice become the thrower's [point]. You know what that is right?" I said I did not, feigning ignorance to keep her engaged. "Well, that's the number you gotta keep throwing if you expect to win. Now you, if you the thrower, you can throw 3, 4, 5 [which is like 7 and 11 in regular craps, automatically winning numbers] or 18, which is three sixes to win. You got that? The game is set up, I should have told you this at first before I was *so rudely interrupted*." She glanced over at the guy, but he was now talking to another man.

> But the game is set up with a banker and other players. The banker is the person who puts the money up to begin the game. The banker might change because if you wanna know the truth about it because any player can be the banker, you know any player can take the position of the banker. There is no limit. The banker can start with $100 in the bank. And at that point, he holds the dice and will usually throw first. Before which the players will place their bets as to whether he will throw either 3, 4, 5, or 6, 6, 6, or crap out. If the banker throws 3, 4, 5, he picks up all the money

> from the table because these three numbers are instant winners. He may also place bets with the same players on the side if he wants to do that. A player may place a side bet on the banker for any amount.

I bought her a drink and thanked her for the information, but she was just getting started.

She pulled out cocaine and offered some to me; when I refused, she asked why I didn't sniff. I used the standard line, saying this was not a good time for me to indulge, and no further explanation was required. She started to tell me about a woman named Blue Bell, pointing her finger for emphasis:

> Blue Bell had a gambling habit, not a gambling jones, because she loved to gamble. She would have her coke to sell—she had a little compact case filled with fifty dollars, spoons, and her money for gambling. She would blow hundreds and more than likely lost more than she ever won. But she had a natural gift for selling coke. First, she is very attractive, I mean a very stunning woman, fair skin, real nice body. She had one of them dreamland-in-Chicago bodies. Duplex. You know. So, most cats would love to buy anything she had to sell. Most of 'em also thought they could hit on her. So that added to her ability to get over. She was a helluva gambler and could hold her own with men or anybody. She smoked them little cigarillo-type cigars and could out-cuss a roomful of sailors. Your man, Frenchy, he knows her, Blue Bell might show here one night, you never know. But I haven't seen her in a while though. Makes me think she stepped out for a while. When Wild Man got out of the joint, he and Bo Peep started a little place in the Bronx. [I know neither of these people.] And for a while they had to close, because they weren't making no money. You see, when the hustlers don't make no money, there ain't no money out there to be made. When the economy is bad,

> the hustler suffers because the more they spend in the spot the more he's [the owner] gonna get. Well, let me tell you something. The spot [the after-hours club] is tailor-made for the hustler. And as you can see, if the hustler ain't got no money, the joint [after-hours club] ain't gonna survive. You see, unlike the regular clubs and bars, the joint thrives and survives on the illegal. Whatever has been taboo in the society, the joint sells it, lets it happen, for a price, of course. For a fee. But the average man or woman, I mean working man and woman, they ain't gonna be in the after-hours every day or night, or whatnot. They can't afford it. I don't mean people who got a hustle has to work there in the "spot." You know, selling shit; I'm talking about the regular worker who makes ninety to a hundred dollars a week. They ain't gonna be there every day. Well, that's true of most people except maybe the professionals who may go there but can afford to go there. The people that come there every day are hustlers. The other people are weekenders or one- or two-nighters. They ain't there every day, but the hustler is. He is there every day and night. Gambling, drinking, snorting. When the drought hit [in heroin that year], a number of clubs closed, mainly because the money hustlers were making off heroin sales declined, and so did their attendance at the clubs.

The revealing aspects of this conversation were not so much the information about gambling but the various functions of the clubs and who supported them. Clearly stated, the "average citizen" was not the main reason for the success, failure, or operation of the club. This was mainly because the average citizen did not frequent the club every night, only visiting on a whim—on a Friday or Saturday or every now and then. It was the players, both men and women, who came consistently and spent substantial sums of money nightly on cocaine, gambling, and alcohol who were the mainstay of the clubs.[29]

2
THE SCENE

She can't even do wrong right.

—Mavis

RULES OF BEHAVIOR

After-hours clubs like Le Boogie Woogie permitted a range of illegal activities, and as a consequence, patrons were required to maintain a low profile. A regular might not feel any qualms about getting into a personal argument or fight with another regular, but they were nevertheless bound by rules of decorum set up by the management. In addition, patrons tended to behave themselves because they were concerned about personal dignity and status. Some behaviors were considered extreme, such as fights between patrons; others were mild infractions, such as sitting on the dancer's platform. Unlike a regular bar, where aggression and other forms of boisterous behavior could be normal, the after-hours regular was expected to exude "coolness."

Coolness was exhibited and defined as poise under pressure; by pressure I mean situations of emotional and/or physical risk. Coolness was the capacity to behave and converse in a concerted, smooth, self-controlled fashion, even during stressful or perilous situations, or to maintain affective detachment during emotionally volatile encounters. It is important to understand the implicit and explicit social controls of the rules governing after-hours clubs. How did management maintain these clubs? Dues? Cover charges? Could regulars bring guests? How were problems handled? And most of all, how did owners of these clubs avoid drawing attention from community members or law enforcement?

Many of the employees I talked with at Le Boogie Woogie described what they did and how they came to work there. Frenchy recruited guys he knew from prison as bouncers and door guards, using street bad boys with tough-guy reputations. Conchita got her job because she met a man at a regular nightclub who knew Frenchy. She was looking for a job, or at least that's what she told me.

I saw the after-hours club's setup as part of an organized system of rules that regulated certain patterns of behavior between and among people, both explicitly and implicitly. While these rules were not always obeyed, they were recognized by everyone in the club, restricting the social behavior of the group to a predetermined range of propriety. Uptown, flashy dress, designer outfits—expensive attire—was required. You could be refused admission if improperly dressed. The finer the attire, the more prestige a patron brought to the club.[1] The rules regarding proper attire at Le Boogie Woogie were not scribbled on the door outside but were unwritten and enforced at the discretion of the door guard. Unless a member was well connected, anyone could be barred from entry, but it was more likely nonmembers who were refused admission. Le Boogie Woogie charged a hundred-dollar membership fee, paid in quarterly installments. Members' names were placed on a list, which was held by the manager, though most members were known by sight. Members typically had street names, and many preferred that their street names instead of their given names be placed on the list to avoid police attention in the case of a raid.

Adventure was at the heart of the cocaine user's lifestyle. There were regulars in the nightlife scene who were not risk takers or thrill seekers, in the sense implied here. People who were part of the night underworld but were not taking a "chance" were considered artists. They possessed some of the same qualities as the "players." They made their money through wit, skill, and guile, and often at personal risk. Street-hustling artist types possessed less flamboyance than players; their ranks included the professional shoplifters (boosters), pickpockets (dippers), and con artists (stuff players). For instance, Dexter was a short, stocky man with a gap tooth and a mischievous look on his face. He went to after-hours clubs for one reason.

> I went to the spot to rob people. I didn't go there to have fun, although I would hang out with the ladies and all of that, but I was basically there to rob, and I had a method where I would rob the one-arm bandit [the slot machine] because I had a little button on the back of those machines that I would press and would hit the jackpot and 777 or what have you would come out and bingo, the cash would flow, but one day I got caught and was damn near killed. But I'll tell you about that at another time. I got caught. But keep in mind when I went there I went to rob.

Hustlers like Dexter were out there to "get over." The dealer was out there getting paid by selling his product, the ho was out to get a trick, the night bandit could be a pickpocket, a stick-up artist, or "sneak freak" (burglar).

At Le Boogie Woogie there was a feeling of community, a sense that sniffing cocaine as an activity was part of the patron's everyday life. I saw a clear pattern in the interaction, the act of physically coming to the club every night to snort, greet, complain, and laugh with people one knew or at least with whom one felt some camaraderie. One of the employees noted that John, a regular, "comes to one particular spot every night. He never misses a night. It's just like his second home."[2]

Some things people can't do in polite society were taken for granted in the after-hours environment. People would openly snort cocaine, smoke marijuana, opium, hashish, or angel dust. They would share cocaine with others, pay for others' drinks, or eat someone else's food. They would seek sexual favors from the dancers, barmaids, and others. They would buy cocaine or marijuana from management or the dealers. But there were limits. "What people don't want is drama." Angela explains, seated on the sofa's edge: "I mean what I don't want is drama." I note her freckled dimples in the light and her attractive braids.

> You have to understand something, because when a nigger is all zooted up it don't take too much to get him all excited; a smile, a wink, a brush up is all it takes. You see, I didn't like some of the bitches in this spot because they be all about drama, you know what I mean? Pure drama, and I didn't want to deal with too much drama. I just go to one or two places in the neighborhood that be drama free. You hear what I'm saying? That's because in my neighborhood . . . you know, what's that word when you afraid to go outside, you know afraid to go to certain places? Agorata? Something like that kinda places. Well, I don't go to places where there's too much drama. You should have a word for that. Places where there is too much drama.

Though Angela saw no need for drama in her interactions, there were other behaviors that were frowned upon at Le Boogie

Woogie. Patrons were not to carry weapons, sit on the tables, lean on the dancer's platform, be on the nod (high on heroin), engage in sexual intercourse (except in specially arranged situations and spaces or rooms), or engage in physical fights. I saw the after-hours regular as the quintessential embodiment of street values: sexual, independent, reckless in character and behavior, masculine, and courageous enough to tell you to your face what he or she thought.

BYRON HALL AND THE BACK OF THE TRACKS

The devil himself lights the lamps only so as to show everything not as it really looks.

—Gogol

Today, so far as I know, there are few after-hours clubs where young musicians can learn through apprenticeship as older musicians once did. What the club lost for the musician, it kept for the street hustler. Byron Hall, a Yoruba enthusiast, wore a kufi, a small white cap, to cover part of his head. He was a twenty-nine-year-old painter when I met him; he had a small dimple in his left cheek, which he touched when he smiled. He frequented after-hours clubs regularly. His father owned one back in the 1940s. Where do street people who become successful through illegal means display their wealth? Hall described the after-hours club as a "showplace" for street people with money. The after-hours club remained an institution for the "fast-money players," those who may be successful for a night or a month. Byron revealed how after-hours clubs bred "nighttime people," the types who became Le Boogie Woogie regulars.

After-hours clubs were and remained diversified in their offerings. Some continued in the cocaine, marijuana, and female sex-worker tradition; others maintained a noncocaine, male-prostitute orientation. At the time of this research, jazz was (and still is) mostly absent from the clubs. Hall recounted how his father's club followed in the tradition of the Storyville neighborhood of New Orleans, where local singers could get their start:

> My pops had a joint called Back of the Tracks, that was located down by the railroad tracks, the old Penn rail lines. That's where the sho-nuff, sho-nuff was happening. People used to come in there—blues singers, jazz players, hustlers. People used to play music, sing and dance. But in your big after-hours joints, you had big-time entertainers, people like Billie [Holiday] and stuff. But you know, every area had its singers. Even Nancy Wilson. She started out in Ohio, but she came to the Bronx and worked in an after-hours club under the name Baby Doll. That's the way she started. She later had a show on TV and was one of the first Black singers to do that. [Thelonious] Monk played in my pop's place too, because he lived up there in the sixties at San Juan Hill. Billie, too. Monk and my father grew up together. Miles [Davis] hung out in an after-hours spot over there on 100th Street wearing a raincoat with a big star on the back, when he was in that exile period from his music. But I'm getting ahead of myself. I wanna tell you about way back in the day. Yeah, you know, so that after-hours had their own entertainment. But my pops and Monk would get all smoked up and stuff. Of course, you'd have to pay for all that. Like, in my pop's place, if they had a gig, a set, with dancing and stuff, then you had to pay to get in. Other nights, it was just like you had to know somebody. That kind of thing. To get in, dig? That's how it worked. You had to dig it to know how it

> got dug. You dig? If you knew so-and-so, then boom, you were in. Besides just the booze, the coke, the smoke and stuff, there would be gambling games going on in there too. And, of course, you had the girls working there. The working girls. This was like their base. They would come on down and they would get a trick and go upstairs or somewhere. All of this was going on, and pops gets a percentage. Because they got protection and rooms. Plus, board. All that.

Thin and freckle faced, Hall wore a dark shirt and black trousers, his small goatee on a frail face with big eyes, his smile bright and intelligent, especially when he spoke about the subjects he enjoyed. His Japanese girlfriend, a university student, sat beside him as if coaching him along. I noticed a pair of crutches next to her, but apparently they belonged to him. He said he had sickle-cell anemia but didn't show signs of illness, though I wouldn't exactly know what to look for. He continued talking, occasionally sniffing cocaine from a dollar bill he had tucked in his palm:

> Every night, my pops and his brothers had to throw somebody out. Him and his brother be everything: manager, bodyguard, bouncer. Somebody would shoot up the joint every Friday night. Everybody got rowdy with all the booze. Yeah, booze was for everybody, but the coke was for the pimps, you know, the people who had the bread. Coke was more expensive than smoke. Even smack [heroin] didn't come on the scene for a long time. The first thing that was on the streets was morphine. Then all the smoke, then coke, then heroin, [heroin] doogie, the "shit" [heroin] came on the streets. But coke was reserved for the so-called upper-class negro Black folk. And everybody else was drinking that moonshine. They also sold clothes and had the numbers in there. See,

> my pops worked in the garment district. And he be swagging clothes on the side. Dig it? And they had something hooked up that if you just tell them what you want, the size, color, what have you, they'd order it, snatch it, and cop it. Like they were running a tailor shop. So, they had that going, and they had the after-hours joint where they be going with the booze, you know, the coke, the smoke, you know. And they be cooking dinners, pig-feet dinners, Southern-fried-chicken dinners, you know. You can just get a platter of any kind of dish you want. Dig? You remember when Billie was singing, "Give me some of that pig feet and a bottle of beer?" That's where that comes from. From the after-hours joint. Give me a pig foot and a bottle of beer. Pig-foot platter, you dig? You get your pig feet, black-eyed peas, potato salad. You dig it? And a bottle of beer. You could eat, drink, sleep, you could stay there all night and the next day if you wanted to. Because this was the street, man. You know the cat who's running the after-hours joint is the dude with the same kind of mentality as the pimp.

He passed the cocaine to his girlfriend, who politely sniffed a bit, then gave it back. A man walked over and asked her to dance, but she refused. Byron then stepped to the men's room and passed us again as he headed to the bar. When he returned with a glass of wine, his tone was more animated, but he stuck to the subject. "There's a more organized element to street culture," he says.

> All the people that I would relate to would be street people. The after-hours joints, I mean, served a lot of purposes. It was one of the best places, sometimes the only places, you could get a meal after a certain hour and the food would be really good. I mean the pig feet and rice was really good, you know. And it wasn't that

> expensive. And if you had some bread to gamble, it was one of the best places to go to. It was even better than the alley and other gambling joints. You get a better deal, you know. If you were going to get a knife in your back, that's quick and can happen there too. Don't misunderstand me. But you see, God don't like no ugly no matter where it taking place. You got to cool yourself, now. But for the most part the after-hours was a pretty cool spot because you got nowhere to run, nowhere to hide if you sending bad vibes. You dig what I'm saying, you understand? All this is going down. More organized. So that the after-hours was the place everything happened. And especially for people that were entertainers and pimps, this was their showcase. This is where they could show off. The entertainers would come to the after-hours after their gigs and they'd be up all night, playing some more. Jamming. It was showcase. You know, the after-hours was full of night-time people. And this is the kind of crowd they be pulling.

This part of Byron's talk was not about making things simple but about making the situation real as it existed at the time. The use of slang terms like "talking shit" is purposely old-school because that was how people talked at the club at the time (although people do still use this expression today).

One of the enduring qualities of Le Boogie Woogie was language, its nuance, and the way people spoke at the moment when no one was around but Black folk. There is a beauty in the way people spoke, especially those with Southern drawls so thick you could cut them with a knife. It's a special kind of poetry. Byron noted: "As a matter of fact them motherfuckers was so bad back then the motherfucker would kill you on Saturday night and come the next Saturday and kill you again." This was the Black folk talk I heard growing up in Mississippi. It was considered bad English by certain middle-class-minded folk who wanted to "ape their betters," but it was the way the language was spoken. And the after-hours club was a place where cursing, loud talking, joke cracking, and bullshitting was the norm. It was a style of artistic expression characteristic of a medium like jazz or blues. It was, after all is said and done, still all about what Ellison called "the idiom." Idiom was our kind of time.

Talk in the club was often laced with laughter, good humor, political and social conversation, discussions about current events, women, sex, drugs, and any and all sundry topics of the day. Tall Sam was a bearded but bald man of about forty. He was sitting at the bar conversing with the barmaid when two other patrons entered the scene. Sam passed cocaine to the barmaid, who took a few quick sniffs. She handed it back to Sam. He took a sniff, then said, "I just left Patrick, and he said he saw a pussy yesterday as wide as one of them tall ships." Everyone laughed. He continued, "That dude reminded me of a joke a cat told me in the joint [jail] one year." The barmaid chuckled, and the other two men sniffed the cocaine and laughed along. "What did he say, Sam?" one asked, and the other said, "Go ahead, man, run it down."

> Well, he was with this chick and they had a few drinks and then they decided to get in bed. The bitch takes off her clothes and the cat takes off his. He decided like most men do to first warm her up, you know, fingering the lower part of her vagina and the clitoris. You know. So, he puts one finger in, and then two, and then three, and goddamn, before he knows it, he got his whole fist and wrist in there. So, the cat don't think nothing is wrong too tough yet cause he's seen some big pussies before anyway, you know. So, he decides to crawl up in there. Well, he gets in there, he gets lost, and runs into another dude walking around with his head

> down as if he lost something. So, the first cat says to the second, "Hey, man what you lookin' for?" and the cat says, "I'm just trying to find my keys, so I can drive outta this motherfucker."

Everybody cracked up—a few people down the aisle were rolling. Tall Sam rubbed his bald head, tilted it slightly back, and took another sniff. The use of profanity and language of a sexual nature was commonplace within the club setting. Management and personnel were not the enforcers of rules relating to language. They were often heard using the rather spicy language themselves. Occasionally, a regular would say to another, "Be cool, there's a lady present," and a woman would tell her male friend to lower his voice and not curse so loud, but these were rare instances.

Speaking loudly, "talking loud," was another taken-for-granted feature of Le Boogie Woogie behavior by patrons.[3] As the club wound down one night, a tall, dark man dressed in white pants, a white jacket, a white hat, and white shoes kept repeating to a young woman he was escorting, "All my bitches go straight to the window at the bank, huh." I noticed the ring on the woman's finger. He was talking loud. It looked alive. I knew him to be a pimp who had recently surfaced from the call-girl business, which was the most highly organized and sophisticated kind of prostitution. It was the kind of prostitution that went on in private places, where "tricks" were turned for fifty to one hundred dollars and up. Whatever triggered this man's outburst was unclear, but the intentions were obviously to embarrass the woman, and he succeeded in doing this. His tone was louder than everyone else's. Loud talking existed among some patrons "on a regular" in the club. The drug facilitates loud talking.

Henry, Tall Sam, and Jody, three regulars, were seated around the lower part of the bar area. The bar was quiet. The jukebox was out for repairs. Jody and Sam were talking about how a police officer had killed a Black kid in Queens, and they discussed the possibility of his getting convicted. When John (called "Snake") came in, the conversation switched to sports. Snake opened a bill (with cocaine), and within a few minutes they were all arguing vociferously about whether the heavyweight champion of the world was going to win his next fight. In the bar, it was customary to hear patrons engaged in verbal exchanges that were simply "talkin' shit" or "bull shittin'."[4] Talkin' shit involved a range of emotive communicating, from feelings of affection to hostility and contempt. Men were often seen talkin' shit before any interesting women arrived, for example, and talkin' more shit once they got there. To talk shit was to exaggerate for the sake of the group interaction, to further the conversation along. The talker was not held accountable for such talk because it was framed within an unserious time. This type of talk between patrons was usually full of wishful thinking. "Man, I'm gonna get me and I woulda . . ." or "you know what I shoulda got . . ." or "I coulda done so-'n'-so." These were common openings for such talk and were referred to as *woulda, shoulda, coulda* conversations, where the person was either totally bullshitting or pretending to be. Patrons often recognized that they may be guilty of "talkin' shit," explaining themselves with statements such as "Yo, you know I was just talkin' shit, you didn't have to take that for real. Anyway, Sammy knew I was bullshittin' from jump street." But more often, the other members of the scene would quickly acknowledge the person was just talkin' shit. In other words, the person was not to be taken seriously by anyone.

Women were not exempt from talkin' shit. Take the talk from one of the recently hired barmaids. She was talking about the people who showed up in the club and the comments barmaids and others made about people unlike themselves. "Everybody wants someone else to be different. I don't like the Arab cause his nose is too long. I don't like the Black because his skin is too dark. I don't like the Chinese because his eyes are too slanty. I don't like the fat one, so they should be skinny. I don't like the short one, they should be tall. Everybody wants someone else to be different. Just leave folk the fuck alone and be yourself."

It was said by patrons that "cokeheads" talked much more "shit" when they were high than when they were not. They were the first to realize how too much cocaine could result in a specific type of talk, referred to as "coke talk." One listening to a patron who has ingested too much cocaine needed not take the substance of the excessive snorter's talk seriously. In other words, the listener needed not hold the person to their word. The "coke talk" aided in concealing identities, and a general ignorance of others' biographies aided in this type of social intercourse. Vagueness was a virtue, since the action was between strangers whose commitments to one another beyond that night was never assured.

One thing that could cause a voluble altercation was spilling someone's cocaine. Although seldom done intentionally, occasionally the patron was confronted with this situation. The upper and lower sections of the Le Boogie Woogie club were often crowded. One of the patrons once said, "It's wall-to-wall people in here, man." In one instance there was at least twice the normal crowd packed in to celebrate a new barmaid's birthday. Around the side tables near the men's room, several men and women were standing, resting on the jukebox. Two women were seated tightly against the cigarette machine, one holding cocaine and about to pass it to the other, when one of the men lifted his arm off the cigarette machine, hit the woman's arm, and the cocaine powder spilled onto the carpet. She looked up in disbelief and said, "Motherfucker, what is the matter with you! Do you know what you just wasted? A hundred dollars of the best high in town!" The man said something inaudibly, and the other woman started to explain that it was an accident. The woman who lost the cocaine continued berating the man and didn't stop until the man offered to pay her for the loss. Cocaine spilling was a rare occurrence, but it did happen. A rowdy patron was occasionally escorted out, but this was rare, too. Gunplay was also unusual, since most people were searched before entering. But if this were to happen, the only protocol was to have the person escorted out. Management accepted only normal trouble. Any regular who started trouble jeopardized himself and every person present, since after-hours clubs were and are illegal. The most common forms of normal trouble I observed were arguments, pushing and shoving, and abusing the furniture (putting cigarettes out on lounge sofas), behavior permissible in the clubs that normally would not be in other settings. All of these issues occurred alongside loud talking. Sometimes, cocaine was offered to appease the antagonists. Unlike other subcultures, where talking simultaneously was part of the norm, club culture allowed for pauses between speakers and hearers. The loud talker, however, took advantage of this pause and continued without interruption until his or her point was made.

SOCIAL ORDER AND SENSIBILITY

Managing an illegal business involves risk, money, and a bit of luck. The time given to the various tasks was exhaustive, compounded by the existential threat of the business getting raided at any moment. Owners of illegal after-hours clubs hoped election years would not bring new "law-and-order" crusades against drugs, gambling, or prostitution. As far as fire codes went, inspectors were obviously paid off. To maintain order at Le Boogie Woogie, some workers were legally employed, including a doorman (who frisks patrons), a cashier (money taker), an armed guard, a manager, barmaids, and several "house girls." How they were hired was different from most legitimate businesses. Frenchy—the owner of Le Boogie Woogie—recruited "tough guys" from the neighborhood or ex-prisoners. This was one of the few places where a prison résumé got you a job when no other business would hire.[5]

One of Frenchy's door guards was Jason, a big, heavyset man with several front teeth missing. He had a habit of continually looking behind him as he talked, and he did not like people patting him on his shoulder. He got annoyed whenever anyone did that. One night I asked him why, and he said it was something that he picked up in the joint. I didn't push him to explain what he meant and never found out why, but one could guess. I spoke to him several times during a slow night. He admitted to being a thief but also said he'd robbed one club too many and didn't do that kind of work anymore. I wasn't sure why he confided in me when he told me how he got one of his jobs:

> I was caught stealing from one of the slot machines, this was a spot on 113th Street called Grants. You got to understand that all them spots had gambling rooms in the back, snorting, lots of girls, and such. Now, you know the joker machines, well, I had a way of pushing a button on the back of the machines to get the money to come out, and my buddy and I discovered this by accident and it came out 777. So, I started doing that in all the machines in the joints. Anyway, I got caught, and the boss held a gun to my head and I didn't flinch and after slapping me around because I wouldn't tell him how I did that little trick with the machines, he later told me I had guts and asked if I wanted a job.

> He said all I had to do was sit in the game room and collect the tickets and he would give me five hundred a week. And that's how I got that job.

Barmaids came from the street, other bars, and clubs. Dancers were from nearby topless bars and clubs, but a few came from the neighborhood. Underage girls were recruited from sources including known pimps. The local public housing projects were mentioned as a recruiting location, but I was not certain of the truth of this or how it would have happened. The "girls" were paid in cash and, depending on the night, received hundreds of dollars per night in tips. Some of the dancers were undocumented and thus unlikely to go to the police should they become unhappy with the terms of their employment. Dancers were not regular employees because they were usually hired for one night or on a contingency basis. A dancer might become a regular employee if she took on the duties of the "house girl," working strictly for tips rather than a flat fee of about fifty dollars for her dancing.

Former inmates were often employed as bouncers. They were responsible for inspecting individuals who frequented the club as they entered. They were acquainted with every member and their guests. The door guard's role was to answer the door each time the bell rang, indicating a new arrival. Bouncers might sniff cocaine discreetly but were generally not to be seen taking drugs or drinking alcohol. Door guards were often armed and unfriendly. They interacted very little with the patrons and were at the ready in case of trouble. A guard told me:

> I worked at a place called the Yacht Club off Convent Avenue for six months right after I got out of the joint. I knew Frenchy and Preacher and they got me the gig. Nothing really jumped off until

> the pimps showed on the scene, and then money flowed. I caught motherfuckers coming in one time with a loaded nine [millimeter] he tried to conceal in his girl's purse. And I got knives off motherfuckers too, but for the most part my job was easy. Pimps would give me hundred-dollar bills as tips, and women would offer titties, pussy whatever to get in or to meet certain cats. My job was boring most of the time until I met a freak who wanted me to search her repeatedly. You know, shit like that.

The bouncer's encounters with patrons were usually brief and stern but cordial. He was one of the few people at the club known to be armed. He searched men and women (usually their purse and bag but not their person) and would inform people of any special events taking place inside.

Management offered customers entertainments such as gambling, music, and prostitution, though none would admit to this last one. Gambling at after-hours clubs was often found set away from the regular patrons; at Le Boogie Woogie, however, because of limited space, the gambling table was in the main room of the club. Anyone could participate if they had enough money. Patrons did not come and go as they pleased, and in some cases, once a patron left, he or she could not reenter. The managers discouraged patrons from leaving by informing them of this rule as they were leaving. The drugs sold were used solely on the premises; in that way Le Boogie Woogie functioned as a private cocaine dealer to its clientele. A final staff character whose job was to maintain order was the house man. He was the individual responsible for making people feel comfortable while ensuring their obedience to the house rules. He offered to buy people drinks or cocaine as a form of social etiquette and worked with the owner to make sure customers had no complaints. I queried the manager about his attitude toward the club's employees. He said, "First of all, this is a business, man; I'm here to see that my workers do their job. If they have fun, I don't know about it. They are here to work any way you look at it. As for the folk that come here, they can do anything they wanna do as long as they don't hurt nobody or bother other people."

An employee at Le Boogie Woogie mentioned how the "working" people (a regular, nonhustling worker) enhanced the prestige of the place and bestowed it with respectability. The employee noted how whites and middle-class Blacks gave the place "class." This employee got tired of "them street folk, ghetto niggers, talking loud and cursing and acting a fool." But when I asked the owner what types of people run after-hours clubs in this city and who supports them, he replied:

> Everybody does things a little differently. I know cats who don't have nobody coming in their places except "carriers" [people who bring in drugs], and when a big deal is made, they may all party and bring a few friends along. But the place ain't for no pleasure thang like others are. I know a bunch of bartenders, hotel waitresses, and they all go to special clubs just for them types. Then there are other spots, gambling, poker, and CeeLo joints. These places sometimes let a few outsiders in and sometimes they don't. As for who owns them, if you speaking about my personal knowledge—I know about some and heard about others. A lot of them dagos [Italians] have 'em in East Harlem, the Bronx, Brooklyn, all over. Puerto Ricans have a bunch of places, too. And Blacks own 'em here [the Bronx] and Harlem. A lot of dudes be fronting for the mob. But basically—hustlers run 'em, and they really are for hustlers, too.

Club ownership was racially diverse but hustler specific. You had to be a hustler to run such a place. But their function was not limited to a "party" category. After-hours clubs existed and likely still exist for all kinds of business reasons.[6] Regardless of style, club owners expected first and foremost to make money, and they believed the economic truism that the higher the risk, the greater the reward. Frenchy sold house coke at the club, but he really was a street dealer of heroin and cocaine. He was a man after money, an entrepreneur who expected to make it rich. As far as I know, this never came to pass. If Le Boogie Woogie was a front, Frenchy took an even greater risk than was immediately evident. He certainly didn't act like an owner. He was low-key and never seemed to be particularly involved in the operation. There was no overt bookkeeping or cash management or that sort of thing. Some patrons knew who he was, of course, but he affected a distant relationship between him and the club. Regardless, club ownership wasn't a long-term occupation. They did not remain in business very long, in part because of financial insolvency and a lack of consistent clientele, risks faced by many types of service businesses—but now add to that an expectation of repeated robberies or police raids. Such problems notwithstanding, some clubs survived the years. Frenchy provided both a description of one such club and why it continued in business:

> Six years—you know that's a helluva long time for a spot to stay open because they go and come every day. The police don't always have anything to do with it. Sometimes, yeah, and sometimes, no. Anyway, if a spot is too disruptive in the community, I don't care how many cops are on the pad [taking bribes], the cops will close it down. If it's a mafia place, it may take longer to shut it [down], but it will be shut too if the noise [from the community] is loud enough and directed to the correct ears in the government. Did I tell ya 'bout Griffin? Everybody, everybody on the street, that is, called him Sneeze because he would take so much coke,

> he would be sneezing all the time. Anyway, Griffin was a two-time loser who had a reputation of being a snake in the grass, a real scumbag at one time, mainly the years on the streets as a junkie. When he didn't have that shit in his arm, he would rob his mother's grave. Shoot, to kill. You know. Well, recently, he had fallen on hard times, and he and his woman went into Jo Jo's place [an after-hours club] and robbed everybody. But the mistake he made was to shoot a dude who some say shouldn't have moved. Tried anyway to be a hero, and Griffin shot 'im in his shoulder point-blank with a sawed-off shotgun. Well, what Griffin didn't know was that Jo Jo's was incorporated [it belonged to a group of businessmen, hustlers, and other associated people]. Well, Griffin hid out for about a week, and while he was sitting at a bar on the Lower East Side, he was hit [killed] right behind the head. The only reason his woman didn't get it was because she wasn't with him.

Frenchy attributes longevity to collectivity. Those businesses that protected one another by offering mutual support, bribing the police, and issuing violent reprisals against those who trespassed and violated the club's space were apparently more likely to survive than those not employing such methods.

Although the owner was a facilitator of forbidden pleasures, he was not above criticism. The patrons questioned, critiqued, and challenged the owner's ability to function as owner. The behavior of the owner was scrutinized by patrons, and just as owners had rules by which patrons and employees must abide, the patrons had ideals and norms that the owner must adhere to—or, at least, that he should have to be aware of. Patrons, for example, felt owners should not indulge in excessive drinking or snorting in their presence. They were more likely to respect the owner if he went about the business of checking on any problems and the overall operations of the place. A patron who had frequented many clubs echoed this sentiment:

> Latin owners are a lot rowdier and more physical in their clubs. If a dude gets out of line, the owners are more likely to try and throw him out. They also get high and drink a lot. They are generally not too cool. I know this black dude who runs a spot uptown. Even though I know he snorts and gets high, I've never seen him take a blow in that place from nobody. He's there looking after the place, taking care of business, and if there is any trouble, he's in a position to handle it. In most of the Black-owned clubs, the owners tend to be much more businesslike than the Latin owners.

This attitude may have been a racially prejudiced account and emblematic of a preference for one ethnicity over another rather than a serious assessment of who was more or less business oriented and responsible. There is little evidence to support any particular ethnicity as possessing any unique business qualities over others. The use of drugs on the premises, for example, was a rather poor criteria for such judgments and was as much a matter of personal taste as it was patron pressure. But race or ethnicity played another role outside the doors of the club.

For the small business in New York City, a lot of power resides in the hands of the local community, be it the corner-store owner, the bar owner, or the residents in the nearby apartment buildings. Whereas the patron will, in most situations, tolerate a club owner's drug use as a personal preference, the community might not. A patron told me about a Latino after-hours club located in Upper Manhattan, north of Harlem. Puerto Ricans, Colombians, Cubans, Dominicans, and African Americans made up the area's population. Columbia Presbyterian Hospital, the George

Washington Bridge, a Port Authority bus station, and major historical buildings like Jumel Mansion give the area a sense of real New York. The new migration of mostly West Indians, Dominicans, Cubans, and Puerto Ricans are evidence of the cultural diversity in this area. At this club, situated in the basement of a mostly Latinx-tenant building, no more than twenty-five people could fit comfortably, although most weekends as many as a hundred people might have been in there at one time. The place had the problems all after-hours clubs seemed to face in this community. During the week of the club's opening, a member of a small gang of Black teenagers threatened to close the place down because it was "one of them all-night joints that would bring drugs to the community." The club was adjacent to Thompson's Garage and posed problems for its manager. Cars were always blocking the driveway. One mechanic, when asked what effect the new club had on his business, replied:

> That place should be closed down right now, if you wanna know the truth about it. One night, a guy pulled a gun on me because I told him he had to move his car from the driveway. Look—there's a sign right there which says, "Please don't park in the driveway." I need to be able to get the cars out when the customers want 'em. As it turns out, the guy couldn't read English. Well, that's not my fault, he ought to go back where he came from. This is America; if you can't read English then go back to school somewhere. This place has fights all the time, too. I've heard gunshots go off in there. Sometimes, on weekends, you won't believe this, but cars are double-parked all the way down the block. This is a long block, too. I've even called the police—but they don't seem to want to do anything until something happens in the act.

These sentiments covered a range of problems associated with after-hours clubs and their effects on the community, but not all of them. Among the most common that I encountered was loud noise, boisterous behavior, arguments, illegal parking, honking horns, and open drug use.

OVERINDULGENCE

They say cokin' is bad / They say it's a sin / They say cocaine will kill ya / But they didn't say when.

—Luke Jordan, "Cocaine Blues"

Overindulging in other people's cocaine at Le Boogie Woogie was never acceptable. Patrons were never permitted to snatch other people's cocaine, or drop it, or mess with it in any way. But still there were those sniffers who would exploit the norm of sharing among drug users. Overindulgence defines the outer limit of the cocaine subculture, and snorters would continue to take "blows" until they either reached a saturation point—for which one must have either a great deal of cocaine or a very powerful product—or until the cocaine ran out, whichever occurred first. In situations where cocaine is the primary source of pleasure, there was always a person or persons, be they sniffers, smokers, or shooters, whose desire for cocaine exceeded the boundaries of good taste. Angela was a heavy sniffer, and you could tell when she was high. Her face was inscrutable, but her eyes were wide open and got wider every time a door opened or someone moved toward the bathroom. She would rub her eyes incessantly after she snorted. This was a "tell." When she was very high, she rubbed her eyes and the left part of her face constantly. People in a club who snort cocaine had a defined, mutual understanding that regulates its use. When Angela approached a table at which sniffers were sitting and was offered cocaine, she would naturally sniff some. But when she took it upon herself to continue sniffing, it violated the norm. Miguel, with a bolo hat on his big head, laughed at odd times, or I should say, he laughed when no one thought what was being said was funny. He was a regular at the Le Boogie Woogie and commented on what he referred to as "vacuum-cleaner snorters": "Some people come to the [after-hours] club just to get free cocaine. Some of the ladies here—they snort and snort without ever asking me if they can have more." He laughs. "They just try and clean me out." Other people laugh but he doesn't. "That's why I only put out a little bit at a time." He laughs again. "But I won't tell her she can't have any more, because you just don't do that here." It is important to note that in the sniffing culture, one must have either been offered the sniff every time or at least ask permission to snort. A patron at another club noted:

> If somebody just sniffs my coke or a friend's coke without buying any or offering to buy some themselves, then it doesn't take long for everybody to ignore them. They just won't be offered no more coke by nobody from then on. You know, I'm funny about snorting other folks' coke. If a cat say, "Here, man, take a blow," I'll take a one and one, but that's it. Now if I ain't got no money, I won't take but a one and one. If he insists, I'll take another blow. But then I'll ask if he has any to sell. If he says no, I'll just put five or ten dollars down on the table and say, "Thanks, Man, that was beautiful," because if the shoe was on the other foot, I would want him to do the same.

These two patrons had different perspectives on the cocaine-snorting norm. Miguel at Le Boogie Woogie didn't wish to inform the woman sniffer of her lack of discretion because he felt it would be improper. The other patron felt he would be taking advantage of the situation if he did not reciprocate in some way. Although we are considering norms in general, it is the gender of the sniffer on the one hand and the variation in cocaine ethics on the other that partially explain the different attitudes toward overindulgence. In the case of the second patron, the physical size of the club played a significant role. That club, near 115th Street in central Harlem, was very small. It held about twenty-five or thirty people, most of whom knew one another from working for the Department of Sanitation. Because the patrons there were friends, the person who violated the cocaine-sniffing rules there was immediately "told off" by everyone because they could see the violation clearly. In Miguel's case, Le Boogie Woogie was much larger, and the rules were not quite as enforceable.

Regardless of the location, women's distasteful actions were more tolerated because their presence was sought after in the club. Women could sit with one patron and sniff cocaine until the supply was depleted. She could then move on to another table where there was additional cocaine. Miguel would not have hesitated to restrict, question, or simply withdraw were it a man breaking the norm in this way. The second patron expressed the expected sniffing behavior among men. Behavior also differed from club to club. Sniffers would strictly adhere to the cocaine norm in the club they were in so as not to damage their reputation in the wider club culture. They, of course, did not wish to endanger either their ego or status position.

At Le Boogie Woogie every person in the place deserved respect no matter who they were, and that's why patrons wouldn't hit on anybody, talk to anybody, or just say whatever they wanted to anybody. Even those who came in with status wrapped all around them, who might be doctors, lawyers, or big shots outside the place, when they came inside, they were just another person. This aspect of the culture had a great deal to do with the respect that patrons had for the club. The club management expected this respect from its patrons. In Le Boogie Woogie, where Miguel was a regular, it was expected that he not become upset if a woman took too much of his cocaine. He was expected to remain "cool" and not become belligerent. On the other hand, the second patron, because of the nature of his club, its clientele, and his own reputation, may be expected to react differently. He might have shouted at the person for overindulging and creating a scene. His reputation remained intact because he had proven once again that he would not allow anyone, whether man or woman, to take advantage of him. These variations of the cocaine-sniffing norm were not as contradictory. They were just variations within the subculture.

At Le Boogie Woogie, offering cocaine to others was done both verbally—"have a blow," "take a hit"—and nonverbally, where the user simply passed the cocaine to the other person by holding out the "package" to the person. Someone in a closed group refusing once may be offered cocaine again in each round of passing. But in an individual offer—person to person—he or she may not be given another chance. Rarely was a person offered cocaine twice having once refused. A man may have offered a woman a few chances to sniff, but men did not generally offer other men more than once or twice after a refusal. Near the bar area, passing cocaine was restricted to a few close regulars near the person offering, usually no more than four or five people.[7]

The act of standing and holding cocaine involves a bit of dexterity, risking spillage. When holding the cocaine in a small piece of foil or, more precarious yet, a dollar bill, all one needs is a steady hand. Snorting was done sitting until the user felt the urge to dance or stand. I rarely saw anyone spill a package, even while walking and snorting the stuff. I assume the reason is, in part, because of its special value, but even those who could

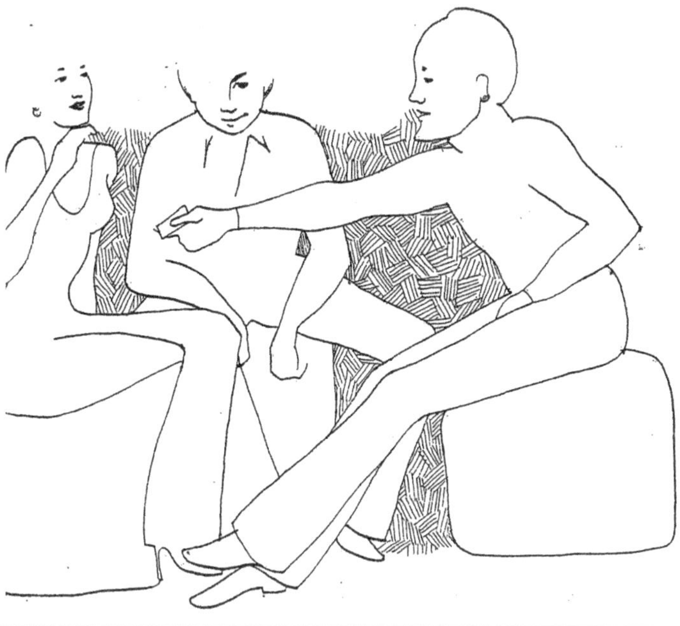

FIGURE 2.1 Cocaine-sharing ritual: Three snorter/habitués sharing cocaine.

easily afford the drug rarely seemed to lose control of it. It was as if it was bad luck or taboo to spill any. One young woman accidentally spilled some and smiled at the man, as if to make up for the indiscretion. “If you don’t have enough, it’s just like being broke,” the dark-haired woman whispered to the man sitting next to her, “but I gave her a look that said I wanted to wipe that smile off her face.” She seemed more annoyed than the man who got his coke spilled. Cocaine was a form of social currency more important than money. You needed the coke to get high; if you’re out of coke, you can’t get high on money. Having no cocaine put the player, the patron, at a decided social disadvantage. If you had cocaine, giving it to others was a normal

FIGURE 2.2 Cocaine-sharing ritual: snorter/habitué.

way to act and was a standard form of behavior. This very basic ritual served a primary purpose. It brought people together. It enhanced the action, it smoothed out arguments, it repaid debts for drinks or marijuana offered, it introduced new friends, it intimated sexual encounters, it stimulated rapport, and it bound the regulars in a ceremonial rite. When a young woman got upset at a man who accidentally stepped on her foot without apologizing, she kept screaming at him until he looked as if he might hit her. One patron sitting opposite the table looked up

FIGURE 2.3 Cocaine-sharing ritual: a male habitué giving a woman habitué a one-'n'-one.

and said to both, "Hey, let's not fight here—take a blow, baby [referring to both], and forget about it," at which point the woman left and the man sat down and had a few "blows" of the offered cocaine.

The barmaid was constantly offered cocaine to sniff and indulged continuously all night. If she did not like the taste of one person's cocaine, she might refuse to accept. If she liked another patron's cocaine, it might be difficult to keep her away.

Not all cocaine offered was high quality, and she had ample opportunity to choose ones to her liking. When Dana was asked if she sniffed all night, her reply was:

> Each night is different, it varies. Some people give me cocaine because they like me. Others because they want to impress me. When you ask me about what my man feels about all this, I say to you which one? Every man that comes in here is my man. Some men will give me coke like a tip, but, listen, I prefer the money. I can always get a blow. Like I said, every night is different. Some nights you get a lotta coke offered, and some nights you don't get any. I tell a motherfucker don't try to play me, play lotto.

Snorters who were in the passing ritual seated around the floor would literally pass the cocaine to anyone present. But as the crowd got larger, the game became who got the cocaine and who did not. People were often seen moving chairs and tables to accommodate additional friends. The other physical components that set the scene were light, sound, odor, temperature, the cigarette machine, the jukebox, the staircase, the lavatory, the mirrors, the bar, and the heating. They all gave order and meaning to the club experience. For instance, small leather stools were installed after people complained about the low seating. The new leather seats were easily moved around, which encouraged patrons to relocate to share drinks, cocaine, or marijuana.

The tables and chairs were set up in such a way that conversation and physical contact could go smoothly. A rectangular table, because it has two long sides and two shorter sides, is inherently directional. The longer a rectangular room, the more it will encourage visual and physical movement parallel to its long axis. A circular table is better. This design was common in the club's main room, off its long rectangular hallway. The round tables allowed each user of the drug equal access to view what the others had to give or display. This meant there was nothing hidden. Most times there were several different circles of cocaine being passed around, and men were seen giving cocaine to women and women to men, as well as men to men and women to women. Many patrons commented on how they liked this arrangement because they could see and be seen, as nothing was hidden.

But when a person was in line for a sniff and was passed over, whether deliberate or not, it was considered a serious breach of cocaine etiquette. Latin salsa music was blasting from the wall-high speakers as seventeen or more male and female regulars were sniffing cocaine almost in unison. People were scattered around in all directions, some with individual cocaine packages, others sniffing in small groups. This scene was not typical. "Do you believe the motherfucker did not give me the bag?" The speaker was looking up in disbelief, fuming, speaking to no one in particular, it seemed, yet loud enough for the person next to her to hear. "I'm sorry I didn't—" "Don't tell me you didn't see me. I've only been sitting here for the past hour-and-a-motherfucking-half." The barmaid looking on said to no one in particular, "But she's not only observing his cocaine, I bet she was also looking all the way to the cash in his pocket." Patrons did not deliberately pass over others unless it was the owner of the cocaine, who of course could use his or her discretion. In this case, the male patron may genuinely not have seen that the woman was in line to receive the drug. She was sitting with her legs facing outside the small semicircle and conversing with a friend. It was understood, however, that being skipped was a violation of the norm, and if a norm is regularly used, it becomes a significant basis for future action. When an act is condemned, its censure reestablishes the boundaries for the group.

STATUS

The dancer said soak my feet in cocaine.

Around midnight a crowd started to form near the stage, while several broad-shouldered men in leather jackets stood around a table in the back corner. A local rapper, wearing gold chains around his neck, diamond rings, and a big gold watch, entered with his bodyguards and started throwing money around, literally. He took money from his pockets as the dancers stood around him wiggling and dancing wildly, catching dollar bills as they danced. This faddish ritual is called "raining," and some hip-hop stars and other entertainers and players in the hustling business have been known to do this in bars.[8] When the women stopped dancing to grab the money, bouncers moved them away bodily and told them to get back on stage, since only dancers who kept dancing and grabbed money at the same time could continue to perform.

Anyone who came into Le Boogie Woogie had a certain amount of status just by being there, and regulars worked hard to maintain dignity while also enhancing that status. A key element in this effort was the attempt to be "cool" at all times. Dancing represented the best or all the most recognized qualities of the street: tension, élan, violence, sincerity, immediacy, pleasure, and style. This matched the patrons' social behavior as cool, calm, trickster prestidigitators. This social behavior and conversation were smooth and controlled.[9] One man was wearing a white, wide-brimmed hat, white fur coat, white leather pants, silk shirt, and white boots. The woman he escorted wore identical apparel, from hat to boots. They wore identical pinky diamond rings. He had a larger diamond ring on his middle finger in the shape of a heart, with little diamonds on the edges and a large diamond in the center. As they walked in, all eyes focused on them. A hush fell over the place. Only the jukebox seemed not to notice. Some people continued to talk as if these bejeweled "players" were not as special as everybody seemed to think they were. There were only sixteen to twenty people in the place, and everybody wondered what could top the attire these two were draped in.

About twenty minutes passed, and things settled back into normalcy. The owner and six or so others were seated at the bar. This new couple, who had remained quiet, sitting over by themselves, were drinking. The doorbell rang, and a young teenager with a black turban, black pants, and a cape came in, holding a small box four inches in width wrapped in a cloth. Again, the crowd hushed. As the tall man in white rose, he revealed beneath the cloth his personal box of cocaine, which he offered to the crowd along with a gold spoon to use for sniffing.

Patrons need not have gold and or silver spoons to sniff cocaine; as a matter of fact, it was common to see people using ordinary objects: matchbook covers called "scoops," fingernails (players grow their pinky fingernail long and paint it), plastic cards and straws, cut-off business cards, pen caps, and two fingers (the forefinger and the thumb) are all used for this purpose as well. One tended to see lower-ranking patrons, referred to as "lames," that is, those with little money, using these latter methods, but certainly not only them, since the use of creative methods to snort the drug depended on circumstances. The patrons with more access to cash had diamond-headed coke spoons or turquoise ones with gold or silver chains, worn as necklaces. In an emergency or in a situation where the regular may have forgotten to bring their diamond-studded spoons, the fingernails or the scoop were readily implemented.

Identifying a clear hierarchy at Le Boogie Woogie may not be possible, but what is clear is that at the club there is what might be called a "status situation." You understand by "status situation" the chance of certain social groups or individuals receiving positive or negative "social honor." The chances of attaining social honor are primarily determined by differences in the styles of life of the group or the person. In the outside world this can most clearly be seen with reference to differences in education—but formal education degrees were replaced in the club by street credentials, time in prison, gang ranking, mob affiliations, and street knowledge, all of which, if used adeptly, could yield some of the same rewards as a college degree. The regular (as spectator) was neither aware nor interested in the educational credentials of a patron who happens to be flush with cash and holding a baggy of cocaine in hands adorned with a diamond ring and gold watch. This was social honor, because the situation in the club, just like outside, was such that patrons linked social honor with the position the person holds in the place—they associate this honor with material display—wealth or power, for instance.[10]

This ranking process was difficult to assess because patrons were constantly shifting from one club to another. Admitting that one patron had higher status over another was made more problematic if one considered the role of "instant wealth," such as what happened in hitting the numbers or winning at cards or CeeLo, which played a significant role in the status system. These "instant-wealth" players held the same status quality as the patron who gave away plenty of cocaine every night. And although the latter got more deference and respect, should he falter in his display, he suffered a loss of status. On the other hand, the instant-money player suffered no status loss because his or her instant wealth was understood in that context, and, in addition, he or she may never be seen again.

We have arrived at some important considerations in this analysis of status at Le Boogie Woogie. First is whether the patron has an advantage over others if he has status, and second, whether the patron maintained status if he or she was inconsistent in displaying status elements.[11] The more frivolous the cost, the better it served to symbolize the buyer's ability to afford it. In this way the regular who could "waste" or give away freely thousands of dollars of an expensive drug to strangers was expressing the ultimate in status because "as an expression of status, waste is efficient." The status hierarchy as developed in Le Boogie Woogie contained the assumption that those regulars who either temporally (one night) or continuously (many weeks) displayed the status elements of money by heavy tipping, sharing cocaine, or both represented the ultimate in status opulence.

3

THE CHARACTERS

But suppose the Devil took to turning up at your elbow day after day, so that, even though you didn't want to take anything, he persisted in thrusting temptation upon you.

—Gogol, *Dead Souls*

CONCHITA AND POWER DYNAMICS

If agency is the capacity of individuals to act independently and to make their own free choices, Conchita certainly had agency. But where did that courage, that moxy, to be who she was come from? I wondered if speaking to her parents would help me gain some understanding. I made an appointment and went to her mother's place of work, which was not far from the university, to meet her. After half an hour of waiting, and just as I was about to leave, a tall, strikingly beautiful woman with large, almond-shaped eyes and hair tucked in a bun swaggered into the room. She had a commanding presence and spoke with a slight speech mannerism. A proud woman, I thought. I asked if she was Preciosa. She didn't have much time, but the brief talk we had was all about Conchita.

Conchita, she said, was a trooper, "a tough cookie," and I didn't have to worry about her because, no matter what, "she's a survivor." I wasn't altogether sure what she meant but gathered she thought I knew more about her daughter than I did. Her mother said Conchita had attended public school but never completed high school. She played piano, she said, "a little bit" and liked music but lacked discipline to be conscientious enough to do anything with her talent. She said though Conchita had taken voice, dance, and acting lessons, none of them had stuck, and she remained uncommitted to anything. Always a rebel, when she was not yet fifteen years old, she struck out for Woodstock with her hippie neighbors and their kids to become part of the 1960s counterculture, thriving on drugs, music, loose morals, and lots of fun. Her mother paid plenty of money to psychiatrists, counselors, teachers, and others to help her daughter become "sane" again. Conchita had alluded to this by saying to me: "My mother thought I was crazy, you know. She wanted to make me have some sense, but I wouldn't hear it."

A lack of interest in things, Conchita later revealed, "except sex," permeated her life. Her mother said Conchita had an office job where she was "rarely punctual but worked well once she got there." The relationship with her fellow employees was courteous, she said, but it was her mother who got her the job and who was primarily responsible for keeping her there. If Conchita had her way, "I'd be out there trying to make some real money. I know I can do that if I really try hard enough." I suspected she meant prostitution by "real money." Would she really tell me about this?

I asked Conchita to write down her thoughts, anguished moments, and feelings about her family in a little diary. In an earlier conversation with Conchita, I had used the word "diurnal," and she asked me what it meant, and in her written account she used the word because she says the people she hung out with wouldn't know what it meant—but she would.

These are snippets from her diary.

CONCHITA'S DIARY

The night is a different life, it harbors its own sounds, people, employment and entertainment. At night I feel I can be anyone I wish. Naturally there are those who maintain a daytime (diurnal)* lifestyle at night, but it's still very different. The night is more serene. You're not faced with grouchy morning people, pushing and shoving during rush hour. Not to mention the intolerable odors of perfumes, colognes, and perspiration combined and crammed into one train car or bus. 9 a.m. to 5 p.m. is not for me. I love the feeling of waking when most are ready to sleep and not being alert, having fun, when the majority are all dreaming. For me, night time is daytime, my hours are only reversed. I live the other half of the day.

My jobs are different perhaps, but still and all they're an income as much as any diurnals. I feel comfortable at night, I'm not afraid, and my mood, I find is less irritable. I seem to be able to adjust better to life at night. For instance, this piece is being written at 2 a.m. It's dark and cool, the moon is full, stars barely revealing themselves and the people mostly secluded in some bar, club or after hours, if hanging out. Nightlife has its own public; gentlemen of leisure, ladies of the night, common workers, hustlers, addicts, musicians, dancers, bisexuals, transvestites, thieves, police, warlords and on and on.

All interesting in their own way, each having a purpose or a goal. To me the night is sweet, refreshing, I trust the night and respect night people. As clean and cool as some may appear, we all work hard. Game running ain't easy! As well, survival for night people holds greater competition, risks, and grievances. As few as we may be. I hate getting up in the morning, it's not laziness, because when one thinks about it, I'm up and about just as many hours. It's more a combination of the seclusion and velvet shelter of the night; the sleazy, unique features of the night; and not having to open my eyes to a shocking sunlight every morning.

I consider night people a minority. We're the adventurers, the type that the average person fantasizes about. We can lead a double life, working during the day and hanging at night, or just be as I am. I don't *work*, I hustle and borrow, I live freely, without many responsibilities, I hangout, party. I laugh, I scream, I cry, I smile, and I fall asleep at daybreak. But with a lot of love being given me, almost all has come to pass.

Conchita revealed quite a bit of herself in the journal notes she had given me. I did not think this kind of behavior was OK, and of course this revealed my own biases as well as my fatherly attitude toward Conchita. But it certainly wasn't my job to tell her what to do; after all, she had parents.

I was taught to record what I saw, what I heard, what I sensed, what I felt, in a word, what I experienced, not be a parent to a runaway woman-child hell-bent on self-destruction. The situation with Conchita did bother me, and I asked myself on many occasions if I should intervene more or not, but I kept strictly to the ethnographer's code, remaining what Walter Wallace called a "producer of knowledge." Don't try and change the behavior of folk, just appreciate the situation.

VITAL AND JULIO

Sniffing at every risk-filled corner for a rhyme.

—Charles Baudelaire

The bullet scar over Julio's right eye cut a prominent niche in a big forehead. He had piercing eyes that never blinked and curled lips he kept pressed together most of the time. The scar was never asked about, so no one knew how he got it, apart from the fact that the bullet had nearly killed him. Vital, one of his oldest friends, found that out when Julio was high and spilled his guts, a rare occurrence. He talked about the scar that one time, then never again. But, on occasion, Vital says, "some virgin chick blurts out the question, 'What happened to your face?' and when she did, he never gives her any cocaine." Men seemed not to ask, maybe because they just knew better, or knew there was a story no man wants to tell behind such a scar, or perhaps it was just plain home training, like as kids you know not to point at people.

The scar cut into the eyebrow, splitting it like a double thought. Asking about it caused a breach, an impertinence, a felony worthy of the most vicious penalty one could mete out in the club—to be denied a sniff while everyone else got one. When the blow got around to the offender, Julio would wave his finger, and the coke would come back to him. After two or three such snubs, the person would either leave or ask, "What's up, can't I take a hit?"—and the answer would be no. Vital said Julio was the only man he ever met who could sniff cocaine with two fingers (forefinger and thumb) in a public place and get away with it.

> This is just like the Middle Ages where you'd see royalty taking a pinch of snuff between their fingers. Anyway, he'd be in a

> restaurant, at the bar or table and he'd take out this baggie while everyone is having a drink and would pinch two fingers and take a sniff with one gesture bring it up to his nose and then immediately point outward as if pointing to someone in the room and with the same hand wipe any residue off his nose. It was so bold a move it would send laughter around the table; he'd insist others do the same.

Julio, a medium-height Dominican, was a very nervous guy. He was also the first patron I saw use a matchbook cover to sniff cocaine. He would take a matchbook, tear off the top part or half of it, bend it into a V-shape, and snort with gusto. He also never used lines; he felt, as did others, that lines were college white-boy stuff. It was more than square; it was octagonal. It was too mechanical and corporate. Plus, doing lines suggested a democratic thing, that all share equally, and cocaine sniffing was not about being democratic. It was about self-aggrandizement, self-promotion, largesse, and individual ego tripping. Nothing more exemplified this than Julio taking out his baggie (which he always carried with him) and pouring a half-ounce mound of the stuff on the table, permitting people to sniff as much as their little hearts and noses desired. As long as no one asked how he got the scar. But he wouldn't force anybody to sniff; he respected you if you didn't sniff the stuff. Julio had a no-nonsense face you couldn't lie to. Because he had so much cocaine, Julio would often feel generous, and you could buy from him, but if you were partying with him, as Vital was wont to do, he'd just tell you to give him a bill.

> What?
> Give me a bill.
> Okay.

You would hand him a dollar bill, and Julio would fill it with cocaine and give it back to you. Vital explained what usually happened next.

> Now, by the end of the night when all Julio's cocaine is gone, or when he felt he'd given out a bit too much and needed to reserve a few grams, he will ask for that cocaine back. If he'd given you cocaine earlier and by the night's end would ask you if you had any left, you had to tell him the truth because he had a way of badgering you, pestering you, he had a way of sniffing out the truth, so that if you had any left he'd find out about it, and he'd look at you and you had to tell him the truth. Of course, after you told him he'd never forget you lied to him and held back on him so six months later he'd remember the exact date, place, and circumstance when you lied.

Some of the people Vital hung out with, like Julio and, on occasion, Dapper Dan types, were mini kingpins or at least thought they were. All the drug money was "nouveau riche," and the Gucci, Louis Vuitton, and Fendi luxury leather on the young patrons' gear was strictly old-school money, symbolized by the street gangster's ghetto-fabulous wardrobe.[1]

I told Vital about the study I was doing regarding after-hours clubs—he was one of the only patrons I told—and he agreed to let me in on a few secrets regarding the trade. He also said I could write about him, and then he introduced me to Julio, whose garments reeked of cocaine. A radical Communist Party teenager back in the day, Vital also learned the guitar and could play beautiful Cuban and Dominican ballads. He was as delightful to listen to in song as he was in conversation. He had a fine voice. I knew him from high-school SNCC (Student Non-Violent Coordinating Committee) rallies and demonstrations.

He was one of several teen rabble-rousers who marched against the Vietnam War and over desegregation in the South. Not having seen him in many years, I was as surprised to see him in an after-hours club as he me. But I was aware he used to sell pot, even during our college days, and I was curious if he now sold cocaine. He told he was not doing either but was just accompanying a dealer friend. Vital was a strange guy, paranoid about women; he never introduced them to his friends, for reasons he never explained. Or, I should say, at the club, if he was with a woman and introduced her, everyone knew it wasn't someone he cared about. His snorting habits were similar to how he was with women: stingy. People said that Vital would keep a gram of cocaine until it turned to table salt before he'd share a grain but that if he had cocaine in a dollar bill, he'd sniff the wig off Washington.

Short in stature, olive complexion, and a quick talker, Vital always took a politically radical stance at the table. Take Castro's Cuba, for instance. In one conversation, everyone sitting at the table was pro Castro. Vital: "Did you know Cuba had a Black presidente before Castro? Well, it was Batista, because Batista acted like he was a white Cubano, with some Black blood, not like Castro, who was white Cubano with some Black blood. Castro was, by the way, a white Cuban, and you know how white Cubans feel about Blacks don't you?" Answering his own question, as he would often do:

> Contemptible, that's what, contemptible. White Cubanos hate Black Cubans. Anyway, before Castro they had a Black president, and this Black president of the country could not go into certain restaurants and clubs in Havana because of discrimination. The Cubans, I mean white Cubans, have a word for Blacks, which is

> worse than nigger here, it's more like excrement, shit, and foreign shit at that, you know what I mean. So, Castro's Cuba is no sanctuary, and if you talk about race in Cuba you will end up in prison so fast it will make your head swim. You cannot talk about race, or discrimination, or nothing like that in Cuba. Nothing, nada about race.

Vital would sniff and talk, talk and sniff, until he saw someone whose manner or dress or behavior he could poke fun at. Then he would begin telling stories:

> I once saw these motherfuckers come in the spot with a set of golf clubs. That's right. A set of golf clubs and who asked people if they wanted to go to the course with him and play with one of the famous golfers, I forgot who with, Palmer or Trevino or somebody like that, and he wasn't kidding. This guy was so square it hurts. And how he got in the club with the clubs I will never know. But he coulda had a machine gun in that fucking bag.

He told a story of what he called a "whack dealer" or someone "who cokes his cut." When Vital started speaking, people would start laughing immediately, in anticipation, because they knew they were going to hear something funny.

> Well, I knew this guy who was wanting to deal and when nobody had anything to sell, he would always have something. Well, you know most dealers go out and buy an ounce of material, some good blow, the best they can get in order to make their product decent or better than decent. Well, this guy would go out and do the opposite, he'd buy a pound of cut and a gram of coke to throw in to it. So, he would coke his cut.

THE REGULARS

In the after-hours cocaine scene, any user who hung out every weekend at the club or even every so often would be considered a regular.[2] If a person came every night to the place, and if their work and play involved the use of the drug, they would be considered a heavy regular sniffer. Heavy regular sniffers' use of cocaine might exceed several grams a day. They might be dealers, who must constantly sell and promote the product, in which case they carried cocaine for "business purposes," known as "calling-card coke." There may have been others who were heavy regular users as a result of their contact with dealers, including wives, husbands, girl/boyfriends, or relatives of the dealer. Regulars were patrons who got off work and visited for a few hours before returning home or going back to work. Transit workers with odd shifts would come in, imbibe, and go back to work. Others, such as bartenders, pimps, hustlers, bus drivers, and hotel workers, worked in nearby neighborhoods. Regulars at Le Boogie Woogie were there to socialize with likeminded individuals in some kind of community and shared space while using drugs and alcohol. Employees, on the other hand, could be considered regular users because their use of cocaine was continuous over a given work night (into the day) and because of the many "turn-ons" they received each night. Cocaine use in this way was a perk of the job—or an occupational hazard, depending on how you saw it.

I had just finishing eating some barbecue cooked by the father of a barmaid, which she had brought from a party, when the man next to me started telling me about the effect cocaine had on him. This was not "coke talk" but a genuine concern about the effect the drug had on him. There is a difference between coke talk and regular talk, and you know the difference when you hear it. Given how much the drug was snorted, eaten, and smoked, it was notable how little talk there was about the drug's effect. "Cocaine has a curious effect on me and I think most men." He was not a patron I knew. I had only seen him once or twice in the club, about a month or so ago before this conversation. He was casually dressed and mentioned something about Washington, DC, though he didn't repeat what he'd said, or at least I didn't hear him. He'd been drinking now for about three hours. When I returned to the bar from the upstairs room, he was sitting at the far end, and he started talking, seemingly to himself, but as I sat down to drink my orange juice and ginger ale he asked me if I knew anything about cocaine. Before I could open my mouth to reply, he continued, "I mean it has a curious effect on men sexually, wouldn't you say? On the strength."

> If I just take a little bit, I get real sexual and can maintain a hard-on, an erection for a long time. But if I take one sniff too much it detracts its power, on the strength, and causes me embarrassment by stopping right in the middle of the act. I can tell you right now I prefer the coke dick to the whiskey dick any day. It's as if the drug is punishing me for overindulgence or overindulging. I had not intended to overindulge, you see. I just wanted to sustain a great experience, like any true hedonist, for as long as possible. I had brought cocaine along with me because I thought it was a welcome companion and wouldn't have much to say about what was going on. I was wrong. You know what I mean? On the strength.[3]

He was a heavy regular sniffer.

While this conversation was "heavy," that is, confessional and personal, most interaction between regulars was unserious. A "joking" relationship existed between two patrons where one was permitted, and in some instances required, to tease or make fun of the other, without offense. It was a "peculiar combination of friendlessness and antagonism. This behavior was such that in any other social context it would not be taken seriously. There was a pretense of hostility and a real friendliness. To put it another way, the relationship is one of permitted disrespect."[4] The joking relationship was common between regulars.

THE WOMEN

I wouldn't trust that bitch with a box of matches.

At Le Boogie Woogie, language was rough, with "bitch" this and "ho" that, "niggah" this and "thot" (those ho's over there) that. I saw a woman arguing with a man, and I realized I'd been noticing a bit more aggression with the women in here these days. It seemed like the women were getting tougher and tougher. Margo, a regular in her mid-forties, spoke her mind and was not afraid to let everyone within earshot hear what she had to say. She started talking about a situation involving a man she'd recently had an affair with but then shifted to discussing envy: "Everybody envied the couples' diamonds, his Rolls, and his stash. But then someone said nobody should envy nobody else's stuff or their life." I thought to myself that, on the one hand, envy was considered an undesirable trait and envious people regarded as suffering some kind of character flaw, but, on the other hand, that our consumer culture regularly, constantly, induces envy, as if it were a matter-of-fact aspect of life for kids and adults alike.

People showed up at the club with various conceptions about what was expected of them there. The patrons, dealers, tourists, house girls, and barmaids all had different definitions of the situation in which they found themselves, based on their role—to say nothing of what women expected from the scene versus what the men desired of them. The sociologist Marcus Hunter sees the black nightclub as embodying the sensual.[5] Regardless, it was important that one maintain one's cool. People could see if a person was too high on cocaine. They often exuded "tells" such as excessive tugging on the nose; rubbing around the face; pulling the chin, lips, and hands; or being jittery. While women tended to see other women as "zooted," "fucked up," or "wasted" on the drug, they were not usually seen as "drunk" from cocaine, since the effect was not viewed that way. One social rule in the club involved the way women were viewed both by men and by one another. Men may have exhibited the same effects and seemed "zooted" or "zonked out," and if completely overindulged, "fucked up," particularly if cocaine was used in combination with alcohol, but rarely were women perceived as anything more than "buzzed." In some ways this could be viewed through the lens of gender, but in the club both sexes were equally permitted to get as high as they desired to be.[6]

CAPTAIN SAVE-A-HO

> *You can't turn a ho into a housewife unless you do a whole lotta turning and a whole lotta housing. And that still may not be enough. Anyway, only some white boy, cap'n save-a-ho would wanna try and do some crazy shit like that.*
>
> —Mavis (barmaid)

Conchita's current boyfriend was a popcorn pimp, a derogatory term used to denote a lowlife lacking good "game." He beat up women to keep them in line and to get money; he lacked wit, charm, and the gift of gab. This boyfriend, who went by the name Silky Man, said to her one day when she told him I was writing about her life that I was probably not a professor at all but a hustler. She was trying to get him to talk with me about kids who were surviving on the street in a nontraditional way.[7] He was reluctant to talk to me and surprised to see me at the club. We were introduced at the bar. If he was a real pimp, would he really talk to me about his woman? Would I hear phrases like "choosing cake" and the like? Conchita had agreed to work with me on a study I was doing on teens and how they survive without working regular jobs, essentially kids operating in the underground or off-the-books economy, and I imagined this little meeting would constitute a breach of some kind, since pimps wanted total control of their women and didn't want them associating with "squares." We talked for a minute, but he was preoccupied with two other young men. We agreed to meet later.

Conchita arranged another meeting for us. I found the whole situation amusing. She giggled the whole time and of course didn't stay to participate; she just told him about me and said it was about time we finally had a sit down. I was mistaken about him in some ways. He was different from what I expected, a boy really, about twenty, with a disposition unlike what I'd heard. He was a bit nervous. It was nice to see my preconceived notions disappear. He said he believed Conchita's behavior—in the club and out—was "not too cool," and "that says a lot about her character, and her development, as these parts of her personality come in increments, slow, in sniffs, dribs and drabs like the cocaine on the table, gradually, even surprisingly." I wasn't so sure I understood him correctly, even after he repeated what he'd said. I thought I heard him say he was trying to school her about life. For example, he said Conchita doesn't know the "power of cocaine," what it can do to her, only what it can do for her. He went on to say: "Take the night after the cops raided a club, she [Conchita] was bartending, two of the barmaids invited her to their apartment, and she became aware of sex between two women and discovered she liked both men and women after that experience." This became a bone of contention, Conchita later intimated, between her and her boyfriend.

JESSICA

I began a conversation with the woman next to me as the other women nearby talked and sniffed. Her name was Jessica. She once had worked at the club, and she gave a vague answer about what she was doing then, saying something about hostessing at parties. Her look, eyes, and face were effective in warding off unwanted conversations and conversationalists, but since I did not believe I fit that category, I engaged with her, though I was careful not to join in too eagerly.

She asked me what I did, and I told her the truth. I was a student most of the time but did teaching as an adjunct lecturer and was interested in what went on in places like this one. A friend of mine had invited me, and I'd been coming to this place for almost a year. She said, "Well you know I've been coming to places like this since Skippy was a pup, so I understand how people get their kicks. So that mean you getting yo' kicks on the sly. Am I right?" I laughed. On the one hand, she's right, because my ethnography was in part voyeurism. My honesty seemed to satisfy her. As we talked she held me with a half-smile and engaging interest. She never actually sniffed any cocaine. She just threw it back against her tongue, rubbed it around her lips, and massaged it inside her mouth. She was dressed like a schoolgirl, with knee-length socks, a short plaid skirt, a white blouse, and high-heel shoes. Provocative, to say the least. Two of her girlfriends joined us, returning from the ladies' room. "Yeah 'society,' they all want what you don't have in society." She says this with a bit of sarcasm in her voice, puffing her lips out to stress every syllable.

> But that is the way people are. They want people to be talented, which is already something out of the ordinary, but when it comes with the other thing, that stuff, those things that society considers bad qualities, the baggage [she dips her pinky fingernail into a pile of cocaine] that comes with the talent, you know, the alcohol, the pills, the ho-ing, the cocaine, aah, then they say, oh she's this or she's that, they don't want to hear about that. They refuse to have any understanding of what it takes to be talented, the pressure, the problems of fame, the stress of it all, as if the bad side of dealing with the stress don't come with the good side of being born with talent. You know what I mean?

Then came the voice of a woman next to her, who turned her head to get into the conversation. "As if one doesn't come with the other. People know enough about your business as if it is a noisy fucking mob, so I want to be the gun and the blood it brings, the pencil and the paper, the kiss and the lips, and because I stay out so late, I guess I wanna be the night and the day. Can you help me with any of that?" The way she listened was just as elegant as her speech. She said something about being an "all-purpose girl." When I asked one of the other barmaids what that meant, she said, "a golddigger." She then said, "Women broker their bodies differently than men. Men broker more as controllers, dominants, all the time, whereas women broker themselves more in a sensitive, less demanding way, don't you think?"

I noticed that later arrivals to the scene were generally connected with others of like circumstances. "Old-school" patrons saw Le Boogie Woogie as a place to continue in a social circle they were comfortable and familiar with. Everyone appeared to be floating in the half-light of the after-hours club. The bar conversation continued as one person after another kept the banter going: "Every time someone walks by this guy [tossing her head to indicate a man passing to the men's room] the funk breezes over me like a short-lived fever." "That pigmentocracy shit don't work in here, cause we don't care if you light, bright, damn near white, or black as coal, cause the only thing that matter in here is green." "We gonna be carrying on." The voice of a Latina in her twenties, a new arrival, was heard. She said she was "capable only of temporary passion" because of her recent relationship with a man who treated her badly:

> He didn't like my girlfriends and called us all lesbians. I made the mistake of tellin' him that I made no distinction between men and women [when it comes to sex], and he took that to mean I was a lesbian, and I only meant that passion for me is passion, it's not gendered or split in two. It's just the way I feel, and lots of Latina women feel this way. In my country, Colombia, women love men, but they love women too. But here it's a stigma if you admit to it, and that's fucked up. I love men, I really do, but I shouldn't be beat up by no man because I say I like women too.

The women in the place were mostly what could be called hustling women, street women of one kind or another, and their friends. But with these kinds of characterizations I tread lightly because the attentive reader should see a few aspects of my subjectivity in the way in which I describe things. For instance, I was out one night in the Meatpacking District more than a decade after my Le Boogie Woogie fieldwork. A transvestite prostitute was standing near Hogs and Heifers, a popular bar in the area at the time. She said, "When I started in this business we were just 'whores,' now they call us 'sex workers.' Now who says there ain't been progress in this city? I beg to differ." She laughed as she said this, and I took her to be making fun. Cultural norms change over time, but the boundaries between what is socially accepted and what is not remain.

THE HOUSE GIRLS

Everyone called the women who worked at Le Boogie Woogie "girls," and they referred to one another that way, too. It did not appear intended to demean. The sexualization of young women is age old in American culture and in cultures around the globe. While older women could get a charge out of being called "girl" at the club, the younger women didn't seem to mind, either. Technically speaking, there were no "girls" there.

A house girl had many roles, primarily working as a waitress and dancer. She was there working for the club owner. She was not just a woman who liked to flirt with men to get offered cocaine like a regular at the spot. Her role as dancer (paid a salary by the house) was to serve customers after dancing. She was to be seductive and was used by the owner as a sexual object to attract patrons who might be interested enough in her to buy more drinks. Her salary, around fifty dollars for a half-hour performance, was not an hourly wage but was based on tips received from patrons.

Jean was a house girl who once worked at the club. She spoke about life on the street to find work:

> I'm the only brown-skin thang in there [the club]. But as a house girl, you get the tips. You work, they give you tips. You go there so they can work your ass off. But they want you to kiss ass too. In Manhattan you can make money. Chicks be giving blow jobs

> on the side. I just wanna make my fifty dollars and go home. See that blow job thang ain't me. See, I don't do that, cause I'm funny about germs. I ain't gonna kiss ass but to a certain extent. I told Scotty [the manager] it's a trip but not for me. I ain't gonna kiss no ass. All I'm gonna do is smile. A house girl is when you just live off the tips, and it depends on the amount of drinks you hustle from your customers.

Jean explained that she did not take a "house girl" position initially because house girls did double duty as dancers and waitresses. While given no guarantee she would earn the standard fifty-dollar fee for dancing when she decided to become a house girl, it was more likely she would receive twice as much on any given night. The fifty dollars was for a half-hour dance, and tips came out to several hundred. It was not uncommon for a good dancer on a good night, such as when big-time dealers came in and wanted it to "rain," to make a thousand dollars.

I asked Jean about drugs, money, sex work, and her role as a dancer. She said,

> I don't know 'bout a whole lotta dancers, but for me and a few of my friends money is the joint. Cause ya see, in Manhattan you can make a fortune. But you gotta sell your soul to the devil. I have seen all kinds of things; chicks be into all kinds of shit. One girl's act includes putting a beer bottle up her twat. Are you kidding me? I ain't doing that kinda shit for love or money. I swear it's the truth. Girls be getting paid in drugs, ya know. Some girls will do anything, they be uptight for money, you know, you understand? But I can't dig it. As long as I get mine, I don't give a fuck. Cause I'm not the greedy type. Otherwise, I would be treacherous. I just wanna do what I wanna do and go on about my business. But there are some bitches out here I wouldn't trust with a box of matches.

The sociologist Kimberly Hoang, in her book *Dealing in Desire*, investigates sex work in Vietnam's Ho Chi Minh City, linking the intimate and complex relationship with the country's new and immense global economic ascendency.[8] Hoang presents Vietnamese sex workers not as helpless victims but as women constrained within the patriarchy and using sex work as a pathway upward. Women like Jean, Conchita, and other barmaids at Le Boogie Woogie saw no problem in doing sex work, and their views also echo more current attitudes when discussing male chauvinism, sexism, and the patriarchy. Jean and some other women who chose not to reveal their identities considered sex work, prostitution, if you will, as empowering. Though none expressed it quite this way, in essence they said, *I can do this thing my way, when I want, get the money I want without some man telling me what to do.* The man was responsible for the pariah status of the profession, the stigma that separated the women into good girls and bad girls as a way to divide and conquer.

MAVIS

Mavis did not speak much about her occupation as hostess at Le Boogie Woogie, at least not the first few times I saw her there. A few meetings later, she began to open up. Despite seeing her at the club at odd times, Mavis, after weeks of not showing up, would appear, do her show, then disappear for another two weeks. I knew her only in outline, you might say. She didn't talk much when I saw her. Things changed when I offered to pay her a standard interview fee.

Though working at an after-hours club, she had conventional aspirations; she was just in an unconventional situation at the moment. She said she was going to school and was looking for security and a new way of life. She told me her situation by way of an anecdote. It was then that I discovered she had a wicked sense of humor.

> I met this old witch, a dancer for twenty years. She was attractive. She had a scar, about my complexion, you know. And ah, she had been doing it here for a year, ya know. She had a little mink on and shit. But, I mean, I can't see it as a way of life. You know. I'm doing it to get over for the nth time being, ya know. [Incredulously] As a way of life? Naw. Now I don't knock it for those who do it, ya know, don't get me wrong. But I just couldn't. My grandma always said, "don't say what you'll never do." But uh, I know I won't. Uh, that's why this school trip got me like this [showing a nervously shaking hand, gesturing with it in my face for emphasis]. But I'm sticking with this thang. Ya know, to get grants and things. Ya know, every three years I work. Then I wanna get this new car. Because they stole mine right off Riverside Drive. Ya know, it's hard, connivin' and jivin'. I just don't enjoy it, even though I'm good at it. Ya know, I like the money in it and all, and—I'm afraid if I don't get over now, I may be doing this next year, but I doubt it, ya know. I don't particularly care for it, really. Because ya gotta learn tricks, ya gotta stand on your head, spread your legs, smoke cigarettes [in the vagina] and all that old shit, and there's only so much of that I'll go for. You gotta be a, uhh, I don't know, a rubber band, the rubber-band man.

Mavis, Margo, and Jessica wanted to have some control over their future, and though they were party "girls" at the time, they seemed to understand that this life offered little more than momentary pleasure. "I used to be a heavy drinker," Mavis said, sipping a glass of white wine, which evoked both mockery and a bit of self-pity. "But what stopped me in my tracks was what happen to my cousin Danny." She gathered momentum and told the story:

My cousin, god bless his soul, who I love dearly but was always a womanizer and this passion created a large family, many kids all unrelated to each other, I'm sorry to say, except by his siring. On or about the night of July 4, this was back in '83 sitting on his parents' porch, evicted from his own house and receiving court papers almost every day for delinquent child support. Danny was drinking rotgut like it was going outta style.

To make bad matters worse the county fair was in town and he had neither money to go or a woman to take him there, so he decided to go anyway in the hope that the excitement and fanfare would lift his spirits. While walking around he heard a barker yell something to the effect that he would offer five hundred dollars to any man who would wrestle his gorilla. Well, the raw alcohol eating at his brain and the reality of no money eating at his wallet led him straight to the gorilla's cage. When I got there, I couldn't believe my eyes. I looked in the cage and there was Danny drunk as he could be with his fists held high mocking and teasing this gorilla. Word had spread, and some of Danny's friends were there cheering him on.

There he was drunk as he could be and who couldn't hit the ground with his hat trying to fight a baby gorilla. Or that's what it looked like all crouched over in the corner of the cage. But as soon as Danny slapped him mindlessly near his shoulder this monkey stood up and grew like King Kong and before you could say "get out" that big monkey jumped up and struck poor Danny with a flurry of slaps and down he went.

That didn't stop that monkey, who stomped and kicked cuz all over that cage until the handlers came in with long poles moved him outta there. That monkey whipped that boy within an inch of his life. I saw Danny later in the hospital, and when

> he got out, standing with crutches, bandaged head, one arm in a sling, the other in a cast. I asked him why he did that, and he just said he was drunk and needed the money. I told him after that I would never be a heavy drinker.

Mavis was effusive and raised her glass to her cousin Danny. One of the women said to her, "I thought you said you'd never be a heavy drinker." "That's right. This ain't heavy, it's light."

Despite the drug use and dealing that existed in after-hours clubs like Le Boogie Woogie, I did not observe young girls being turned into prostitutes in these spaces or people being robbed and killed. This is not to say that these things didn't ever happen, but they were uncommon occurrences despite the talk. And for the most part, after-hours clubs draw little attention from the daytime public and the law. I heard from reliable sources about incidents relating to this particular club and how it spawned a brand of renegade profiteers, "choke-and-rob" boys who preyed on unsuspecting patrons who displayed large amounts of cocaine in the club. This gang not only robbed the person but often followed the "vic" home to burglarize the apartment.[9] This kind of activity was and is tough to verify.[10]

BARMAIDS

She was the shape of a pipette, long and slender.

—Overheard

Once called "serving wenches," "hostesses," "cocktail waitresses," and "bunnies," the barmaid role represented an extension of the traditional female housewife. In the club they were simply referred to as "servers," and their role was often as an overseer of the club's activity, maintaining a smooth rapport with snorter regulars at the bar while selling alcohol and drugs (cocaine, marijuana, hashish). There were no bar nuts, chips, pretzels, or straws; only napkins were available to patrons with their drinks. The barmaid was friendly and cooperative most times but at others was cool, reserved, and curt. She indulged in snorting, drinking, flirting, and smoking along with the regulars, both strangers and friends. To perform well as a server, one must be patient.

Barmaids were the only ones I've seen in the place reading a book (on a slow, snowy night). Reading must have been difficult, since the lighting was quite dim. The brightest it got was right before the club opened and when patrons left in morning. This was perhaps the most startling feeling because the club's ambience made you feel as if the light of day had been forever lost. Leaving and walking out into the daylight was always a bit shocking to the senses. "It kind of sobers you up," one patron was overheard saying.

Maria, a Latina barmaid hired from another club, when asked how she felt being around so many men who constantly flirt, said,

> Well, it's okay, because most of them are coke heads anyway, and I know it's the coke talking most of the time. They say little things like asking me out, but the owner he don't like me to go out with the customers. Because if I go out with a guy and I'm in here talking to another guy, he might get mad and start something. So as a rule, I don't go out with them. But if I find a guy who is real nice to me, I might go out with him, but that depends on the guy.

Barmaids wore provocative clothing, low-cut blouses that sometimes exposed their breasts when they bent over, and tight pants or short skirts. The physical appearance of the barmaid was a crucial criterion for the job. According to Frenchy and others, the barmaids used their charm and flirtatious behavior to short-change patrons and ask for cocaine from patrons who gave them "play." A barmaid talked about hustling the "joint":

> We don't have no cash register here so all I got to do is give the money to Barry [the houseman]. But when I need a little something, I just don't give it all to him, and I put some in my pocket as my tip. It looks like I should be making a whole lotta money here, but I don't. People don't be giving away money like they used to. They give away a lotta coke, but not money. If Frankie [she meant Frenchy, the owner] catches any of us stealing, it's all over; you might never be able to find another job in these joints, 'cause he knows everybody and every joint in town. The best hustle you can make is to be nice to people who be nice to you and don't take no shit. People respect that. Sometimes, when a group orders drinks, I may shortchange them an extra dollar or so, and unless they bring it to my attention, I get away clean. Often people are high, and I might shortchange them more, but this is not unexpected since every waitress in here do that. I think customers don't very much care either.

But sometimes the patron did notice. One woman told me while shooting a glance at the bar, rubbing her hands together as if to wipe the disgust away, "I went to a club one night and somebody, I think it was that damn barmaid, stole the little purse out of my bag. And I thought that was a pretty lowlife thing to do. So I haven't gone back there since."

Another barmaid was discussing two men who were within earshot of her conversation. Her voice was obviously pitched so they could hear:

> Well, they've been here all night, and one doesn't drink and the other has snorted up all of Jake's [another regular] coke. But Jake don't know it because he's so fucked up, he don't know his head

> from a hole in the ground. One of 'em had a little teeny-weeny bit of coke in a well-used piece of foil [implying the foil had been opened and reopened a number of times], and earlier, he had given me some. So, me, like a fool, gave them a little package of what I had. Well, they both sniffed and sniffed, I was expecting them to give me more of theirs, you know, but I guess they didn't have any more or else didn't wanna bring it out. But that wasn't the kisser. You know, they left without leaving me a tip? Not one Franklin Delano Roosevelt. Can you believe that? I work here, I serve them, and they don't give me nothing. That's not only gross, it's downright disrespectful.

Le Boogie Woogie was a place of continued emotional release and discovery through drug use, fostering a collective sense of being. The drug use. The conversations. The sex play. The competition between the "girls," each trying at times to outperform the others for tips and attention. Whatever took place in this club was an alternative to life as many people knew it. The drug use, for example, was complicated: people were high in a way different from an alcohol-induced high. They were stimulated, talkative, nervous, paranoid, sexually excitable, and thirsty. The barmaid role was complicated, too: she had to take on the crowd and deal with the bartender and all the hullabaloo going on around her. She had to take orders while the jukebox was blasting, with the crowd pulling at her coattails, with men and women feeling her ass. The guy who just gave her a hundred-dollar bill was now locked on, and whatever he wanted he got, including a body bump and rub when he tried to get past her.[11]

Conchita felt she was doing a good job as a barmaid and was oblivious to all the talk surrounding her. Maria said of Conchita: "The only reason he [Frenchy] let her [Conchita] handle the bar is when Jake [the regular bartender] is too fucked up to come to work. He gets drunk and doesn't show sometimes." Jake is an alcoholic, but he is very popular with the barmaids, and they respect him; he never says anything derogatory about them, even when they make mistakes. The main reason Conchita was called "a fuck-up as barmaid," Maria explained,

> is she was too busy flirting trying to get the guy with either the biggest dick or biggest dollars in her in some way, so she either ignored the little tippers or just pissed them off in one way or another. She never really got the job right any way; I mean she don't know how to do her job, or maybe she doesn't care the way she do her job.

Jessica and Mavis said pretty much the same thing. As Jessica put it: "All the girls, for example, must learn the skills to do a good job, and that means doing the work in the midst of a crazy, excitable crowd where the drug is affecting everyone." Mavis:

> A lot of these newbies are really there for show. They are there because they have big tits or big asses or just eye candy for the customers, so, I hate to say this, but some are pretty, alright, pretty dumb. You know. So, Jake has to put up with some who can't count, or who get the drinks mixed up or some who are just clumsy, dropping shit, spilling shit, short-changing customers either on purpose or just because they just don't know any better. Jake is very patient with them. But Conchita is none of that and constantly gets into hassle with them, and that makes for a very long night for everybody.

Woman patron: "She had a tight-fitting skirt, a big ass, perky titties, and what-the fuck-you-looking-at brown eyes." Mavis and I both heard this statement and gave a big laugh. The woman was a weekend customer and had seen Conchita for the first time. Mavis said, "You see, Conchita when acting as bartender is even more difficult because she keeps small change and gets pissed off if barmaids try to rush her into serving people. She forgets when taking on the bartender role that she was once a waitress just two days before." Conchita approached the women, wearing a pair of cuffed dungarees, loafers, and a butch haircut parted on the side. She had a habit of looking the women up and down before saying anything, throwing her lips up and raising her chin at the same time.

When Conchita was behind the bar, a person who complained about not getting his change of fifty cents was generally shunned and ignored. Big tippers were given the royal treatment, including the "brush," which was a slow rub of the barmaid's ass. Barmaids were known to keep the change even before the customer told them to do so. Most patrons knew not to ask for the change if it was less than a dollar and in some cases less than two or three. "It's better to be single and get paid than to be married and fucked for nothing," one woman was overheard to say. There was no doubt the division of labor was strictly in favor of the bartender. The barmaids worked very hard to get in the bartender's good graces. The bartender's power included the ability to offer free drinks to patrons, demand patrons leave if disorderly, evict patrons they didn't like, admonish workers, and hire and fire workers.[12]

In Le Boogie Woogie, women barmaids were confronted with issues of gender as soon as they entered the door. "Girls" was the label they accepted because, as they said, it made them feel young when they were called that, and the boss preferred "girls" over other designations. And while the women reflected on and critically engaged with essentializing ideas of womanhood, they also "dive straight into the gendered expectations."[13]

Looking at the dynamics of women and men at work together is significantly crucial for understanding any kind of gender relations.

One of the regulars I've spoken about at the club said she would speak to me only on condition that I not reveal her real name. She said, "Whenever I meet men in the bar, they always want to know if I was hooked up with anybody and assume I would hook up with them because I like coke, but they were always disappointed. Though I wasn't married and wasn't interested in getting that way, it was always an issue when I said no thanks to their offers." The various skills each person in the bar must have mastered, whether they were a doorman, frisker, manager, barmaid, or bartender, were interpersonal. Of these roles it was the barmaid who had the most to contend with. Speed was required to assuage egos, know the prices and recipes of drinks, make change and rearrange orders, talk to customers, move back and forth from the bar to the tables, and avoid unwanted advances from men and women who wanted to rub, grab, pinch, and touch. These were just some of the concerns of the barmaid.

Despite the jealousy, envy, and bickering, the barmaids managed to get along. They helped one another out by cleaning tables when they didn't have to or when another barmaid was too busy. One night, Dana found a fifty-dollar bill under a table after Conchita and a new barmaid had just got off their shifts. The new barmaid worked the table where the money was found, so Dana said, "listen, honey, this belongs to you." The new barmaid gave her half the money and blew a kiss at her. She said something to the effect of "I give up a lot of things, but I get them back." This kind of comradeship among the wait staff was not uncommon but was not always the norm either. It's a dog-eat-dog world in the club sometimes, but obviously not always.

Conchita's youth, beauty, and the special way she carried herself attracted many patrons to the bar area, and she knew it. This caused tension and jealousy from the newer and older barmaids, who resented the special treatment she got. Jessica, for instance, says this was one of the reasons women didn't like to tip her. "It's because of her high-and-mighty attitude. That bitch does not have to say 'I'm sorry' for anything she does, and you know why, she [stops short of saying Conchita's name]—Mavis told Jake she would pay for the broken glasses. Well, we know she's [Conchita] is either patting that pussy or want too because everybody sees how she hit on her [Mavis] every chance she gets." The question of who Conchita really was as a person puzzled me for some time, and I began to account for her behavior in a more through way.

THE BARMAID, PLAYERS, AND A HUSTLER

Conchita was the barmaid the men in the club felt they had to do something for. Like Fern in Jean Toomer's *Cane*, men felt they had to buy her a gift, find a ring that fit her finger, buy her a house, or give her as much cocaine as she could snort. Once you had her on your mind, you'd want to give her whatever you had. Everyone seemed to be drawn to her attractiveness. Men lost their selfishness because of her. Women lost their ambivalence, though it wasn't all women who felt this way. The young women who worked as barmaids sometimes came from the local housing projects; they were highly desired as barmaids at Le Boogie Woogie because they could be paid the lowest wages (basically working for tips) and not complain. "You see they are

Mexican, Dominican, and Puerto Rican, and don't know any better. The Mexicans and the Dominicans just got here and don't wanna leave, and them Puerto Ricans been here too long and still don't know what time it is." Conchita told me that although she's not from the projects, she tended bar to supplement her income, as the other girls did, but she said she did it for other reasons as well.

Conchita's smartness was what got her into trouble and why she was only used in an emergency at the bar and as a barmaid. She had a reputation for being a "fuckup" as well. She was curt with customers, changed the rules in dealing with them, kept loose change for herself, and complained about women who never tipped. She said that men were the best tippers and that women never tipped "unless they're dykes." She said she kept the change because "I can't be bothered with making change when six or ten people giving me a bill to change." What she meant was when a party of six or more came in and each one wanted to buy an individual drink rather than pay for the whole tab. She told people, contrary to the house rules, that she wanted only one check because this made her life easier, and the bartender's, too. This meant patrons should work out the details among themselves. There was lots of money in the club, and big tippers abounded, but women, according to her, are notoriously "lousy" tippers.

> Men are all big tippers. These guys get off on trying to impress, and they pick up tabs, pay for drinks even for people they don't know, but try to get a decent tip from a woman in here and it's like getting blood from a turnip. Women just don't tip like men and that's a fact. I like the older men because they're my best customers. All you gotta do is smile at them and they tip you really big. They just be the best because they always looking for a young

> "thing" they can get their hands on, but most just want some young pussy around because they think more about sex than actually doing it.

I later learned that Conchita did not fully understand the dynamics of bartending and how her relationship with other barmaids and the bartender affected the situation. "You can't have the bartender mad at you and you can't have the barmaids pissed at the bartender because both can make life miserable for the other," Margo said. It was only after the manager recognized this that he decided to stop allowing Conchita to bartend except when there was no other option. The manager understood that profit was made from alcohol, entrance fees, cocaine sales, gambling—and by keeping labor costs low. Barmaids like Conchita and the wait staff made more in tips than in salary per week. She made $300 a night on a good weeknight and as much as $500 a night on weekends, though this could not be verified. The bar was the biggest moneymaker, since much of the liquor was watered down, except the champagne. There was no requirement to provide food, no taxes to pay, and the jukebox rental was minimal and paid for itself. Food was served on occasion, but it was brought in by catering services. The barmaids cooked and brought food in for Christmas, a birthday, or the New Year's Eve party. Club rooms were often rented out for special events. The most popular were the wedding and bachelor parties, and on one occasion a post–pimp's ball party was arranged.

PLAYERS

The player used cocaine as an ally and friend. He wore dark shades because daylight offended. He was the quintessential underground being. Even though the powder was supposed to stimulate, he rarely danced; everyone was aware that he's beyond the reach of certain stimuli. The walk of the player was a symbol of control. It was boplicity personified, a cross between a scream and a poem. The walk carried the body like a concealed weapon, a gangster lean, every step a schizophrenic motion, and he stood just a step away from the crowd. His eyes shrewdly narrowed, mouth and body poised as if anticipating a response from an unasked question. The gestures, palms upraised, fingers pointing downward, a form of greeting that meant some previous misunderstanding was now rectified. There was no need to say a mumbling word; a head nod, a flip of the thumb, a slap on the palm, a push up of the lips, or a wink of an eye would do.[14]

All of the practice players got "talking shit" played out at Le Boogie Woogie. It was there, standing at the bar, feet wrapped in gators or suede, shoulders squared, elbows in, hands at one's sides, fingers spread out, eyes open like a paranoid policeman. The music they liked was soft, not hard or loud, and when the whole place was in full swing and everybody was dancing, singing, sniffing, profiling, or all four, the player stood watching and waiting for the right moment to pounce. Players were usually patrons who had made fast money or, thanks to their occupations or other advantages, consistently had money. Cocaine dealers, gamblers, owners of businesses, pimps—these regulars possessed qualities beyond the bounds of polite society, which set them apart from others. They were in the "big time" as opposed to small-time, nickel-and-dime "popcorns" or pimping punks with weak game. It was the difference between the true professional and the amateur.

An old man now, Sam had a mischievous face with a trace of the comic in his cheeks. He had big hands, a deep voice, a scar under his left eye, and chapped lips, the bottom red and the top a purplish black. I was struck by his walk. Ralph Ellison called it the most elegant walk in the world. You see it less and less nowadays. You might see an occasional bop here and there, but it is rare. The "hip hitch," "pimp roll," or "strut" was what pimps used to call it, and the TV character George Jefferson was the last time I saw it on screen in a way that wasn't pure parody. I asked Sam to describe a typical "player" to me.

> Well, I always say you can tell a player by the way he dresses and the way they talk. I must say this is a kinda superficial thing, I mean, a stereotype thing because not every player dress well or talk well but I would say the vast majority do. They are fast talkers and wear elegant, expensive clothing and jewelry. Most are intelligent, and I would say, and they show some ingenuity in their game, which reflect a strong personal style.

It is not too much to say Sam was really talking about himself, since he considered himself a player. He rapped poetic as Frenchy and two others stood near the bar:

> A player is a cat who's been there and back, picked it up, put it down, slammed it, jammed it, threw it, blew it, tossed it around, swung with it, laughed at it, loved it, hated it, stole it, sold it, bought it back, put it away, took it out, lost it, found it. Done everything there is to do and then some: booked it, crooked it, made it work, hired it, fired it, rented it, consumed it, held it in, made money on it, sexed it, and played it, till it was no more.[15]

Everyone called him Sam, but he said his name was Samuel. He remembered his first encounter with cocaine in a speakeasy many years ago:

> I was going to a spot, keep in mind that white folks call 'em "speaks" and Black folk call 'em "spots," and the police called them "speakeasies," and to "speak- easy" was a way of defining the spot as location for secrecy, but whatever you call them they were the places all the players hung out in them. At that time, I was with a ho named Chickie. Back at that time we call them "ladies of easy virtue." She was black, cold, and built like a marble shit-house. This spot was around St. Nicholas and [1]45th Street, if I remember right. Smooth Tate and a friend of mine owned this ho. I say owned because in them days, a pimp was a ruthless, dangerous motherfucker who would shoot and cut somebody in a minute. And them bitches knew it, so they stayed in line. Chickie took me to this spot which was about fifty/fifty: fifty Black and fifty white. We sat in that joint and I didn't know what this cocaine stuff was all about. I was sniffing and sniffing, smoking reefer and drinking that booze. Well, before I knew it, I'm getting sick, you know, so I asked the owner of the joint if I could lay down somewhere. She took me to another room and I slept until later that day. When I got up and went back out in the room, the crowd was still there just like I hadn't left. But that was my first time sniffing coke. And Chickie—I was with Chickie last, about six years ago—no, maybe five years ago. And you know, she'll still make a hound dog break away from his chain.

I found it strange that Sam's reaction and first encounter with coke was the opposite of what most people feel, but he didn't say much more about this. But as we can see from his story, Le Boogie Woogie offers the patron a chance to live on a stage built of cocaine and pretension. Le Boogie Woogie provided a carefree zone, where those who saw themselves living a thuggish, contrarian, "unsquare" lifestyle could find an outlet. Everyone in the club had hopes of taking part in the world outside but needed some time and space to reflect on that decision.[16]

STRAIGHTEN OUT THE SQUARES

I works the bars, not the street.

—Happy the Hustler

One type of regular was the kind of person who goes to a party and never wants it to end. Where do you go when everywhere was closed but an after-hours club? These patrons did not want to get high alone and preferred to share with others. Regulars tended to be hustlers who visited every week or several times per week. The squares were regular workers who visited once every few months. Tourists came only on social-events nights. Party patrons were there on special nights such as birthday parties, Christmas, and New Year's.[17] Patrons, regardless of type, usually stayed an average of three or more hours. Most patrons did not on any given night know one another, aside from those they came in with. For the most part, they came to the club to get high because their husbands, wives, or partners did not indulge or did not approve of their using the drug. A club night out was the only time to get high without interference. Many times, this was a girls' night out, and women would show up with girlfriends to engage in risqué behavior they might rarely have had a chance to do otherwise.

I had not seen one regular known as Happy the Hustler, a cheerful fellow, for months. He mostly hung out at the Cozy Bar off Morningside.[18] As he strolled into the bar he rhymed: "I got the rags with the tags, money is tight, times are hard, here's your fucking Xmas card." He had a specialty: he told Frenchy he never worked the street, just the bars. There was a clear distinction to be made between common street hustlers and Happy; he implied he's a cut above the rest because he doesn't sell in the street or just to anyone. Though there was no selling in the club normally, Happy was the one exception because of the high-end goods he had to offer, including mink coats and hats, expensive designer perfumes, and the like. Le Boogie Woogie permitted a range of illegal activity and behaviors to transpire, and patrons were expected to maintain a low profile in the process. In all things patrons were bound by rules of decorum set up by the management and enforced by one another.[19]

On a personal level, everyone was expected to exude "coolness." As discussed in the previous chapter, coolness is poise under pressure. On one occasion, the patrons were sitting around the dance floor intently watching a young woman who had snorted too much cocaine. She was stripping on the stage. One of the men at the club was screaming at the top of his lungs, "Where is the dancer? Where is the dancer?" Most of the other patrons responded, "Shut up." When she got off the stage, several men went up to her to offer cocaine. While the young woman had clearly overindulged and was engaged in transgressive behavior, it was the man who had failed at being cool by drawing undue attention to the young woman and to himself in the process. It took me some time to discern social status without stereotyping. For instance, people would say "oh he's a player," or "she's a player," "he's a ho," or "do you mean that lame." Coolness was definitely a factor. Jim, the super at one of the buildings on the block, was a tough one to read. He bragged about having known the owner of the "spot" before Frenchy took over, and he visited "every now and again" to see what was going on. He at once understood the rules of discretion yet openly violated them in his conversations with me. "I met him [the owner] twelve years ago," Jim told me.

> Long before he opened this spot. As a matter of fact, he wanted to have it in the building I was the super at, but it was too big and had too many of the wrong people in it. You see, to have a good spot you need to have either a building you own or a small building with an accessible entrance, that people can get in and out of in case of po-lice raids. Short of that, a spot with a discreet location, off the street, kinda, you know, on-the-down-low-type spot. But I like the freakiness of this spot because the girls do get freaky in here. People let their guards down in this place. Man, the things I've seen in here you would not believe. And if I told you twice you wouldn't believe it again. One broad, listen, one broad, she was sitting right across from where you are now, and she got buck naked after taking some shit and a few drinks, I mean buck-I-don't-got-no-clothes-on naked, right there.

Le Boogie Woogie was largely a "time-out place" where hustlers went when they got off work. Of course, if an opportunity arose to "catch" (acquire a woman or man), they would not hesitate to do that, but for the most part spots were places where everybody was just out to have a good time. They were not expected to control their urges for cocaine; on the contrary, they were expected to indulge to their heart's content yet in doing so remain "cool."

After-hours clubs were the major socialization sites for cocaine dealers, and they were treated as "cool-out" locales where pimps could relax with their "ho's." This was a male and misogynistic point of view. Cool was male. The following is characteristic of a cool cocaine encounter at the spot. A man approaches a woman with cocaine to offer. Then, as the woman sniffs, he watches how she did it to see if any teachable moments are possible. In situations where no teaching was necessary, he would wait the appropriate number of seconds before looking into her eyes and beginning his standard "rap," employing the latest cues, taking words from a song, commenting on a recent hit record, the atmosphere, or the quality of cocaine. His initial approach would be an interrogative sentence, one in which a question was asked to elicit a response. This made the encounter reciprocal and opened the person to react and engage. Sometimes this would work, sometimes it wouldn't, but it was within the bounds of male cool.

Patrons at Le Boogie Woogie who frequented only on weekends were seen as "squares" or "weekend warriors." They would spend several hours sniffing, drinking, smoking, and dancing and were attracted to the place by street gossip and curiosity. They were obviously uncool. Take, for instance, Maria. Like many cocaine users, she began her cocaine experience with close friends or intimates but developed and matured as a user in an after-hours setting. Most cocaine users did not begin their experience in after-hours clubs, nor did they all begin them in a positive way. She lived in Brooklyn and remarked how it was only in the last six years or so that she had learned what cocaine was like and how to appreciate and recognize its subtle effects:

> Listen to me and believe me, I'm gonna tell it to you slow. You see when I started sniffing coke—a long time ago, my old man was into gambling, you know, buying loaded dice and cutting games. He used to bring in a little coke every now and then after he'd won a little money during those days. I would keep a ten [of coke] for a few days, that's how good it was. But now a ten I don't even bother with, it's so little and so cut up. It's just a waste of money. But also, I didn't know what coke was like, either. I would sniff a little and taste a little, but basically leave it alone. I guess

> a few years in between there, I didn't have any at all, but I know around 1970, I met Harry, and he took me to this spot [after-hours club] on [1]23rd Street. Well, in that place, we sniffed and got turned on to so much coke I was flying. I mean I had never felt that way before on coke. I don't know whether it was the place, the club, the people I was with, the quality or the quantity of coke that did it, but I really enjoyed myself. It was only afterward that coke has meant so much to me. For some reason, I had always expected a big bang or something from it, but that's not what it's about.

If Maria were a man, in the game, from the neighborhood, or hit the spot with greater frequency, would she have been cool? It's not for me to say. You be the judge.

THE OLDER MEN

You could say I had some unfulfilled ambitions.

Some frequent visitors to the spot were middle-aged males, mostly former hustlers, certainly not all, well dressed and married at one time or another or "shacking up." All were in search of younger women for sex or to gamble or just hang out with. The men were not far from a full table of women and stood or moved within striking distance, where a wink or the flash of a diamond ring could be seen, a quick tug on the crotch, leaning in a special spot, posing with a certain poise, a suavity, hat with a certain symmetry, shoes matching trousers, trousers matching shirt, shirt matching jacket, jacket matching everything. If they were anywhere else, the appearance would be incongruous, but here they fit perfectly. In this location, in this spot, at this time, where time stands still, every gesture has meaning for the standing background players. "To each his own" is an adage that suited Le Boogie Woogie. The women in the club understood how the drug affects men, and that could work in their favor, by exciting the man to the point where she can easily get to him. She knows overstimulation from the drug can turn the man to "butter" in her hands.[20]

FRENCHY

Frenchy, fifty-one years old, lived in a run-down section of central Harlem, where garbage cans dot the street, overflowing with refuse. On the corner, a small cluster of men stood around a huge can, fire roaring up and smoke disappearing in the sky. Every few minutes, a new face walked past and asked one of the men in the group, "What's the number?" or "What's leading?" Frenchy lived in a centrally located block, opposite Tom's Bar, a local "jook joint" or "bucket of blood" where drugs were bought and sold like a pharmacy. As I walked into the building, I thought about Frenchy's reputation for not building friendships too easily. I felt he had allowed me to see part of his life mainly because I was not a part of it in that way. It was not incumbent upon him to tell me anything, and that made me feel somewhat privileged at times but uncertain at others. I knew, for instance, that this was his work "crib": a spot he dealt, mixed, and packaged drugs but not where he and his wife lived.

In the early 1970s, Frenchy made a tentative entry into the legal labor force. He got a part-time, minimum-wage job but held it for only a year before losing it. He had not had a legal job since, nor had he sought legal employment. He'd been out of the labor force for fifteen years. This was common for most hustlers of his ilk around this time. They had short job histories, then dropped out of the labor market. "You could say I had some unfulfilled ambitions, because when I came up hustling was the way, regular jobs were for squares." Only Frenchy's brother has "gone good," and that was only because he got a job in the Armed Forces.

JAMES

When I first sat and talked with James, his eyes had a look as if they wanted to reveal more than they were able to tell. And the more he told me, the more I understood why. I could have sworn I had seen him before, but as he talked, saying he knew Frenchy from back in the day, I realized I didn't know him. Although I remember seeing him, I can't say I knew him.

The week before, I had seen Frenchy hand him something near the bar, and that, I guess, was the only thing that stood out about him. He had short stubby, hairy fingers. I saw an everyman kind of face, and I suppose an artist would have caught the nuance of his personality, but I wasn't sure I could. He told me:

> When I first got out [of prison] I had nowhere to go really. My old lady had left me long before, hadn't visited me but a few times over the years, and plus I didn't really have much to do with her anyway. So, when I got out, I met up with an old buddy, but I didn't wanna get back into the game, you know the same shit I was in before but what else was I supposed to do. I had been down for more than a deuce and a quarter for one rap and wanted a fresh start. You know. He brought me here [Le Boogie Woogie], and I admit this is the best place I've been into for a while. I wanted to see some chicks but like my buddy says I gotta learn to get outta

> my own way. You know what I mean? Everybody I meet wanna know about my past, and I wanna move and talk about what I'm gonna do from here on in. I made some bad decisions and I can tell you I been living outta magazines, man, and been living a magazine-type life, you know what I mean? I wish I hadda, I wish I couldda, I wish I wouldda, and I wanna get outta that magazine. You know what I mean? Because I believe every time we go in [prison], we take some culture away from our community and I wanna give something back.

He held cocaine pressed into a dollar bill and offered it around. He wiped his nose with his other hand. The barmaid walked over and asked what I wanted to drink. He wore a black, wide-brim felt hat, though it was July, a blue/dark gabardine double-breasted suit, white shoes (polished), and white socks. The polish ran down onto the brown heels. He held a black, Italian-looking man's handbag. "I gotta de-lay myself sometimes. Nobody run, nobody bow. I taught that horn to talk Creole." What he meant I wasn't quite sure. Perhaps he was a musician? But this was outlaw talk, and James was just back from "vacation"—in a word, prison. He was wearing the clothes that had been returned to him upon his release.

He was garrulous about prison, policing, and what he called the "slow death of the community" if people like him didn't start being more activist oriented. "I think a Marshall Plan for prison returnees would be good idea, and I think we, ex-convicts, have a lot to teach people in our community because after all we help fuck it up, you know what I mean? And if we fuck it up then I know we can help build it back up." I wanted to speak with him again, but I only saw him at the spot once. This was one of the frustrations with this kind of study, where people are extremely transient.

Many would have called him a "playa," and they would be right. Though players usually refer to men, many women were players too. Both men and women knew exactly what the game was about. They dressed in fine clothes, suede shoes, and snakeskin boots, and although the wealth was evident, they were not trying to ape their betters but rival their compeers. The silk shirts and shimmer of lace, the sweet perfumes, the delicate aroma of champagne amid the hidden world of money, drugs, and sex, the ability to hang out in the after-hours clubs on the regular—all were part of the allure and mystique of the "spot." They were the predominant type of patron, certainly the most frequent visitor. "I live in New Orleans, and when I come to the Big Apple, this is my standing place. And what they do in here wasn't did like that back down there." I found this use of Ebonics phrasing interesting from a McWhorteresque point of view. "What they do in here wasn't did like that back down there." This usage, to me, was utterly poetic. These were the hustlers who knew a thing or two about human nature, about the opposite sex, about trouble. Who exactly they were and what they represented was what I was trying to find out.

OLLIE

I talked with a guy who worked as a painter for the super of the building where the spot was located. He said he was sixty-three, retiring soon, but couldn't afford to stop working altogether. He was reminiscing about life. A muscular man with bright white teeth, a few scars on his face, wearing a painter's white overalls over white painters' pants. His shoes and shirt white, with a white cap turned straight ahead. He looked like a Santeria priest.

His beard was whitish, too, hair greased with a special pomade, like Dippity-Do, though he had a youthful face. He said his name was Ollie, and he'd been working for the super for twelve years. "I was a junkie for twenty-one years," he said, matter-of-factly. "Yeah, I started taking 'junk' when a girl I knew gave me a snort one night before we had started fucking and it was the best fuck I ever had. And for a long time, I couldn't have sex with nobody else. But then she OD'd one day in the park and that was it. You won't believe this, but I've had a recurring dream with this woman for thirty years. What do you think that means?" I told him I thought it meant she's every woman for him. He looked a bit puzzled, so I continued. No matter what woman comes into your dreams, she replaced that woman for you. "Well you know that makes sense to me," he paused for a moment. "Listen, you a young man and pussy is easy for you now but wait until you're my age, around fifty, yeah that's the number, fifty. At fifty you're be happy to buy some pussy. Because at fifty that's when the baldness starts in, the dick don't get hard like it used to, the rejections set in. People start to call you sir. Your body gives way. The dick gives way to the tongue, unless of course you're Mickey Mouse."

I learned later that the white clothing was not for painting but because he was becoming a "priest" in the Yoruba religion. This white clothing was a requirement: he had to wear all white from head to toe for one year. I also heard he was not supposed to be "touched" during this period. I found that puzzling, since he was touching every girl he could get his hands on. A person sitting alone would usually be approached by the barmaid: "What can I get for you honey?" Once the request was satisfied, be it cocaine, marijuana, or a drink, she might return to chat for a few minutes. Others would approach the table to talk about the weather outside, the latest political event, one's clothing, the crowd in the club, or any number of topics. It was difficult to be in the place and not engage.

A FREAK

A young man and woman were sitting alone in the corner near the door of the club one night. The music of Monti Rock and His Sex-O-Lettes was heard blaring under the smoke-filled atmosphere of the club. As the couple sniffed cocaine, one other woman standing nearby came over and said to the man, "Listen, baby, can I have a little bit? I been waiting for somebody to come in with some all night." The woman, obviously a little high already (or "lit," you could say), was not met with hostility or cold stares but was given cocaine by the couple.

A few minutes later, the doorman came over to them and said, "Don't give her no more of your coke, man, she's a freak." The woman came over again and asked the man what he liked to drink. He said, "Scotch." She ordered a drink for him and his companion. After he received the drinks, he gave her another "blow" from his cocaine, and she walked to the other end of the club, winking to him and saying goodbye.

The doorman's warning indicated that she was there to take advantage of the cocaine offered. More specifically, she was a "freak," meaning she loved cocaine excessively, but when few patrons had cocaine, as was the case this evening, any regular who had cocaine was often approached to share, to sell, and, in general, to be generous. I might note the man kept his coke spoon in his hand and fed her instead of allowing her to do it herself. In this way, he controlled how much she took. She looked him up and down and stared for a moment at what he thought was his crotch, but he later determined it was to see the size of his "wad"—his bankroll. You might think her behavior would cause friction between the women, but this woman was a player, and she did not respect the young girl he was with; plus, it is part of the norm to approach patrons in this way. I was curious when I saw the doorman intervene. Were employees not expected to discuss what the patrons did? What happens to disgruntled employees? I assumed patrons could do no wrong unless they caused serious disruptions, but basically a patron who did not want any contact with others could refuse to engage, lay their head on the table or the bar, stare motionlessly for a time, or give neither verbal or nonverbal cues to others.

There were instances when snorters didn't wish to share their cocaine with others, but since not sharing was considered rude and contrary to the norms of the cocaine scene, some snorters might go to the lavatory to sniff when not feeling generous.

Snorting cocaine in a somewhat secluded area like the lavatory, even within the privacy of the club, was an interesting aspect of cocaine culture, especially since the club was a place where cocaine was sniffed openly. But if the patron had very little cocaine—or cocaine of exceptional quality—they might prefer not to be in a situation where they felt obligated to offer or have to field requests from others. In addition, by sniffing in seclusion, the patron did not suffer any loss of status by sniffing openly and not offering. Cocaine users were under no enforced obligation by management to share cocaine. Passing cocaine was not relegated to any special party mood but took place as an everyday course of action, and such rules were established by the group. However, as patrons mingled and a certain party mood was created, snorters would pass their cocaine around more freely.

THE PLAYER AND THE DANCER

The following observation took place between a dancer and a man I heard Frenchy refer to as a player: The dancer wanted money, but the player wanted the dancer to make him money—a crucial distinction. After arriving this night, I went upstairs, where about eight people were sitting in two semicircles. I had not been to the club in about a month or so, and I was struck by the changes that had been made. Upstairs had in the past been off limits, except for gambling and the occasional private party. The upstairs was now nice and plush, with circular seating. The dance stage had been moved to the center, more or less adjacent to, or opposite, the fireplace. It was now in the middle of the room, and there was a certain amount of congestion as a result. To me it affected something in the room.

The same dancer I had seen a month or so earlier was there. She was conversing with a man who a barmaid told me was a player. He had his hair sort of semiprocessed and was wearing a whitish-green suit with a tie and a sharp stick pin. His fingernails were well manicured. He revealed a large pinky diamond ring on his right hand. He had a machine-gun rap. There was constant wordplay between him and the dancer, who at one point said, "Will you buy me a drink?" He replied, "Of course, I'll buy the little things like the drinks, if that's all you want. I'll buy the little things if you buy the big things, like the house, the apartment, the car. The little things are on me." At that point, she stopped talking.

After a while she said, "Let me show you my legs. You're my man, and I want to show you my legs." He backed up and said, "Wait a minute, baby, I'm *not* your man." She said, "But I thought you wanted me to sit here." He said, "Yeah, I want you to sit there, but I'm not your man."[21] She pulled her chair back a bit. She was wearing black stockings, a longish black dress, an almost formal affair, and what looked like a gold neckpiece. She had a Vuitton bag, in which she kept her clothes. Her hair was wrapped up in a black scarf, and her shoes were high heeled. She continued showing him her legs. The talk between the two of them was easy to eavesdrop on, again, because the stage was in the middle of the room, so there wasn't the kind of intimacy that was present before between the dancer and the patrons, the "starers," the men who often sat right next to the stage, eyeing the dancers, offering cocaine to entice. It is not clear to what extent the dancer played the house ho or sex worker, but the possibility existed, and the interaction between the player and dancer was an exchange between two individuals intent on not giving up anything without getting something in return.[22]

ANOTHER DANCER

It was a night not unlike others; the bar was not crowded, but the owner brought in several new strippers (dancers) for the show. The interaction between the dancer and patron was usually a sexual one, since the dancer was literally enticing the patron. Four Latin men sat in the corner. One was Vital, a regular. One guy in a short overcoat asked the dancer to pose with her breasts in her hands. She sashayed from one side to the other, and one of the men said, "No . . . like this. Like this." Every time she would move one way, he would point or gesture the other way, until she got tired of the game and sat low with her legs spread wide. This same man sitting directly in front of her shouted sarcastically, in a querulous voice: "Show me something. Show me something." The music started, and she got up to dance again. An Eddie Kendricks song echoed through the sound system, repeating the phrase "Boogie down, boogie down, baby," and others in the room sang along. Vital gestured and threw cocaine wrapped in a dollar bill over to the table across from him. As the dancer finally started to dance, people were snorting cocaine with white McDonald's coffee stirrers, which had long stems with a small tip.

One man was snorting from a straw with the edge cut out of it; he was snorting from it, not through it. Three women were sniffing with a lone male, also from a dollar bill. The dancer was young, five foot one or two, about ninety pounds. Her ass was extended like a Koi Koi woman. It seemed the one criteria of management was to have women with big behinds as dancers. Her body was draped in a black leotard, with a black scarf wrapped around her head with the edges draped off to the side. Black flat Chinese slippers covered her tiny feet. She had a small silver bracelet on her left arm and wore two rings, one on the pinky and the other on the index finger of her right hand. Acrobatic and exciting, she lifted her legs, put matches on her nipples (after abandoning the leotards), and lit them while singing "Happy birthday to y'all, happy birthday to y'all!" After dancing exotically and sensually, she descended from the stage platform and danced near the customers. The vociferous man in the overcoat reached up to grab the dancer's breast. She stopped as if in disbelief and immediately slapped him. His friend said, "I don't see why you had to do that, baby. You see you got the man all hot and shit." Her dancing carried her off the stage several times; she would dance around the floor on the chairs, extending her body like a contortionist. She would come off the stage near the chairs, spread her legs and buttocks to fit the size of the chair.

She later felt it necessary to further punish the guy she had slapped earlier, who by now was very high on alcohol, cocaine, and god knows what else. He had his head tilted to the side, with his coat still on. He seemed quite dazed, or at least engulfed in his stupor. She noticed his behavior was at a low ebb and danced off the stage. She moved over to him, dancing, wriggling, and shimmying her body. Once near him, she removed her G-string and started grinding her pelvis around his shoulders, making his body tremble and jerk with a tremor. She carefully, methodically, and rhythmically placed her legs around his left shoulder. She now straddled him, with her abdomen against his ear. Her crotch pressed gently downward against the fur on his shoulder. She did what might be called the "bump," "grind," and "hoochie coochie" all at once.

His body was now shaking the chair, moving almost out from under him. And whether from the impact of her body, the amount of drugs he'd taken, or the shock of her being so close, he was now mesmerized by what he had earlier wanted so much to touch.[23] He seemed in a state of shock during the whole dance episode. He never really tried to touch her or move away. She twisted and grinded her crotch against every part of his neck and face. When she removed herself, the people in the club applauded and laughed, all the time urging her on. The starer never got up to touch or stare again, perhaps out of sheer embarrassment or just too drunk to care.

DEXTER

One night Dexter, a regular of sorts who I only learned later made his living by robbing people and burglarizing homes, including those of patrons of after-hours clubs, described being caught in an after-hours spot breaking into a slot machine. The owner pointed a gun at his head. He admitted he cried because he felt he was going to be killed. This information was volunteered to me unsolicited; talking and snorting are complementary actions, and one goes hand in hand with the other. You talk and snort, with occasional stops to take a drink or just sit back. Because the drug must seep into the brain, the repeated doses produce occasional relaxed moments. If you were in a good little group, the ritual could go on for hours. Comfortable seating is appreciated.

COOKIE AND FRENCHY

Late afternoon, 6:40 p.m., I walked into the hallway. Graffiti written in purple magic marker was scribbled on the first three steps. It read: "Fuck you, Santiago." Frenchy had no children, no close friends to speak of. He did have a brother, a notorious womanizer, gambler, and all-around scoundrel, according to my sister, but Frenchy was reluctant to say much about him. I knew quite a lot about his brother, thanks to my sister's constant complaints about his gambling problems. Frenchy, meanwhile, only saw his former wife, Cookie, when he needed bail money. At the moment she answered the door and told me to take a seat. She "babysat" in the apartment occasionally, and I saw her at Le Boogie Woogie with Frenchy on occasion. "Babysitting" refers to a person who sits in apartments where drugs are kept for pickup at a later date. It is an important but often overlooked role in the drug trade, somewhat like that of a drug mule. Cookie is an attractive, easy-going woman, but she also has a jealous and possessive streak. Frenchy said he was annoyed with her but tolerated her because he liked the attention.

The railroad apartment had green walls and linoleum floors. Frenchy sat at the kitchen table. His bathrobe, draped around his two-hundred-pound frame, was untied at the waist; the belt was missing. "How the hell are you, T.? What's cookin'?" His voice had the inflections and rhythm of a dignitary, a politician, and a gangster all combined. "Wanna beer? Some wine?" An uneasy silence covered the room; usually Cookie was more talkative and Frenchy less loquacious. He was preparing "product" for night sales. The table was littered with plastic bags, spoons, aluminum foil, a scale, a sifter, and scissors. He reached behind him and pulled out from a drawer a plastic bag containing about two ounces of cocaine. He opened the bag, poured its contents into the sifter, gently tapping the side of the sifter with his thumb. After all the powder had filtered through, only pebbles were left. He took the back of a large measuring spoon, crushed these hard crystals onto a separate piece of foil, took the scissors, and cut long strips of foil until he had a pile of neatly arranged squares two inches across. He scooped up various amounts using the measuring spoons, depending on the size he wanted, tens, twenties, fifties. The phone rang. She answered and put the phone down. "Who is it, doll?" he said. She didn't answer him. He got up and mumbled, "Let's get out of here before I have to kill this bitch."

Cookie had held no legal job since the early 1950s, although she occasionally earned money babysitting for neighbors. As a small-time peddler, Frenchy had to turn over large volumes of cocaine and heroin to make a profit. He once made as much as six thousand dollars a week on cocaine sales. Two years earlier, he was busted for possession and served a year upstate. He had not made the easiest of transitions back to the streets. He had to "regroup," that is, reestablish himself by finding a new "connect" and new clientele. His old connect, from "home base" (meaning the police department), was no longer available. He used to get his drugs from a man named "Piggy" (a pseudonym), a cop.

But these days he had a young man, a "pup," according to Frenchy, from whom he got his drugs, but because of old habits, sniffing, consuming, and giving away cocaine in volume, he made little profit, about $800 to $1,000 a day at the most, and more often than not he merely broke even. He got his "material" on consignment, which meant he was given drugs on loan by a higher-up merchant and was required to repay as soon as he sold it. Frenchy would then take part of the money that was left over as profit from the sales. The consignment package need to be turned over quickly to pay off his "connect," or everyone would get nervous. Cookie once opined that "he never really makes any profit but just enough to repay 'Goat,' the young connect. The rest is snorted up and given away."

Frenchy didn't talk about his sales at the club, which I assumed were quite large, for reasons that are unclear, and I was uneasy asking directly about the money he made. I waited until either he told me about it or I heard it from Cookie. I tried to estimate some of the economics of the trade, but I know that's not very accurate or scientific. Considered a low-level dealer or pusher, Frenchy preferred to be called a "merchant."[24] He took daily risks and needed to make a volume of transactions to make money. Additional money came by fencing "hot" items, that is, items stolen by heroin addicts or professional "boosters." He would sell typewriters, tape recorders, radios, television sets (he owns three), calculators, fur coats, and jewelry. You name it, and he'd have sold it.

While the ultimate player was the pimp, second to him was the dealer and his "girl," woman friend, or lady. In white gangster lingo, it was his "moll." I asked Cookie what she was doing. "I'm just chillin' with the villain," Cookie liked to say when in a good mood, when her smirk turned into a smile. She generally found street language vulgar, but she liked to drink rum and coke, and whenever a street phrase came out of her mouth, you knew she had put one too many R&Cs into it. She liked that I was in school and held my head up when I walked, in contrast to Frenchy and other "hoodlums who must hide and creep, so they can't be seen." I have a wonderful photo of her with Frenchy at the club one night. Frenchy was seated at the bar (a .45-caliber pistol in his coat), Cookie sitting next to him. This was during the good old days when I was a student and Frenchy and Cookie were on good terms. They often fought over money, over women, over men, over food, over drugs, over her friends. There were arguments over whom she let in the house, whom she kept out, arguments over anything and everything.

Frenchy even got jealous of me one day when he came home. I was there with Cookie, who had asked me to help her count some money, but before I could do anything he came in and said, "What the fuck you doing here?" Cookie jumped up, fuming, and said: "Don't you dare talk to that boy like that, can't you see he's gonna help you out and me. I can't count all these bills by myself and plus he came over to give you something." It was Frenchy's birthday (though he'd been out all night and it was now the next day). He apologized. "Don't mind me, T. I didn't mean no harm." "Frenchy was just paranoid because he'd been sniffing all night," she said. As it turned out, I never got to help count the money; Frenchy just gathered it all into a bag and left.

Many professions see paranoia as endemic, inherent, a central part of the job. Think of police officers who believe it's them against the world or store owners whose wary eyes treat hoodie-wearing teenagers as thieves, not customers. These vocations have built-in radar detectors for the unusual behaviors, the idiosyncratic movements, the nervous twitches, the pulses of fast heartbeats, the cast of the leery eye, the hesitant walk. No doubt the cocaine dealer fits into the category of professionals paranoid by trade. While this incident quickly blew over because I understood what was going on, I was nervous for a minute because Frenchy was high, hadn't slept for twenty-four hours, and probably was paranoid. I later learned I was one of the few people he really trusted to be in that location—and that I was one of only a handful of people who had ever visited him while he was in prison.

Frenchy was sent to Dannemora, a notorious prison near the Canadian border. Cookie and I went there to see him on more than one occasion. I visited him at Ossining Correctional Facility (Sing Sing) too, and he never forgot that. He said of all his so-called friends not one came to see him while he was on "vacation" for those four years. He spent time in Rikers first, then Sing Sing, then Dannemora. It was a tough prison for tough prisoners. He said he didn't deserve to be there, but he had been convicted "so many times." It was "too crowded downstate," and he and two hundred others were moved to upstate prisons. Heroin and cocaine were getting a bad rap at the time, and he knew he had to keep away from all of that if he was to stay on the street. He said, "I've got no place to go, and I'll be going there tomorrow. I'm just waiting for the lobster to whistle. You could say I have some unfulfilled ambitions." This kind of talk was typical when Frenchy got too high, not just off cocaine but also Remy Martin cognac, his favorite drink. He was lamenting because Cookie was talking about leaving him (again). Despite his macho attitude, this situation obviously bothered him because he kept returning to the subject. He said she was leaving but that she had no bags packed, no clothes changed. "You call that gone?" When she did finally leave him a few months later, she rented a U-Haul. He commented, "We'll, I'll be damned, the bitch moved in with a shopping bag and now she's leaving with a Mack truck and has the nerve to tell me she didn't get nothing outta our relationship."

Frenchy was sitting in the club now, reflecting. He had the kind of face that went with a baritone voice, but his voice was not too deep, just strong. "Well," he said, glancing over with an Orwellian smile, part glee, part sinister. "I'll be a motherfucker, T. You know, a used-to-be is like a never-was. And I can tell you reason is always inadequate against affection, or reason can never win with affection." I wasn't quite sure what he meant by this. I can't recall him using this phrase again, but there was disgust, or maybe cynicism, in his voice when he told me Cookie was leaving him and had written a letter to that effect. The club was packed now. The time was about 5:10, Sunday morning. It was Mother's Day. He looked over at a table of women and said, "How are all you m-o-t-h-e-r-s doing?" He asked me to go with him back to his apartment. I did. He picked up something from the bedroom, and then we were back on the street. I told him I had to go home because I had a noon meeting. He left his apartment around 5:30 a.m., got into a waiting gypsy cab, and headed back over to the spot on 148th Street, ten minutes away. He later told me what happened, and it was just by fate or luck that I had decided to go home that morning instead of back to the after-hours club.

He said when he got to the place, though a little high, he felt uneasy, a feeling he usually listened to but because he was high, ignored. He walked in. His doorman was not at his post but down the long hallway, conversing with a man with a sawed-off shotgun resting on his shoulder. As he moved further in, he saw two other men with guns as well. One of the men hit him in the face with the butt of his gun and knocked him to the floor. His pockets were emptied. Bleeding and semiconscious, he could hear them asking: "Where is the shit? Where is the shit?" I saw the bruise on his head, still visible a week later, and asked him how much he'd lost. "Plenty. I know those gorilla motherfuckers, but they think nothing can happen to them because it's all contraband, but they made a mistake." Frenchy said he wasn't the only one they'd robbed. They took something from everybody. As long as I have known Frenchy, I've seen him beat up on junkies, knock a man down who called his name in the street, and slap women around, but I've never seen him beat up on men of his own stature and reputation. As kids would say, he never picked on anybody his own size. I guess he didn't want to hurt or shoot or harm anybody that might be able to harm him back. But he was wrong about the contraband comment. Even though nobody reported to the police about these matters simply because it was in an illegal place where almost everyone is "dirty," it depended on who was robbed. There was a brand of street justice associated with this kind of brigandry.

After taking Frenchy's cocaine, heroin, and money, the stickup men rushed out. The patrons retrieved whatever valuables of theirs they could and talked about what happened. I've never been in a place that was being robbed. I'd heard many stories told to me by different people about robberies, but I considered them rare events. Perhaps they were not so rare after all. Dana the barmaid applied cold towels to Frenchy's head. After an hour passed more people arrived, and the party continued. Cookie said what happened to Frenchy happened because of how he treated her, and when she got mad with him later, she said that "the chickens had come home to roost." I kept my counsel on that point.

Frenchy never bragged about owning a club, and one reason was the toll it took on his life. At one point he practically lived in clubs, staying long days, gambling, fucking, dealing, and devouring everything, as he put it, "to know I was alive." But this living caused problems at home, and this was what Cookie was talking about, the way he treated her. Frenchy also didn't brag about owning a club because he didn't want people to know, precisely to prevent situations like these. Robbery, kidnapping, whatever. This is why Frenchy never let me know where his other apartment was located. He didn't tell me, and I didn't ask. As far as the robbery at Le Boogie Woogie was concerned, he said if he had his way, he'd eliminate the long hallway, so people could see who was coming. Patrons, however, said they liked the place because it was full of mystery, including that long dark hallway. Sometimes that mystery came at a high price.

Robbery was nothing new to Frenchy in or out of the club. This was his third, though the first at Le Boogie Woogie. This particular robbery was an embarrassment and he vowed to do something about it. He'd thought this place was above that sort of thing. I guess what he meant was that the type of clientele he had coming there seemed safer, but that didn't make sense to me, since the clientele was not exclusive or anything like that. Even when he was on the lam he'd hung out in these places. He knew these spots like the back of his hand. He hung out in them on the regular, picked up women all the time, and most of all knew about the stickup boys because they'd robbed another joint. One gang came back the same night to rob again. They didn't quite make it. Some said the guys were contracted to Preacher for a fee and were never seen again. Nobody really knew where Preacher hid the bodies. Rumor had it he cremated them in a local mortuary; others said he buried them in abandoned buildings. This cannot be proven, but Frenchy said Preacher had taken care of the problem.

4

AFTER-HOURS NOW

RETURNING TO AN AFTER-HOURS CLUB IN THE 2010s

I'm hit with the smell of tobacco and marijuana smoke as soon as I get inside. Though not suffocating, it permeates the rooms. The odorama is made more powerful by the harmony of colored walls, blending with the patrons' bright clothing. Everything here is charged with an energy, frenetic plans to do wrong the right way. The sweet tobacco brings back memories of my uncle, who would smoke on my grandmother's porch, the odor wafting through the house and down the road. This memory mingles with the sights and sounds of the club, and for a moment I am caught up in a powerful wave of nostalgia.[1]

I wrote *The Cocaine Kids* in 1992; since then much has changed about the cocaine scene, though much has remained the same. The self-conscious cocaine fetish was certainly a feature of the 1980s, but the drug is still used by and popular among hip-hoppers, jet-setters, the middle class, and the poor. Many misusers, some of whom are baby boomers and upper-class hedonists, turn the cocaine powder into freebase and smoke it in pipes and pipettes. While sales and busts of the drugs no longer make the headlines they did in the 1980s and 1990s, the production of cocaine and cocaine-related products, including crack, remain drug-culture staples. But there are signs of change. Some changes are subtle, like the closing of large retail locations in favor of smaller locales or the shift from outdoor cocaine "cowboys" and "street-corner boys" to home-delivery services and mail-order services, some using cryptocurrencies. This harks back to a time when cocaine and heroin and other opiates and stimulants could be purchased via mail order or in wines and in local bars. There are fewer after-hours cocaine houses, or "spots," as they were once known, now because of law-enforcement efforts to close them down. Police raids are more frequent, and in many cases busts are for smaller amounts of the drug. One recent drug bust of a single kilo took several years to complete. Street dealers are harassed, and many are arrested on minor charges unrelated to drug sales. This follows general trends in policing in New York and changing demographic expectations.

Some dealers do not want to be "big time" anymore because of the propensity for "big" dealers to "go down" or be targets of police. Yet several levels of sales remain prevalent, particularly for low-grade cocaine, which is sold at low prices, about $40 per gram. High-grade cocaine sells at $100 per gram. Mixed cocaine products of varying quality are often referred to as "empanada," and their sales often take place at homes, apartments, and on the street. Calls are made to dealers, who respond by alerting buyers where to meet. The new phone technology gives an advantage to dealers over the police because dealers can change the transaction location quickly or stop the transaction altogether. They can switch phone numbers at will and discard phones altogether. One dealer told me: "I'd rather stay off the radar by making a little money that pays the rent, not dealing anything too big because they come after you. The biggest fish in the ocean gets that way by never getting caught." He says this with a wry and pleased look on his face, as if no one had ever said this before. His name is Spencer, his street name is Tweek, and he is a little chubby guy with a small teardrop tattoo under his left eye.

He tells me he's been in the hospital but wanted to see me about something he heard. I often get these kinds of calls when the street word is out about a new scene or when a new drug, such as meth, also known as crystal, K2, Tina, or, like his namesake, tweek, hits the street. He said "meth," or "speed," or "crystal" was "taking over downtown" because, as he tells me, "the white boys were distributing and want to own the street." I asked who the white boys he refers to are. "I heard white boys [cops] want to take over all the blow spots uptown and flood the market with crystal. My woman works, so she says to me don't be out there too long after midnight, and I stay low because I don't want to be busted. I got kids, and I wanna be around to see them grow up." Tweek tells me that the police have instituted neighborhood snitches, meaning police informants (in the negative sense), who act as buyers and point out to police where drugs are sold.

The cocaine kids of today are largely high-school dropouts, like the unemployed teens of yesterday. Over 50 percent of New York City kids do not finish high school, according to recent census statistics. As in past years, these teens are still in search of respect, money, power, and prestige through one strategy or another, including the illegal economy. It is important to note that drug dealing still expands in direct proportion to the rise in unemployment, and unemployment is still the highest it has been in years in poor neighborhoods. Black and Latino teens are hardest hit, particularly since even the many low-level jobs in places like fast-food establishments and other such locations are out of reach. In New York City, unemployment remains extremely high for Black and Latino teens, and there is a great deal of stress in the community at large, since living in poverty limits healthy lifestyle choices and makes it difficult to access health care and resources that can promote health and prevent illness. Unemployment and unaffordable housing are closely associated with poverty and poor health. More than one in ten central Harlem resident adults age sixteen and older are unemployed, and nearly half of these residents spend more than 30 percent of their monthly gross income on rent. Whereas downtown (Greenwich Village, SoHo, and the Financial District), where other clubs are located, unemployment is at 5 percent, which ranks fifty-eighth out of the fifty-nine community districts in New York City. In central Harlem, unemployment is 13 percent and ranks eighteenth, and 29 percent of residents live below the federal poverty level, making it the second-poorest neighborhood in Manhattan.[2]

COPPING ZONES

Distribution patterns, or the way buyers purchase, or "cop," the drug, have changed since I first began studying cocaine culture. Rather than walk to drug locations or into drug zones, buyers now use cars to pick up drugs from prearranged destinations. The foot traffic of the past that once characterized cocaine "copping zones" has diminished. Because most cocaine sales are in cars, which can move from location to location, a major part of the old culture, the social etiquette of the snorting ritual, no longer exists. This act, where dealers offer the customer a snort of cocaine to "taste" before purchasing, was a much expected and pleasurable ritual for the buyer. It signified trust and, in general, produced good feelings between buyer and seller. It is equivalent to the sing-song greeting of customers in French shops or how the customer gets to taste a piece of cheese or meat before a purchase at a deli.[3] As the ritual of snorting before buying goes extinct, it gives a distinct advantage to the dealer. Customers no longer see the actual weight of their purchase, nor can they test the product for purity. This allows dealers to "beat" or cheat customers, and buyers typically are not in a position to complain when the dealer "shorts" them on the sale. Usually, if the buyer comments on the smaller "package," a dealer will simply say they will make it up next time. This may or may not happen. The ritual of "snorting" has become a game of "shorting."

As older neighborhoods become gentrified, abandoned buildings where crack houses once thrived are no longer available. Nevertheless, addicted users will allow their apartments to be used as locations for crack ingestion. In some cases, dealers use intimidation or bribe users with free crack to get apartments in "time-sharing arrangements." These arrangements are set up so people can use apartments during certain hours. My contact Tweek maintains that "police have the drugs now, and they own the streets, they got the spots now." I have no verification of a claim like this, but it does give the sense that dealers no longer feel as in control as they once had.

At the street-transaction level, increasingly pure cocaine is being replaced with pseudocaine, lidocaine, or other synthetics. It is safe to say that most of these transactions would not be considered criminal at all, since what is being sold is not illegal. The "pseudocaine" is more likely to appear in small "nickel-and-dime" transactions, that is, a purchase of an eighth of an ounce or less. Though buyers who have regular dealers of some standing are less likely to "beat" or cheat their customers consistently, defrauding customers occurs for many reasons. Tweek tells me:

> I admit to you but I'd never say this to anybody else, that sometimes, and I say sometimes, if I'm in a tight, my rent is due, my kids needs stuff, my wife's birthday, or maybe it's Christmas and I need to buy something, well, then I might throw in a little som'n'-som'n' that ain't real to make a little cash. I can't do that shit all the time 'cause if I do, I might lose my customers. If he's a good customer, I mean if he spends a hundred or something like that every week, then I won't do that to him. It would have to be an unusual situation for me to beat my regulars.

Other reasons "pseudocaine," or "fake" coke, is sold is lack of genuine "product" on the street. This occurs a few times a year, and though dealers don't know exactly why cocaine dries up, they offer several explanations: "It too hot out there." "The cops just busted a big shipment." "The president is in town." These explanations are given, but the real reasons are anyone's guess. Law enforcement states the reasons as drug wars, battles over turf, both here and in the producer countries. Nevertheless, cocaine is one of the most reliable commodities in American history. It rivals such mainstays as Coca-Cola, Bayer aspirin, and Ford automobiles. Cocaine has maintained its price of around $40 per gram since the 1980s, and it has been available twenty-four hours a day, 365 days a year, for over one hundred years. It is the standard for all illegal products, and every country, including Russia, Saudi Arabia, and China, have cocaine markets. And despite all the bad press, scare tactics, drug wars, and congressional hearings, it has caused fewer deaths and physical harm than almost any other drug, legal or illegal, aboveground or underground. But all of this may be changing because of the introduction of superchemicals like fentanyl and OxyContin and many homemade concoctions, including methamphetamine syrups and Ecstasy tablets, which are altering the toxicomanic landscape in ways unimaginable a few years ago.

THE EFFECTS OF GENTRIFICATION

In the 1990s, when I published *Crack House*, the neighborhoods where the majority of the crack houses existed were full of drug-addicted street life. Many after-hours clubs converted to—or became by default—crack houses. This was both because so many users stayed in these places all night long and because the old intranasal, or snorting, culture was giving way to smoking. Though the crack house had few of the characteristics of the classic after-hours spots, it was in fact an "after-hours"-type place in so far as both revolved around drug use.

Today, renovated brownstones and new and refurbished apartment complexes dot the same once-abandoned landscape. There is the hustle and bustle of street life. The rehabilitation of buildings and the lack of any vacant lots reveal an active, vital community. First and foremost, whites have joined the vast number of Dominicans, African Americans, and Africans in these neighborhoods. Most are not newly arrived immigrants but a middle-class and upper-class population. This constitutes a new mixture of ethnicities in a community that was once the reserve of Blacks and Latinos. There are one hundred thousand Africans in the area, which is now being called "Little Africa." What I see is the new "hood," a place that is changing before our eyes, with cameras and surveillance everywhere, a spic-and-span environment, a place where fewer poor people and more police are seen.

There are no specific locales for after-hours clubs in the city, but whether admitted to or not, they are still part of the recreational needs of city dwellers and entertainment industry of the city. Given the changing demographics and the increasing influx of new money, I think it is only a matter of time before after-hours-type spots will return to this gentrified landscape and cater to the new residents. In Times Square, for instance, a cluster of clubs were raided by the police, and in Harlem's Strivers' Row, several clubs were discovered. But in general it is the low-rent areas of the city where the clubs usually proliferate. Transportation can be an issue. Subways and cabs, both regular and unlicensed, have always been the go-to ways to get around the city. Today "greenies" (green cabs) and Uber hired cars permeate the city, including above 110th Street. There is now a hybrid taxi world between yellow cabs and for-hire cars operating in all boroughs and beyond.

MURPHY'S BAR

All the women see coke as a high-class act.

—Nellie

In search of an after-hours club of today to use a comparison, I looked for a high number of double-parked cars during the early morning hours. This is an indication of some sort of activity, but it is not always indicative of after-hours clubs. Because of problems with neighbors, clubs tend to have "Members Only" signs on the door. After-hours clubs usually operate across the proverbial tracks, in places where communities are known to tolerate profligate behaviors or at least look the other way. This brings to the surface the inevitable reality, a reality mainstream people would wish to deny, which is that every city—indeed every society—is like an onion: there are layers to peel back, decipher, and understand.

Realizing that after-hours clubs are less easy to stumble upon as they once were, I visited a few clubs in the capacity of friend of the owner, as a guest of patrons, as a stranger, or as a pretender, using aliases like "Slick" or "Slim" and telling bouncers and doormen "I've been here before." This often got me into places, but not always. The average time I spent in these places was a few hours, usually from 4 a.m. to 9 a.m. I went every two weeks or so, with the number of visits totaling several hundred.

The clubs can be broken out into categories, which the patrons used when describing the types of establishment they frequented. For instance, when I'd ask what kind of place it is, people would say, "This is a dive, man," or "This is a real nightclub," or "This is a ho's lounge, and the problem with ho's is you get attached to them bitches." Such designations did provide a clue not only to what kind of place it was but also to what went on inside and what type of people you would expect to find there. A dive is usually a funky place, no cover charge, with little or no decent service to speak of, an unflushed toilet with a broken seat, watered-down liquor, and cheap furniture, but usually you can find drugs for sale of the "wack" (bad) variety. Over the course of my search I found and focused on a place I call Murphy's.

Murphy's is located in a popular neighborhood known for bars, clubs, and music venues, on a short street bustling with nightlife, four bars, two on both sides of the street, a bakery, head shop, pet store, and coffee shop, all jammed together. The Chinese laundry, with two old bicycles chained to a stop sign, sits next to a graffiti-covered storefront window. The movie theater is closed, but a pair of chairs sits in front, as if waiting to buy tickets. The 99-cent store, once boarded up, is opening again, with a sign: "Baker's Dough." Across the street and down a few yards on the left is a sportswear store with blue awnings, low enough that kids can jump up and touch it as they saunter by. Murphy's and Le Boogie Woogie are both hidden in plain sight.

I chose to study Murphy's because it is not typical of the Harlem spots of the old days. I wanted to offer a more contemporary place for contrast.[4] New York City was changing in crucial ways when the scene of Le Boogie Woogie was dying out. It was a time of fast gentrification, including in Harlem, northwestern Brooklyn, parts of the Bronx, and western Queens, and there was a sharp decrease in crime, and those transformations were accompanied by new policies aimed at regulating behaviors in public spaces, such as the "broken-windows theory" and stop-and-frisk policing under the mayors Rudolph Giuliani (1994–2001) and Michael Bloomberg (2002–2013).[5] As this pro-morals code began to take hold, after-hours clubs were seen conjoint with sex-related businesses by some politicians. Our understanding of the role of sex in the public sphere has shifted as the meaning of sexual contact has changed. One sex policy included the "60-40 rule" (not more than 40 percent of the material sold in any sex shop can be sex related) and the "five-hundred-feet rule" (which states that no sexual establishment may be within five hundred feet of a school, church, park, or another sex-related business), both of which went into effect in 1998.[6] Not only has the city changed, but so have our attitudes and ways of viewing sex.

Two of my street contacts provided me with my initial entrée to Murphy's Bar, and for six months I got to meet and greet people who made up the key group of patrons there. I spent another six months getting a better sense of the local community Murphy's was located in. People said Murphy's operates differently than other clubs, including keeping erratic hours and management by a quirky bartender and owners who had unusual rules about who could come and go in the place. I started to get a feel of the twenty-four-hour day and began to pay attention to the scene on the Lower East Side, where a group described as "Millennials" are making their presence felt.

These patrons are white, young, well-to-do, and engaging in a cocaine ritual called taking a "bump," the term used by this group. This made the after-hours scene different from previous spots like Le Boogie Woogie. The contemporary after-hours club has changed, just like New York City has. I tagged along with a

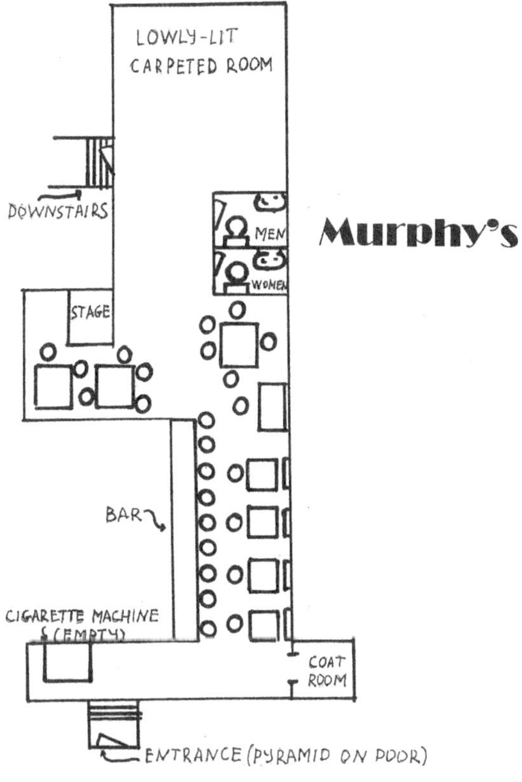

FIGURE 4.1 Murphy's Bar.

regular patron and talked with other patrons, hanging out with them to chronicle their movements.[7] It could be argued that Murphy's and Le Boogie Woogie could be seen as a legitimate marriage, an amalgam of uptown and downtown.[8]

Murphy's members-only club is different from Le Boogie Woogie in that patrons are not allowed to reenter once they leave the premises. In Le Boogie Woogie, patrons were allowed to reenter as long as they were a member. This barlike situation was more similar to the original and visionary "improvisational arrangement" of certain hotels and bars in the late 1980s considered boutique hotels, such as Ian Schrager's Morgan Hotel, which did not advertise their names on the outside.

THE CHARACTERS

The people I know at the bar include Sonny, a talkative, sharp white male in his mid-twenties, and Dustin, who wears cut jeans and boots and has a conservative accent, a white male about twenty-five, tall and lanky. Alice is a regular who knows everyone in the place but could be considered an outsider, since she chooses not to be the center of the action all the time. Buddy is a white male, twenty-something, informative, witty, and smart. Nellie is blonde, aggressive, talkative, and intelligent; White Mike has a receding hairline, wears caps, is short in stature, and is in his mid-twenties.

The duo who introduced me to the place described it this way:

> When you walk up to Murphy's, most times I'm greeted by White Mike or the bouncer. Most of the time he's outside having a smoke, talking to a different girl. I tend to bring a group from the neighborhood and from school, often times with many girls.

> Outside the bar you can also normally find some of the dealers that call this place home, usually having cigarettes or even joints outside, often times standing just over the side of the entrance arguing about one thing or another. If you approach them, most people will be met with instant hostility. These guys are what you would consider the old-school Lower East Side people, the kind of people who if you don't already know them then they don't really give a fuck about you. For me though, it's fine as, again, I often bring groups of girls or guys happy to buy [coke] off of them. I tend to have a smoke with Nellie before walking in just to see what the word for the night is, and of course that means if the after-hours is going down that night.

This is an important point because the after-hours doesn't always open at 4:00 a.m., for a number of reasons. It's up to the discretion of the bartenders, and if they are not in a good mood, not making money, or simply have other plans, then that's it, no late-night partying for anyone.

NELLIE

Nellie is attractive, twenty-three, blond, talkative, knowledgeable, dominant. One night I make note of a young, attractive model type and her lively girlfriends; middle-aged, casually dressed white men silently drinking whiskey; and a group of young Black men conversing among themselves and the bartenders. They were all sharing the small, dimly lit space. There's no common dress code here, no homogenous slang. Diversity of every kind is present in the after-hours scene as well. It seems as though the only common thread among the individuals of Murphy's late nights is a shared love of cocaine.

"Nellie," White Mike tells me, "is always down to have the 'afters,' and I'll check to see if she and others are too and will immediately give me the rundown on how the night's going and how many more people we need inside the bar around 4 a.m. if we want to convince [the main bartender] to stick around." Cocaine is present before Murphy's closes for its exclusive "afters" customers. One particular night while sitting at a secluded booth, I watch a young woman hand her nearly passed-out friend a bump in hopes that it will "wake her up." It was the friend's twenty-first birthday. Often during regular bar hours there are a couple of people in the men's or women's bathroom snorting, chatting, and laughing. Once Murphy's doors close to outsiders at 4 a.m., these bathrooms become more lively, loud, and clouded with cigarette smoke. Men and women gather in the bathrooms to piss, smoke, and sniff cocaine together in comfort. When I see people sitting around the bar or downstairs taking their "bump" on the bathroom counter, I wonder what they must be thinking as they chat throughout the night. I think how many days I have been doing this kind of work—and if it can be called work, because the work is not so much right now but later, when I have to write about the people standing in front of me, the why of why she's doing what she's doing. For instance, there is the woman I see after taking a bump, wearing a purple blouse, holding one side of her nose so tight it must hurt. Why is the tall skinny guy sweating so profusely? Though I think I know why, I shouldn't assume anything and just engage him to find out. Why is the woman behind her not sniffing anything? I should stick to an analysis of the situation: I could see two essential elements involving cocaine rituals. The first element is viewed directly, as obligations, that is, establishing how people are morally constrained to behave; the second element is viewed indirectly, as expectations, or establishing how people are morally bound to act in a like regard.

When I asked Nellie what she thought of the "afters" scene, she said, "People have certain desires, and this place offers them a chance to do them. I think the reason they come here is because they are essentially friends, though I see more and more people I don't know, but the coke is thrilling, and I think everything that is illegal for people is always going to be exciting for human people." I did not expect Nellie's analytical take on the situation and was surprised at her clearly expressed view, since once people start snorting, the talk can be difficult to follow.

SONNY

Some favorable light might be cast about a situation at Murphy's regarding a rumored heroin overdose. Sonny, in his mid-twenties, a tag-along contact, street-smart informant, and funny man, has short black hair, a nervous look, wiry appearance, five feet seven or eight and perhaps 125 pounds. He explained that the rumor about the overdose came from a woman: "She's a professional dancer, which gives me access to parts of New York that typically aren't open to a middle-class guy like myself." He tells me she has only been in the city for a few years but knows the dope scene well. I wanted to know more about the overdose rumor, so I asked him about the drug scene at Murphy's, though I was careful not to mention meth, dope, or ketamine, because I was hoping he would tell me if cocaine was becoming more popular in the late-night scene. Instead he started telling me about an overdosing incident in the bathroom:

> I had run into this girl at a bar uptown, since I knew a friend of hers from school; after an uncountable number of gin and tonics she convinced me to take a cab downtown to one of her late-night spots. The interesting thing for me about Murphy's is unlike many

> of the other club VIP kind of places and events she historically would bring me to, Murphy's operates just like a regular bar, but attracting a very diverse crowd both ethnically and economically. This is the kind of diversity in New York I enjoy most, because it reminds me of my high-school party years, rich kids from uptown, the trend setters from the Village, and then myself and our crazy crew from Brooklyn all getting down. There is very little meth in the social circle that I travel in. I have only known four people who were part of the social life centered around meth. One was a cook who learned about it and was from California. Another one was a cook who got involved with it and was from Arizona. The last two people were both from Jersey, but they developed their habits while living in other places. One developed his habit in Maine. My friend's girlfriend developed hers while living outside in Kentucky. He met her in rehab.

Sonny continued, "People shoot up in bathrooms all over city these days because those are places where people feel safe enough to do that. You know there are no cameras in bathrooms, and the stalls provide privacy from other people peeping in. The more heavily used the better." This is a way to avoid suspicion and blend in with the crowd as they stream into and out of the bathroom. I should note that one of the regulars told me that they too had heard about someone shooting up (cocaine) at Murphy's. This I thought was hardly possible because there is no place for people to do that, but then I realized it was in fact doable, since there is a room next to the women's room that I never saw anyone go into. He also reported how public restrooms were being used more these days as places to shoot up.

I went to Murphy's a handful of times throughout the late spring, but I would always be with NB and her little crew, which limited my exposure and kept me away from really mixing with the other regulars. I started thinking about exactly what the contact's role in all this is. I think of their role as basically someone who helps me gain entry and acts as sponsor, someone who helps me understand and translate a world that I am only beginning to understand, since I am new to the street scene around the Murphy's neighborhood. I was interested in the downstairs area, especially regarding the gender-neutral bathrooms. Once coke is introduced to the night, these gendered labels on restroom doors become meaningless to users; men and women crowd into one stall to share cocaine and gossip. During the "afters," people gather in the open space outside of the stalls to smoke cigarettes, use drugs, talk, and generally bullshit around, laughing, joking. During this time, bathrooms are as animated as the bar upstairs and, often times, more crowded. Coke can rarely be seen in the upstairs bar—only on very busy nights. Smoking cigarettes is only allowed downstairs and outside. I noted this is referred to as the "hook up," which no longer means with girls or sex but with drugs as well. Those you become friendly with at Murphy's foster a sense of membership in the cocaine after-hours scene.

BUDDY

When I left the bar at Murphy's to go with my contact Buddy, I found myself submerged in a different part of the East Side "uptown," as the bar crowd liked to call it. This location, the Carlyle Hotel's bar, is so upscale I was asked to take off my hat when I entered, which I found annoying. Buddy called it "uptown," which I always find a bit disorienting because whenever I hear Black folk talk about uptown, they mean above Ninety-Sixth Street. When these folks say "uptown," they mean

"Midtown." I also visited the Café Boulud and, one time, the Hotel Plaza Athénée. I'd not seen many of these locations, though I had been to Café Boulud for dinner with my editor. I knew these were places the rich gathered—and that the cocaine followed them there. Buddy and I talked about his business at Murphy's and the people he liked there. Talking with him I got some information regarding the typical prices dealers used both inside and outside the club. Buddy was referring to the "uptown" trade, and he told me how it works. Murphy's was for the most part a place to relax for most of the dealers. "These were provided by Alice and her friend Nellie, both of whom said they were selling most of their product on the Internet these days." Buddy held his hand out and snapped a photo of six colored vials, three two-hundred-dollar vials and three one-hundred-dollar vials (figure 4.2). Some dealers at Murphy's use this setup. The sales and distribution of these small vials resembles the color-coded vials of crack that "back in the day" used to mark a particular dealer's product or territory. Cocaine at that time became a major form of employment for out-of-work youth. But now as the underground economy continues to fuel the cocaine trade, it's not just teenagers selling the drug anymore. By most measures, cocaine use is increasing among young white youths and adults. Buddy said he was all stocked up.

He sent this text:

> Here's the rundown: read it then let us know exactly where you're located & what you need. 1 of the partners will take care of you. We are around Sun-Wed from 5PM to 1AM & Thurs to Sat from 5PM-3AM. Large Lindsey Lohan "shirt" = $100 (Below 38th Street). 39th-48 Street requires minimum 2 Large "shirts" = $200. Anywhere passed 49th St. requires min. 8B (Little over 5gs) = $360. Anywhere below 48th Street 8B = $260. We also carry Molly

> "shirts" = $80. Below 38th Street requires min. 2 Molly "shirts" = $160. Anywhere passed 49th Street requires 3-4 Molly "shirts". We also visit BK, QNS, Alaska, lol as long as the Min. requirement is met. Every time you refer someone to us who calls more than TWICE, you will get a TREAT on your next order. WE NEVER 4get!!!

I wanted to know about the quality of the cocaine they were getting and about the fentanyl scare going around the city. "Well, all you got to do is get a tester set from Amazon, and it can be used to determine if your coke has fentanyl in it. A number of people at Murphy's live in Brooklyn, and they issue alerts in the neighborhood whenever they hear about fentanyl-poisoning cases and warn people not to take anything while the alarm is on." I got him on the subject of the rich kids "uptown" who hang at Murphy's, and he mentioned Malcolm Gladwell, and we switched to talking about *The Tipping Point.*

After we left, I thought about the sociologist Robert Merton's article on the "Matthew Effect," which suggests that those who are successful are given special opportunities, leading to even greater success, and that success therefore is the result of what Merton called "accumulative advantage." The compounding of advantages amplifies as a person continues through life, furthering a person's likelihood of success. Though we didn't talk about all of that, our conversation reminded me of the advantages accrued in housing, for example, when whites were assisted by the GI Bill, which denied Blacks and other people of color the chance to buy homes in postwar suburban developments such as Levittown. This was government-sponsored discrimination. They enjoyed huge advantages over Blacks, who were not allowed to buy homes there, even though many could have afforded to do so. Is this what Buddy was alluding to when he mentioned how his parents first moved there? Why would a rich kid want to deal in street drugs? Was it ego gratification? A need to beat his father at the money-making game? I didn't have the answers, but I thought I would eventually find out if I talked to him long enough.

"I heard mention of Bitcoins," I say. Buddy relates a few facts about Bitcoins, cocaine, and drugs as a commodity. "And someone asks what it was, and in 2016 Bitcoins, that's real money, man, real currency, and I mean real money used by regular, normal people to buy drugs, sell sex, gamble, hide from the authorities, some say they can evade the genome and such." Buddy asked, "Did you see *Vice* on TV last night?" I said no, and he said, "Well, it was about what you was talking about last time about Bitcoins. It's real, and I can tell you a lot more about it if you wanna hear."[9]

DUSTIN

On any given night at Murphy's I've seen at most five different coke dealers. Some, like Dustin and a few others, are more of the regular crowd, but others just come in and out, either looking for business or bringing it with them while they stop to have a drink. This creates an interesting scene at the bar for a number of reasons. To begin with, most dealers bring in their own clientele, which is what creates the diversity in the crowd that Murphy's attracts. The second reason is that on any given night most of the dealers will be selling more than cocaine, particularly MDMA (Ecstasy, also called Molly),[10] ketamine ("jet" or "Special K"), or meth. I have no doubt if you wanted something else you could find it for sale from someone hanging about the place. Some events and happenings in the club have to do with social dominance, influences in the Foucauldian sense of crafting one's own personal technologies of power and the need to have a crew around. This is especially what I saw around those who were not just dealing with cocaine. Dustin, for instance, took the main floor, as he personally didn't do very much of his own product, whereas other dealers hung out in the bathrooms for most of the night, blowing down lines and making sales.

Who gets the sales from those who are considered newcomers to the after-hours bar? That seemed like a bit of a tricky issue. Dustin: "It depends on who they are first introduced to and what crowd they end up with, as in most cases a specific dealer is attached to that crowd of people. There is a level of competition though, if someone isn't making sales and sees someone else getting them, they will either leave or have a word with [White Mike] or one of the other regulars to work something out." There is never any violence because most of these dealers know one another very well, but I have noted some underlying hostilities among them. It's an uncomfortable situation when people in clubs are agitated with one another but not acting on the tension overtly. Occasionally it does lead to violent acts, but rarely. Money is important, but cocaine is even more important because it gives people like White Mike, Dustin, and Buddy a power over others that they'd never had before. Buddy, for instance, said he knew money was there for him because he could get it if he wanted, but he didn't really want his parents' money. Nor did he really want to get busted trying to get rich selling coke. He was out for the power more than anything. While some of what is said here may be true, it is not true that there is never any kind of violence involved, since there are always elements of violence in these kinds of places; it's just not always seen or talked about.

THE NEIGHBORHOOD

Early morning. The smells of fresh pastry emanate from the Sugar Sketch bakery. Sights of dog owners corralling their pets, sounds of kids laughing, playing tag near the school: this is not just a place where folk live; it is a community where people find their social life. It is not just the bars but the churches along the avenue and the many business enterprises where people purchase the things they need. The daytime is when there is the most foot traffic in the area. It is when the sun is up that people mostly go to and come back from work. It is also when they walk their dogs. There are always a lot of dogs and their owners. Most are small and are obviously not guard dogs, and in winter all those dogs have coats and sweaters. I have even seen a couple of dogs wearing hats and shoes. At around three in the afternoon the area fills up with children. There are several schools in the area, and the children range in age from elementary school to high school. Some are in Catholic-school uniforms. But after three in the afternoon, the neighborhood changes. This is most apparent after dark. When the sun sets, the foot traffic shifts as the bars fill up.

Happy hour usually starts around three, but the bars generally do not get busy till around five or six. The restaurants, especially the more expensive ones, fill up around this time too, and most of the patrons appear wealthy, based on their clothes and given the prices on the menus posted in the windows. The only restaurant that seems to have a particularly loyal clientele is the Italian one. One night, after talking to a crowd there, I was told the place has special drinks.

The bars stay pretty full well past midnight, but most of the people will have left before then. After midnight, a different set of street people began to congregate. They are generally Black and not dressed nearly as well. A fair amount of transgender, cisgender, or transsexual Latinx groups cluster around a corner bar near the projects and can be seen conversing near several homeless men who are trying to find places to sleep. There is a man I see occasionally who talks to himself and appears to have mental problems. He is coherent enough to ask me for a lighter and cigarette, but we have never been able to have a conversation beyond that. Regardless, there are not usually many people I recognize as not disengaged from some form of work, hustling, begging, or working, such as pulling the late shift in the corner store, in the city that never sleeps.

I stand in front of a store. It is open twenty-four hours, seven days a week, and is on the west side of the avenue. Next to it is a tiny shop with one employee. It is a little more run-down and does not sell nearly the same quality of foodstuffs, but I've gone in because next to the register are two cases. The first one contains phone chargers and adapters, but the second one displays various types of pipes. Besides the standard pipes for smoking marijuana, it has some glass roses, used to smoke methamphetamine. The difference between meth pipes and crack pipes is that pipes for meth have a bulb at one end instead of an opening. There are two slightly different sizes of pipes. One day I asked if they had "the other kind of pipe." The clerk opened a drawer and had to search for a couple minutes, but he eventually found one used to smoke crack. This pipe had no pretense of being a glass rose. It did not have a box, a rose, or stoppers on each end. It was just a glass pipe. He offered to sell it to me for a discount. I asked him if this type of pipe was sold in the area.

The owner, who appeared to be an immigrant from Southeast Asia, said, "This one is a big seller around here just like all the others." He seemed annoyed with my questions and that I was not buying anything. "Are you crying or buying?" he asked.

I pointed to some Bambu rolling papers. I am not sure if he was willing to risk selling paraphernalia like the rose pipe because it was late at night, and I wondered if he might recognize me, since I often buy candy from him. At any rate, this little transaction was a clue that meth was perhaps still more common than I had assumed.

From 10 p.m. into the earliest hours of the morning, people congregate just outside the front door of Murphy's to smoke and socialize. Like the bathroom, this informal place of social life often seems more crowded than inside the bar. Step outside the front door of Murphy's, and you are standing on a small concrete patio raised about a foot up from the sidewalk. The patio has a metal handrail that customers lean on. Along this handrail bar patrons smoke, chat, and watch who might be getting out of limousines, the general comings and goings. During the normal business hours of ten to six, people bounce between the bar and the street and call out to women passersby.

Having gone to Murphy's at least once a week for the past five weekends, I've gained back my status as a regular, an important factor in whether I am allowed to stay for the after-hours portion of the evening. I set out to know more about Murphy's workers and regulars. I came to know the club workers and regulars as risk takers, thrill seekers, nocturnal transgressors, unconventional outlaws, and paranoids. They were socioculturally diverse with respect to age, race, ethnicity, class, and sexual orientation. They are sexually charged, high-on-drugs individuals.

THE "AFTERS" SCENE

Alice, an outgoing, affable woman in her early twenties, is the keeper of the coke. Being a long-time regular customer and a favorite of the club, Alice asserts herself as the gatherer of cocaine for the rest of her small friend group. She collects cash from the group, disappears to trade with the house dealer, and returns to her friends to let them know they can only come to the women's restroom two at a time. Those friendly with Alice take turns sniffing one of the lines she's cut on the bathroom sink counter, always sniffing with a rolled-up twenty-dollar bill. Those upstairs waiting their turn look out for their friends climbing up the stairs, buzzed and still sniffling. She talked about when they were kids. When they wanted to buy liquor, they would bribe local winos from the street to get liquor for them. "The girls loved us because they could never figure out how we always got liquor without being carded."

This type of participation by women is one of the ways the scene has changed from back in the day, particularly in terms of the way women are viewed. But this is also something I heard upper-class kids do to get alcohol. At Murphy's, like Le Boogie Woogie, drug taking is done with impunity and without regard for the police or state laws. While you could not see cabaret or liquor licenses posted behind the bar at Le Boogie Woogie, they are prominently displayed at Murphy's, which is to say that this club is licensed by city and state agencies to dispense drink or hold cabaret entertainment on the premises. Even though hustlers make up a large portion of the clientele at the club, only a certain kind of hustling is allowed. Hustlers selling "boosted" items are not permitted here, and bartenders are told not to sell anything from the street. The club poses a number of intriguing questions of perception: how do you understand what is hidden in plain sight? More importantly, to my way of thinking, I need to see the city as more akin to Dante's Inferno—its social existence is layered and cannot function or be seen solely through the context of a priest's eyes.

In the case of Murphy's, where patrons from various walks of life congregate to use cocaine, most patrons hear about the club through word of mouth, and guests arrive for the first time either because they bribe their way in, know a member, or come with a member. Some locals are aware of the club because of its proximity to their residences, but most people don't even know the club exists; it hides in plain sight. The proprietors may obtain leases from landlords who look the other way; others own the buildings themselves and are not concerned about fire codes and emergency exits. All that means is as a citizen you are not forced to look at the nooks and crevices of the city as layers upon layers of social interaction and existence. It looks just like (and is licensed just like) any other bar. We are to a large extent pedestrians who rarely attend to what is hidden right out in the open. And the places we see every day but never think much about what they really are may have been there for years, operating in broad daylight, at street level. Since the club closes in the early morning, no real activity is seen besides patrons leaving the club, going to work. Patrons maintain their anonymity from the peering eyes of community members because most residents are asleep when the club closes. On occasion there is noise, but most clubs I've seen have padded, soundproofed walls, and the outlandish behavior within does not usually come to the attention of law enforcement.

As a social scientist, "immersion" implies my being there, and here I go deeper into Murphy's to describe the world I came to see and know. In Murphy's, after saying hello to a few people, I'm always greeted by the bartenders, one of whom is John, the other, James. I get them mixed up because they're both very Irish, from Dublin, have thick accents, and are in their mid-twenties. The bartenders are perhaps the key to Murphy's because not only do they obviously control the flow of alcohol and music, but also, as mentioned before, it is their decision whether Murphy's is allowing the "afters" scene that night or not. It's in everyone's best interest to be buying drinks and tipping the bartenders generously throughout the night. Also, depending on the situation, if the bartenders happen to be in a bad mood, this can be remedied in a number of ways. One night, John was fighting with his girl; she came in and wanted him to leave even before his shift was finished. I asked Mike about this, as I was hoping to stay for the "afters," and he told me to make sure the girl had a drink or two and then have someone give her some coke. After that she would probably chill out and want to stick around. I explained the situation to one of the many coke dealers that came in and out of Murphy's, and because having the after-hours actually take place is crucial for the dealers' business, he quickly solved this problem.

Clubs like Murphy's and Le Boogie Woogie are illegitimate institutions that give regulars and workers access to a wide range of illegal activities (selling drugs, buying drugs, sex work, and the like). Places like Le Boogie Woogie exist because people create them. What is it about cities and people that produce and allow this? I imagine that cities are attractive to people for many reasons—jobs, transportation, culture—and people, once there, continue to build on the city's infrastructure in ways that suit them.[11]

I started having conversations with people around the bar, and I noted how cocaine use has become institutionalized in both pattern and consumption in the city's after-hours scene. It is distributed and marketed for consumption there, and in this sense it is the privatization of an illegal enterprise. Part of the institutionalized function is to set up ways to make members who form the cocaine subculture behave. What I see is how this subculture has not only survived but been nurtured by the city—though it is showing signs of decline. Yet groups of people with similar ideas and lifestyles find active involvement in their subcultures necessary and socially rewarding, and it could be argued that urban life still continues to intensify these subcultures.

My contact's knowledge of street life and culture helped provide some of the first clues about the increasing presence of methamphetamine in the area, and while Murphy's is a cocaine spot, it is clear there are many kinds of drugs being used in the neighborhood. I decided to find out more about the contemporary cocaine scene in the after-hours clubs of the city, and both my main Murphy's contacts and other bridge persons provided key information.

THE "AFTERS" REGULAR IS A LIMINAL FIGURE

Dustin, one of the regular popular dealers, says: "There are regular customers I've seen on every occasion at Murphy's. We recognize each other in the bathroom, talk about cocaine and who we know at the bar." The far-back corner feeds into a tight hallway. You find the men's and women's restrooms down a flight of stairs. The dim white walls of the hallway are decorated with a dozen photographs of hockey players, leading along the wall to two other rooms, neither of which indicates a gender save for the cartoon face of Mickey Mouse etched in the bottom-right corner. No one pays attention whether it's male or female, since only one of these rooms is open. The other is locked and opened only by special permission. The state of the bathrooms is typical "dive flavor"—double seated, graffiti scarred, and masculinity signified. Ironically, this is considered the women's room. It consists of four stalls lining one of four sparse white walls, a double sink counter that is later used to cut lines, and a large, soap-splattered mirror. The men's room upstairs is almost identical, with the addition of a few urinals. Dustin took the package, poured about a gram onto the porcelain side of the sink, and took out a credit card in order to draw a few lines. He then took out a fifty-dollar bill, twisted it into a funnel, and snorted two quick lines. A small tear crawled down his cheek. Neither of us said anything, then after a few seconds Dustin said, "Good shit. Really good shit."[12]

Both Murphy's and Le Boogie Woogie appear to be a-spatial and perhaps to some extent a-racial spaces, meaning race matters are less important than cocaine in these locales, and since cocaine is a social drug, it actually seems to unite people in a social way. As such, I thought it worth delving more deeply into examples of how members of this subculture sustain membership in their community, and as I moved throughout the city, I could see that many of the club members are transient, living alone together. And of course, I could see all the ways they sustain group membership during transient periods, by buying and selling, sharing and imbibing, hooking up. I could see how group membership functions here, too, what it looks like, how it works, and if there is such a thing called community. It is basically because the main currency that makes it work is the drug—cocaine—or the "drug community"; essentially, this is a space/place where people are instrumental to one another.[13] Cocaine has a long history as a global commodity; it is one of the long-standing natural-stimulant commodities, along with tea, coffee, and tobacco, despite the social, political, and legal ramifications it has always borne. At Murphy's Bar, a gram of cocaine is $100.[14] The other drugs at Murphy's people talk about but that I have not seen personal use of include ecstasy, meth, ketamine, heroin, and OxyContin.[15]

At 4 a.m., Murphy's is officially closed to the public, and only individuals familiar with the after-hours community are allowed to stay. All other customers are given the boot. A queue of after-hours-goers forms outside the closed front door, waiting for the bouncer's approval to enter. After 4 a.m., entrance is based on knowing someone who is already a part of the community. I was introduced by two patrons who had known about Murphy's for several years. After 4 a.m., later in the night, the bouncer can be seen drinking and using cocaine alongside everyone else.[16] During weekends, the after-hours scene at Murphy's hosts anywhere from twelve to thirty patrons, and on busy weekday nights the stuffy bar is filled with chatter and whatever music the bartenders feel like playing. The Murphy's crowd tends to stick to cocaine. Once the "afters" at Murphy's actually starts, one of the owners will close the door, draw the blinds, and turn the music up. Everyone immediately relaxes. Like most after-hours spots, once you leave, unless you have one of the bartenders' cell numbers, you're gone for good, and unless you're a regular or have been brought in by a regular, you will be asked to leave before the "afters" comes into effect.

NIGHTTIME

The real night people live at night not out of necessity but because they want to. They belong to the world of pleasure, love, vice, crime, drugs. It is a secret, suspicious world closed to the uninitiated.[17] I took notes during an interview I had with a former Murphy's patron (he asked I call him Mr. Z), when the scene turned for the worse. I was only able to use the camera on my phone to take one picture, and Mr. Z asked that I crop him out. He had to be in a court-ordered twelve-step meeting in an hour and a half, but he was generally open to talk about any topic I asked about. We had breakfast at the school cafeteria, which was mostly empty. In hindsight, this was good, since he was nervous whenever someone walked past us. On the street his demeanor was much more comfortable and confident. Ironically, he suggested I come to his meeting in order to recruit people. He said there were many still-active users at the meeting, some of whom used to hang out at Murphy's and who could probably tell me more than he could. I was thought it was unethical to recruit at an anonymous twelve-step meeting, so I did not attend.

Our first conversation was about his personal drug use and routine. "So what drugs do you use? What's your drug of choice?" was my first official question. "Everything. Whatever I can get my hands on. But I have a dope habit. Obviously, I do cocaine when I can." He reported that he had a "dollar-a-day" habit. A dollar is slang for a hundred dollars. Dollar amounts are rendered as cents. For example, a ten-dollar bag is a "dime." The use of the term "bag" is a generic term for a unit amount of a drug; no weight or dollar amount is assigned to it. His preferred dealers were "uptown." (Again, "uptown" does not mean what most Le Boogie Woogie patrons meant by "uptown." Here "uptown" meant "midtown.") He was vague about where exactly uptown was, but he assured me uptown had the best heroin. It comes in paper bags that are folded and stamped. This stamp lets users know which dealer the heroin comes from. The market is organized enough that dealers have what amounts to a trademark that distinguishes their product from others'. He did buy drugs in the area where Murphy's is located, since he knew there were a lot of users in the area from his meeting. Stamps are not used uptown among black dealers anymore, because there such advertising was bad for business; police used trademarks as a way to arrest people.

I asked, "How do you pay for your habit?" "I fly a sign on the street. I spend most of my day attempting to raise the money to score." "Scoring" is the general term for purchasing drugs. "Flying a sign," he explained, is holding up a sign with a message asking for money. Flying a sign was an important way to avoid contact with the police. Statutes against aggressive panhandling meant that he could not approach a person to ask for money. Instead he had to hold a sign passively and hope that a person approached him. He reported that he makes a couple hundred dollars a day this way. His first priority was scoring, which includes subway fare, since he usually has to travel between where he scores and where he flies his sign, but he did not have a set place. It was only after he scored that he worried about other things. Food was second, and cigarettes were last. He would score cocaine if he had extra money or needed to counter the effects of the heroin.

I also asked him how he got in touch with his dealers. "You got a phone? Do you have to call him, or they got spots up here?" I asked. "Nope, no phone," he said. "I don't need one. I know where to go." "So spots, then?" I asked. "Yeah, they're everywhere uptown. But the dealers don't trust white people they don't know," he replied. He agreed to show me one someday, but there seemed to be a racial divide where the dealers were either Black or Latino. He did report using Link NYC to make calls if he needed too. This is an unexpected use for the city's new "smart" infrastructure. The changing urban space produces a need to reconsider the interaction between the rights and responsibilities of the individual and her society. As the physical and emotional spaces between people diminish, what happens to the right to be left alone and to do what you please with your own body and mind? How can these rights be reconciled with the regulatory duties of the state to protect us from drugs too hazardous for unrestricted availability?[18]

FRANK

NB, my key contact at Murphy's, had known Frank for four years. I was ignorant of his involvement with drugs other than in the "afters" cocaine scene. One common thread is that of after-hours clubs as a second life, a secret life, separate from work and other parts of one's social life. "Frank kept that part of his world secret from those who didn't share the culture or those he wasn't close with. Smart move. Every occasion I spent with him he reminded me that what I was witnessing was special, that he was privileging me with those parts of his life he protected. The closer our relationship grew, the more he indulged in drug use openly with me. The last time I saw him, we talked at 1 a.m. on a street corner. He was so high on ketamine—eyes glossy, hunched shoulders, nervously smoking a cigarette—that his words trailed off. Many of his sentences were incoherent. He promised to let me know the next time he went to 'afters.' He warned me it would be dangerous, but he promised he'd try to protect me. His eyes darted all around the street, watching out for something. Cops? Paranoia was prevalent in this study before my research work could even begin. As I desperately searched for other contacts into the after-hours scene, I was shot down again and again by near-strangers, friends of friends, and people I'd been close with for years. Fear of getting caught, documented, and analyzed stalled my inquiry of contemporary after-hours spaces for months. Once in the scene, I could see that after-hours spaces were protected spaces but not entirely safe ones. Frank fell into a coma, and two weeks later he died. As I process the feelings of sadness, guilt, and anger, I also have gratitude for the time I was so lucky to spend with him, regret that I didn't get more, and frustration with the circumstances that led to a young man leaving the world so soon."

One could argue that the changes in American drug culture is about macro social forces, such as a shifting economic base, housing revitalization, gentrification, resegregation, and a drug-economy expansion that all have created national-level crisis situations for those with low incomes, whether living in rural areas or the inner city. But drug misuse is not just limited to these locations, as increasing statistical evidence suggests. Since white suburbs and white rural communities are possibly the most insidious abusers of opioids and other drugs—and always have been—this is really an American problem affecting the entire country. White kids were once immune from the nasty sting of heroin in the 1970s and 1980s, as media focused on black and Latinx populations. This all changed by the 1990s, as rural whites became major users of pharmaceuticals, especially OxyContin, methamphetamine, and cocaine. Most of those users were white males between the ages of fifteen and sixty-four. The numbers bear this out from 2010 to 2016. Opioids and other pharmaceuticals became the most popular drugs used by whites in the United States, and in 2014 close to fifty thousand opioid users died of overdoses.[19] Today, as I pen this text, more will have died, and the political will to do more about this situation falls on deaf ears.

CONCLUSION

A Culture of Refusal

I want control of my own peculiar altered state.

Drug behavior is only one example of present-day resistance to conservative values and of the desire of human beings to seek pleasurable ways of being regardless of risk. In Norbert Elias's *The Civilizing Process*, what constitutes this process of "civilizing" is basically the concealment of what is repugnant through the invention of manners and etiquette as a social form of approbation. If the act is distasteful—urinating or defecating in public, nose blowing on the sleeve—then such acts should be hidden from sight. This culture of refusal is one of the ways our society began accepting contrary ways of being as normal, particularly in the form of behavior that rejects sobriety and embraces a "chemocratic order" where better living through chemistry is accepted and endorsed throughout the culture.

The after-hours cocaine culture of the present-day Lower East Side of New York and central Harlem of the 1980s, as exemplified by Murphy's and Le Boogie Woogie, respectively, functions as a rite of social exorcism. Patrons expel the virtues of sobriety, righteous living, and convention, what Howard Becker might refer to as "conventionality." This occurs in an opposite manner to a Catholic confession, in a sense. The owner of the club creates a space where people can practice what they preach, which is to act in defiance of the values of so-called mainstream society.

The after-hours club, by its very name, suggests a happening outside the constraints of time. Patrons are forced to abandon what is expected of them, reject the moral object, forsake the home for the jook joint, exchange the wife for the whore, rebuff the husband for the hustler. The social exorcism in the club is a ceremony, one replacing those used in certain religious traditions to expel demons in persons who have come under their power.

The regulars at Le Boogie Woogie were expelling the social constraints and laws that constrained them from acting on their own free will to live life to the fullest. This rite of social exorcism was easy to succumb to because it was wrapped in such finery, such lush elaborations, that it tested the person's will to resist. To some degree, Le Boogie Woogie and after-hours clubs like it sit at a confluence of anonymity and narcissism. It is hard for people to exist in a vacuum of anonymity. Even the street hustler who should remain as low-key as possible cannot resist the temptation to be known.[1] In Nikolai Gogol's "The Night Before Christmas," the Devil produces elaborate schemes to entice people to sin. He goes around the town disguised as the tax assessor, who has the power to peep and creep into people's lives. Gogol depicts the young girl Oksana admiring herself in the mirror and uses this act of narcissism as the hook to get her to reject the blacksmith, and thus the sin of narcissism is planted.

Le Boogie Woogie was not just a place for bohemian swagger types; it was a cross section of folks, regular everyday people, mingling with hustlers and housewives, teachers and tarts, sex workers and swindlers, cops and robbers. It was an organic grouping and certainly more interesting than a gaggle of hippie party-time pleasure seekers. This is not to say there were not upper-class after-hours places too, but the diversity I witnessed in those places was minimal. In the after-hours club, the drug-use habit was "untheoretical" as a focus of a subculture that indeed crisscrossed the classes and was more subversive than one would like to admit. Much of the fascination for me lay in the distance between then and now. It is one reason I revived this study after several decades had passed. The events taking place in the after-hours club are for the most part are now historically invisible, and little has been written about this particular culture of civil cocaine use during that time or since.[2] The after-hours club is another example of disappearing social worlds. At a time when demonizing drug use was a media pastime, in these underground "dens of iniquity" it was imbibed civilly, though not always without incident. Nevertheless, it was ingested the majority of the time with a certain degree of dignity and élan, a life-world lost a decade later when crack cocaine became the rage.

To see the details of the action in the after-hours club, I focused on the subtle gestures, glances, nods, winks, body movements, and nuances of language. And while these observations are decades old, they are not subject to memory lapses. They are recalled from field notes and tape-recorded accounts. Only the framing of the work is newly formulated. Le Boogie Woogie may have closed, but the concept of after-hours spots still exists. Semipublic cocaine use still occurs, as the existence of spots such as Murphy's Bar shows. The after-hours culture changes over time but remains part of the urban fundament.

Cocaine has been called a woman's drug (historically speaking) because of its power over the "fragile female." The myths surrounding the effect the drug supposedly had over women were a major reason men came to the "spot." The coquette Conchita shows the foolishness of such an idea. Marek Kohn wrote in *Dope Girls* that "the creation of a drug underground was a specific instance of cultural modernity and it disrupted several sensitive social boundaries of sex, class and race, and packed these destabilized ingredients into a confined space."[3] In many ways this was true of the after-hours scene, since Latina and white women were commonly escorted by Black and Latino men, and integrated coupling was considered the norm. This was a location where integration was accepted, expected, even glorified, because the after-hours club was part of a drug and sex underground. You could argue this kind of "vice resort" has always existed in the African American community; white immigrants have always used the ghetto as a haven for prostitution, drugs, and illegal alcohol.

In New York City, the institutionalized after-hours club developed and nurtured the cocaine user and nonuser in a private and vibrant social world, the boundaries of which were not rigidly defined in terms of who is a member and who is not. To gain entry you must be a member or an associate, but these clubs can be best characterized as a flexible, adaptable place or social setting that allows people from widely disparate backgrounds to come together in an underground, forbidden location to have a good time, exchange ideas and opinions, and engage in the unconventional practice of drug use. In doing this work, I found all kinds of night people. Eccentric vagabonds, street walkers and talkers, criminals on the prowl, cyclists, and men and women with putrid odors, sometimes called "the great unwashed" by poets—or "stink people" by the police and insensitive academics. I have met drug addicts, transgendered persons, people with physical deformities, and undercover police officers, all parts of a coherent, subterranean, nocturnal world.

In what I call the "soft city" in an upcoming volume, the after-hours world extends the "time zone" to twenty-four hours, since patrons can and do stay all night long.[4] This is about "time-out" time. In the city, for example, there are all-night supermarkets, peep shows, restaurants, taxi limousine services, movie houses, radio, TV broadcasting, rent-a-car agencies, hotels, gay pornographic film screenings, gas stations, candy stores, banks, laundries, film-developing centers, and bus and subway transportation. Murray Melbin hypothesized that "the forces of expansion into the dark hours are the same as those resulting in expansion across the land. That is, a single causal explanation should account for the spread of people and their activities whether in space or in time."[5] Le Boogie Woogie was a fort on the frontier of time, a settlement in the darker regions of the city, and time and place together make up the stage on which people do what people do. Cocaine sniffing, as a form of popular culture, reflected the privateness, rebelliousness, and decadence of the times: low-key, individuated lifestyles as opposed to mass demonstrations, rallies. Cocaine culture is political only in its defiance of laws that dictate behavior that people feel should not be regulated.

Marek Kohn has written:

> Drugs have lost their history. A few antique episodes remain in popular consciousness: opiate use among Romantic poets, Freud's unwise dalliance with cocaine, Britain's Opium Wars against China, the drug fever of pre–Hays Code Hollywood. But there is little sense of how certain drugs came to assume their special role, corrosive and Dionysian, in twentieth-century culture. Despite the political and social saliency of the issue today, public understanding of drugs rests on unsophisticated assumptions. Principal among these is the belief that drug laws reflect a sort of natural law; that the illegality of a number of chemicals is the

> necessary consequence of their inherent pharmacological properties. Indeed, drugs that remain within the law, like alcohol and tobacco, often go unrecognized as drugs at all.[6]

Every community has good places and bad places, places for work and places for play, places for sin and places for atonement, places for hiding and places for showing off. The city community is a complex place, and all sorts of people occupy this urban terrain. Like all communities, vice of all kinds is a reality, whether overt or hidden. Once upon a time, the illegal drugs of today, such as cocaine, heroin, opium, and hashish, were legal, and this demonstrates that whether a drug is legal or illegal is nothing more than a historical coincidence. Today is a time of much cultural unrest, a time when cocaine use is considered a menace. It is seen as a dangerous drug by law enforcement, pilloried as a peril to society by segments of the scientific community, and demonized by the press. While this has been a familiar refrain for many decades, I present a retrospective look at the cocaine phenomenon by focusing on a particular point in time and space in the drug culture when cocaine use was "civil" and when the "rules of engagement" insisted on a set of manners: a site where people actually shared in the use of the drug in a natural setting, a venue situated above the hype and hysteria and where cocaine was used with impunity, calmly, with proper etiquette and good manners.

I evoke here a little-known place, one that has all but disappeared. A place where modern-day gangsters were regulars, such as Nicky Barnes, Frank Matthews, Pee Wee Chadwick, Bobby White Boy, and Alberto "Alpo" Martinez, to name only a few. I look back at a time when cocaine was certainly illegal but regularly used, part of our everyday lives, still bearing the stigma of a "hard drug" yet not quite as nightmarish as its derivative progeny crack was to become a decade or so later. I believe it's important to look back, four decades back, and set the record straight. Cocaine was not the most addictive drug in the universe. Using cocaine did not give the user superhuman strength or trigger violence in Black men that justified police using larger-caliber weapons to shoot them. Cocaine was not predominantly located in ghettos. These and other stories were just that, stories, myths, not true then and not true now. This story is not only about drugs. And as our drug history in America has shown, this story has never been only about drugs. Drugs are the smokescreen for racial injustice, sexism, scapegoating, stereotyping, demonizing, and a host of other issues: power and profit, expanding bureaucracies, selling newspapers and movie scripts, increasing television ratings.

From a methodological perspective, most urban ethnographers do not imagine themselves to be historians in the classical sense of the word. Yet there is an inherent and unavoidable historical framework to all ethnographic work. It need not be strictly archival, in the sense of bibliographic research, yet setting and place are archives too. What do they tell us? This is precisely what is sui generis about the narrative I present here. It explains a complex history of cocaine use, both personal and commercial, that is really a basis for how Black life in poor communities would be reshaped by the so-called War on Drugs.

A class analysis exists here as well, a story about regulation of use. This is the setting the club provides. There are other analytical ingredients that must be used to transcend the symbolic, and those are touch, smell, taste, and sound because they are essentially nonsymbolic pathways toward a culturally meaningful experience. The club provided decorum and its patrons a marked departure from the depiction of "crackheads." With the advent of crack, the chemical nature of cocaine use was altered both by new technology and its accompanying street lore to create greater addiction and, thus, profits. This chemical history is part of the story and, in a certain sense, is alluded to at least in the case of powder cocaine. The "bazuco" method of smoking cocaine was part of the history of cocaine use even before it filtered down to the masses during the crack era. Crack cocaine and the War on Drugs would forever alter the geography of poor Black communities and reshape the criminal-justice system. It is a history of production and use and is a significant parallel argument. But there is also a complicated idea of free will and drugs, that is, the personal desire to alter one's consciousness and the idea of spaces where those desires could be safely permitted but regulated, which after-hours clubs sought to do with their patrons.

My journey concerns the after-hours cocaine-sniffing club and associated bars that catered to drug dealers, hustlers, sex workers, gay men and women, and others who saw the club as a second home, an extension of the living room. It would be unfair to assume that except for their being high on a more regular basis, be it on pot, coke, dope, the whole toxic-manic cornucopia, these folks are in no manner, shape, or form any different from others in society. The question is: What separates the after-hours cocaine sniffer or the regular user of marijuana from the rest of us? Is there such a thing as a real deviant or unconventional bogeyman who is somehow different from the rest of us? The sociologist Kai Erikson states there is a positive function in his concept of unconventional behavior and viewed the "differentness" of deviance as one of the oils that keeps the machinery of society functioning. Erikson reasoned unconventional behavior as conduct that is generally thought to require the attention of social-control agencies, that is, conduct about which "something should be done." "Deviance is not a property inherent in any particular kind of behavior; it is a property conferred upon that behavior by the people who come into direct or indirect contact with it. The only way an observer can tell whether or not a given style of behavior is deviant, then, is to learn something about the standards of the audience which responds to it."[7] Cocaine users, that is, users of unconventional drugs, do this on a regular basis to satisfy both their own desires for pleasure and the demand made upon them by their needs. As a result they find the location or the spot where the activities they most prefer can be realized in as composed an environment as possible. In this sense, the cocaine sniffer is no different than the three-martini luncher or daily happy-hour patron; the sniffer's actions parallel legitimate drug use. The big difference is that one is legally sanctioned, yet the consequences for both can be just as problematic. In the case of the hustlers at Le Boogie Woogie or the dealers at Murphy's, it is safe to say that after-hours life is an essential part of doing business.

The sociologist Howard Becker has an interesting take on the matter:

> Deviance is the product of enterprise in the smaller and more particular sense as well. Once a rule has come into existence, it must be applied to particular people before the abstract class of outsiders created by the rule can be peopled. Offenders must be discovered, identified, apprehended and convicted (or noted as "different" and stigmatized for their non-conformity, as in the case of legal deviant groups such as dance musicians).[8]

In Becker's view, the social system is situated around people doing things together, and in some places the most interesting behaviors are deviant, since they represent the most extreme kind of conduct. But Becker posed the most poignant question related to deviance several decades ago when he asked: How is theory derived at, given that there are so few studies done of specific kinds of unconventional behavior? There are no studies of cocaine clubs in part because most social scientists cannot access such illegal and occasionally dangerous places. After-hours life was not conducive to what became freebase or crack use, because of the repeated doses and the obsessional behavior associated with freebasing. Dysphoria sets in quickly for the freebaser, and the smoker's desire is to recapture that particular high to avoid "the crash." Sex became the most obvious response/reaction to the "hit." This did not mean there were no places where people could smoke, hang out, and have sex, but these were not popular spots, like the old after-hours clubs had been. These new places became "freak houses" and "base galleries" where "basers" or crack users could pay a one-time fee for entering, then another fee for the drugs they would need to stay high.[9] The freebaser was a loner, only interested in smoking the drug until satiated, while the after-hours club snorter was a mixer, a person wanting to mingle, dance, and have a good time with others. These were two different kinds of users. The real task in the Le Boogie Woogie scene was to acknowledge the complexity and humanity of human beings and depict it wholesale—the good, the bad, and the ugly. They all work to tell us something about the whole society. As one late-night patron said to me, "I want control of my own peculiar altered state."

By mapping human behavior—or the idea of the complexity of urban manners, which is to record what people do or decide to do regardless of their class in the club setting, you find the hustlers coexisting with the preacher and the con man, chatting with the rock-and-roll singer, the cop hanging out with the crook, the doctor partying with the patient. The club can be seen as a reading on human desire regardless of social class and accomplishment. All these lives are equally complicated in a community or a neighborhood, and in this sense, I redefine frameworks of deviance. Each new generation has a different take on what drugs mean and what they can and cannot do to the individual. The Baby Boomers saw drugs as panaceas, Generation X emerged when various pharmaceuticals became de facto legal for the middle class, and now the Millennials, those born between 1980 and 2000, are seeing opioids raging out of control but drugs such as marijuana legalized or decriminalized. Yet these are some of the same drugs that were the scourge of the earth before they were born.[10]

Whites are now the predominant users of opioid-based treatment modalities. A recent *Atlantic* article by Ta-Nehisi Coates stated: "And so an opioid epidemic among mostly white people is greeted with calls for compassion and treatment, as all epidemics should be, while a crack epidemic among mostly black people is greeted with scorn and mandatory minimums."[11] It was the sociologist Robert Merton's functional analysis that "uncovered a world layered in ironies: evil producing good, good producing evil, a variety of evidence testifying that benign intention, in emergencies or otherwise, never ensures favorable results."[12] The after-hours scene was and is part of the creation of a drug underground and is a specific example of "cultural postmodernity" because it challenges more than a few social boundaries of sex, gender, class, and race and situated these elements into a small, hidden, secret underground space where a tiny coterie of users could act out their own senses of narcissism. The crack house was mistakenly viewed as mostly lower class, but in fact it had always been mostly middle-class white, as the present opioid crisis reveals today. Even during the heart of the crack era in the 1980s, I met many folks at the crack houses who were upper class. I remember when a poor person who drank alcohol to excess was called an alcoholic but an upper-class person in the same state was considered a "social drinker." These distinctions are class differentiated and also made by those who have the power to define what is and is not deviant.

The difference between a crack house and an after-hours club is perhaps one of degree, and the two places may be more similar than dissimilar. To be "zooted" in the crack house is to be totally fucked up, where as to be "zooted" in the after-hours club is to be pleasantly intoxicated, a condition not always determined by looking at the person, though there are telltale signs. The snorter's lips and face become slightly distorted as the person shows the effect of "the freeze," as it is called. Another sign of being high is excessive talking, rubbing of the face, twitching, and/or grinding the teeth, which is pretty much universal: the central nervous system is stimulated, and the person feels disinhibited. The teeth grinding seems almost to suggest that the person wishes to talk but does not. The crack-house regular is more solitary in his or her drug use and prefers a quiet place to get high and take that "first hit," which is best experienced alone. There are manners associated with both places. In the after-hours club, passing cocaine to others, including strangers, is common, whereas in crack houses, sharing a pipe with strangers is not done at the beginning of the smoking ritual and, as one's drug supply runs low, never done. Crack pipes are usually viewed by crack users as sacrosanct. In a certain way, all of what you see and hear about crack-house culture still exists, yet in other respects it's all quickly disappearing.

The description of the intimate domestic universe still corresponds to the object status of the "get high" and, in turn, to both the higher levels of temporary ecstasy and to the lower depths of despair and inaction. The evolutionary link between the two locations can be found perhaps in the legacy of the "jook joint," which was the institution in the community where both bad and good people went to indulge in vices of one kind or another. The crack house and the after-hours spot are two of those places. The other evolutionary link is with the drug itself. The roles of new technologies and street knowledge played out in the way cocaine was and is used. In one way, the drug took on a life of its own, shaped by different forms of consumption, switching from sniffing and snorting to inhaling and smoking, as a result bringing about new rituals of use.

In some ways, the change in the drug's chemistry or chemical outcome altered the way people responded to the drug, and this alteration may have a lot to do with the brain and how the brain responded to this change in chemistry. Taking a "hit" of cocaine via inhalation drastically affects the "high" a person receives because this hit is so much more powerful than a "snorting hit" of the same amount. The instantaneous high from a smoked hit will produce a strong demand from the brain for another hit, and unlike snorting, where the user of cocaine can reach a satiated point, with smoking cocaine that satiation point is fleeting and more difficult to sustain. This need to consume more of the drug took away the niceties of snorting culture. The difference between inhalation and intranasal use created a different type of response to the drug.

Scarcity also played a part, since one needs more of the drug to get high on crack than on cocaine powder. This scarcity creates a paranoid effect as the drug begins to wear off, and most users began to develop a "me-against-them" mentality. Users tended to hoard the drug as it disappeared. The snorter of the drug, by contrast, can more easily reach his or her limit. They may have nosebleeds or begin to sneeze or gag—one way or another they know they have had enough. The crack user does display symptoms of overuse too, such as vomiting and gagging.

The after hours club and the crack house historically attracted different types of people as a result of the kind of use both places saw. There is also a bit of interest here from the users of both types of drugs, who do not see eye to eye on the issue. Upper-class or even middle-class cocaine users have lives outside of the club, and though those lives may be thug-livelihood bound, they see proper manners and decorum as virtues.

ACKNOWLEDGMENTS

The work related to this book has taken many twists and turns over the years and has benefited from the assistance of many friends, mentors, and colleagues. The original research was made possible by a number of fortuitous events, family connections, and people I met in the after-hours world. A number of people became famous and did not want to be named in the book; others were so eager to be involved they shared their field notes. The assistance they offered provided an important contribution to the making of this book in more ways than they know.

My former students are deeply thanked: Dr. Anahi Viladrich, Dr. Beverly Yuen Thompson, Dr. Cristina Dragomir, and Dr. Shatima Jones. Others who played a key role in the making of the material for this book: Isabella Bauso, Scott Beck, William Borstell, Frenchy Charleston, Jane Ciampa, Marlene Kim Connor, Leo Craig, Paul Craig, Patrick Devitt, Natalia Filippova, Selina Fulford, Rezvaneh Ganji, Tom Gerry, Monica Gomez, Alexandra Harocopos, Hakim Hasan, William B. Heimreich, Yukiko Kimura, Audee Kochiyama, William Kornblum, Jana Leo, Adrian Leung, Dara Levendosky, Noah Lucas, Ye Lui, Carmen Martinez, Jules Ostro, Jackie Oberlander,

Phillip Oberlander, Yvette Pipers, Denise Poane, Dave Ray, Donald Smith, Sergeant Floyd Smith, Jason Smith, Sandra Smith, Teun Voeten, Conrad Walker, Diane Williams, Janice Williams, and Charles Winick.

At Columbia University Press I want to thank my anonymous reviewers and warmly acknowledge the help and guidance provided by my editor Eric Schwartz, Lowell Frye, Marisa Lastres, and the able art staff. Special thanks to James Alicea for his keen assistance and masterful art and to Sandra Smith and Kahlil Zulu Williams for their assistance.

People who remain anonymous by only one name: Alice, Buddy, Caprice, Conchita, Cookie, Dexter, Dustin, James, Janie, Jayson, Jessica, John, Madeline, Mavis, Mike, Nellie, Preciosa, Sonny, Tina.

All my students who assisted in the book with ideas, comments, and suggestions: Patrick Devitt, Dade Dodson, Isabelle Durbin, Tabitha Liucci, Lily Majteles, Jordon Marco, Nina Moss, Sarah H. Pitt-Cort, Mia Pumo, Hailey Redd, Amir Sharif, Amber Shooshani, Jacob Yusufov.

Although all of the aforementioned assisted in some way in the completion of this book, I take complete responsibility for any of its shortcomings.

Appendix 1

METHODOLOGICAL APPENDIX

1980s AND 1990s

The day was warm but not hot in the city. I left downtown and made my way uptown, going back to Harlem, where I did my fieldwork. I live in two worlds, the world of the academy by day and the life of the street by night, and I felt I had to reconcile them if I was ever to be the writer—the sociologist—I wanted to be. I lived in Harlem but spent much of my time downtown in Village eateries, bars, and clothing shops, often mingling with people who I felt at times did not understand or always appreciate "uptown" hoi polloi. By the same token, the academic world only came in contact with my uptown compadres when they became the "subject" of some scholarly inquiry, poor people to "study." I had not thought I'd be following the advice of a bunch of professors telling me to ask questions of people in a Harlem nightclub, but that is what I was intending to do.

My brother-in-law's "connect" to the club made it easier to gain entrée, but he did not assist me in getting into all the places I visited. But my being a "social scientist" is more or less intimately, organically, tied to the lifeworlds and communities I study. Thus, the issue concerning "getting in" raises the bar to a great degree because of what I was learning from doing this kind of work, where much of the worlds I decode is literally hidden in plain sight. I did not walk in with a notepad and start writing down what I saw and heard, but I did record when people were not around or in the bathroom, in my car, and on matchbook covers—part of my "Malinowskian imponderabilia thing."

I did record only the people I knew well and those who asked I tape their stories. These taping situations took place outside the club proper and only a few times inside, when the place was empty. Had I not gotten permission, taping would have been foolishly difficult and dangerous to do covertly—plus it may have gotten me shot, even if I was the brother-in-law of the proprietor.

I believe the reconstruction of what I saw and heard can be considered another methodological tool, and since I am not trained as a professional court stenographer, most of my notes were only an approximation of what I heard and saw. Regardless, in order to write about what I saw and heard outside the limited formal interviews and to maintain a detailed, systematic journal of events, I had to be there. The account of what I saw and heard outside of the formal interviews with people is akin to keeping a detailed diary.

This is part and parcel of the ethnographer's trade, especially in view of what is taking place at the club—much of which is illegal. As an ethnographer, I sometimes start with a question, but when it came to this work, I had many questions. What institutions in the community support a thuggish lifestyle? Where in the ghetto do people who make illegal money go? Where do they spend illegal money? Where are some of the places those who make illegal money hang out to show off their illegal finery? What goes on in these places where thug life is vibrant and active? Where do you go to do something indelicate and off-color or risqué, something illegal, something wrong? Where do you go if you are looking to visit Sin City? A few years ago, you might have gotten a glimpse of this world in the HBO series *The Wire*, in the scene where the boxer, Dennis, goes to a place that resembles an after-hours spot, where all kinds of "deviant acts" are taking place.

My sociologist colleague Paul Willis clearly makes several important points. In brief, the question is: What goes on here? But for an ethnographer, to find out what's happening means going "out there" to find out what's happening *there*. Willis writes about what he calls going "half-native" in describing the ethnographer's role in field research; he says the role engages bodily presence. In other words, you must be there on the scene in body and mind; you must live through the event and have face-to-face contact or bodily traction, a kind of bodily interaction. This means you always have to go half-native, what he calls "bodily implication"; you had to have access to the action and pick up meaning as it happens. I soon learned that the after-hours club is one of the places that supports thug life and hustlers of various kinds, who go to such places to spend their money, so that's where I went.

2017

Once I was in the after-hours world, most people did not know anything about me except that I was a patron who hung around the spot. Most people I only saw one or two times; a few regulars came back once a month or so, but I basically spent little time with patrons after the first night. People did not know I was doing any kind of study. My note taking was never obvious, though I always had a notebook or journal with me and would capture conversations or snippets I'd overheard. I developed several strategies; one was to listen to two conversations taking place on either side of me.

This meant my hearing was quite selective; the approach here is to "reconstruct" the conversations. I would piece together parts of the speech and make whole sentences as needed. If I heard a joke, I would just jot down the punch line because recalling the punch line made the rest of the joke easier to remember.

I was aided by the work of my contacts, what Hakim Hasan calls "bridge persons," who provided notes, introduced me to further contacts, and showed me around areas I had not been privy to. In going over my Le Boogie Woogie material, I realized I needed to provide a snapshot of what the after-hours world is like today (2016–2019), for contrast. This made it possible to gain an understanding of cultural meanings and provide necessary details of the intensive period of the work. In that sense Murphy's is the shadow of Le Boogie Woogie.

I use the field notes from my contacts at Murphy's to visit the current after-hours scene, to give readers both a better sense of what's happening now and a nostalgia for what used to be. This provides better support for the "historical" argument, and since the course of people's experiences with cocaine-related behavior is intermingled at several points with two different locales—Murphy's and Le Boogie Woogie—it will probably be better if I recount both of these places separately. In that way I avoid the error of getting too far ahead of my story, which I might find myself doing, since I am so moved by both accounts.

COCAINE USE AND ECONOMY

Cocaine use has declined in established markets, where per capita consumption was high, and has increased in new markets, where per capita consumption is still low. The cocaine epidemic in the new markets is still at an early stage. The number of cocaine users showed a marked decline in the United States and less significant decreases in Europe over the 2007–2014 period.

Based on the amount of cocaine available for consumption and the number of cocaine users, table A1.1 suggests that the mean amount consumed per cocaine user may have increased over the 1998–2007 period, from 37 to 41 grams per user, before declining to 29 grams per user by 2014.

The estimated global coca-bush cultivation has been shrinking since 1998, showing a decrease in cultivation by more than 30 percent over the 1998–2014 period. It is estimated that one in twenty adults, or a quarter of a billion people between the ages of 15 and 64 years, used at least one drug in 2014. Over 29 million people who use drugs are estimated to suffer from drug-use disorders, and, of those, 12 million are people who inject drugs, of whom 14.0 percent are living with HIV. The impact of drug use in terms of its consequences on health continues to be great.[1]

Despite these regional fluctuations, the annual prevalence of cocaine use remained largely stable at the global level over the

TABLE A1.1 PER CAPITA CONSUMPTION OF PURE COCAINE AMONG COCAINE USERS, 1998, 2007, AND 2014

Year	Amount of Cocaine Available for Consumption (tons)	Number of Cocaine Users (millions)	Average Amount of Pure Cocaine Consumed per User (grams)
1998	512	14.0	36.6
2007	747	18.2	41.0
2014	537	18.8	28.6

Source: UN Office on Drugs and Crime, Division for Policy Analysis and Public Affairs, *The World Drug Report* (2016).

1998–2014 period, fluctuating at between 0.3 and 0.4 percent of the population aged 15–64. However, as the population has grown, the number of cocaine users has increased, from some 14 million in 1998 to 18.8 in 2014. Meanwhile, it is likely that there has been a decline in per capita consumption of cocaine, promoted by a decline in the amount of cocaine available for consumption over the 2007–2014 period, mainly linked to a drop in cocaine production in the Andean region. In parallel, the number of heavy cocaine users in the United States has declined. These facts point to an overall shrinking of the cocaine market, although the number of recreational cocaine users in several emerging markets continues to rise.[2]

Appendix 2

FIELD NOTE SAMPLES

NEW YORK CITY 1

I have gotten to know Conchita these past few weeks more closely. She calls me at home; we discuss her family issues, politics, her sex life, drug-related matters, and the problems of growing up. For the second week in a row she and I have gone to after-hours clubs or discos where she once worked; we've also gone to her place, where a host of friends, mostly male, hang out. I find myself jealous at her teasing and flirting—then in a second, I ask myself how ludicrous I am being. She says maybe she's got a crush on me, and I tell her maybe I've got a crush on her. We both laugh at this banter, but she has begun to show real interest in my ethnographic work and how I go about doing it. She said she's willing to write some of her own views concerning teenagers in New York and agreed to meet up on Thursday for a short time to discuss her life story.

She's seventeen years old (going on eighteen; she will be eighteen in two months). Conchita lives on Manhattan's West Side these days, part time, since the man she sees (her "sugar daddy," as she calls him) pays for the apartment and occasionally visits. Or, as she says, he stays around while she's there and leaves when she wants. I could not get the story straight about what exactly she was saying about this situation; she appears to be hiding something or at least leaving something out.

Perhaps she just doesn't want to say what the situation really is. She is a kept woman or girl, any way you look at it. I met her at an exclusive teenage after-hours club in Harlem, though I did not know she was the "Conchita" I would later know. She used the name "Nana" at that club. Many teenagers who are young lieutenants in organized crews or who are well-established drug dealers have clubs such as Patsy's, where I met Conchita to hang out in. They sniff cocaine, smoke reefer, gamble, and dance. Conchita is a party girl, one of the many young women who frequent these and other clubs to have fun and engage in illicit activities.

Conchita and I met on several occasions at Patsy's, and during one visit around Christmas, we discussed a study of teens I was involved in at the university. She and I began to have regular telephone conversations about the research I was doing. She developed a genuine interest in ethnographic research, methods used, interview strategies, other studies I was involved in, and basically sociology-type questions. I asked her about writing down thoughts of her life, her friends, and her hangouts, and she did. This issue of how much intimacy and empathy the researcher should give to the subject remains an unresolved ethical dilemma, and no definitive answer comes readily to mind, other than to use common sense and judgment.

To say you are married would be one of many possible answers to this question; another would be to use the standard rule, which is never to date the people with whom you work. Questions relating to sex with contacts, or even simply during fieldwork, are rarely discussed publicly. The anthropologist Ralph Bolton, who recounted his sexual life in the field while doing

HIV-AIDS research in Belgium, noted in his account how much it speaks to fieldworkers who do not settle in a community with lovers and informant partners.[1]

But the field is our standing place, too, and most of us work alone—even though the "couples" approach is evident in fieldwork in both anthropology (Margaret Mead and Gregory Bateson) and in sociology (Betty Lou and Charles Valentine, Patricia and Peter Adler, and Robert and Helen Lynds, who conducted the Middletown study).

Sarah Daynes and I wrote:

> Getting into the field single is a lot more complicated for the ethnographer—the companionship helps in having a sense of purpose from the beginning, but being a couple also largely deflects questions and reflections about sexuality. Most of us enter the field single, though, or at least without our partner. Some of us will choose to form emotional and sexual attachments in the field; others will decide on an ascetic route. . . . No matter what decision you end up making about sexuality, it remains that once in the field people attach themselves, and so does the ethnographer. Because people hold on to you and you to them for one reason or another, disengaging must be reckoned with as the ethnographer exits the field; but not all ethnographers actually "get out." Punctual studies, or faraway studies, might be easy to leave behind, for there is a spatial distinction: one day the ethnographer is there, the next, he's gone. Keeping contact, in this case, is a choice rather than a fact of life. But getting out is not really an option if you live in the community where you happen to be doing your research. . . . Daily reminders of my field work greet you in the street in the morning or see you coming from a party late at night.[2]

NEW YORK CITY 2

Lulls, those short periods of quiet in the club, are usually around 4 a.m., before the place has many patrons; or during bad weather, when few people show up; or early morning or midday, when everyone has left. I would try to take the opportunity to chat with Frenchy during some of these down times as we waited for the action to start.

Frenchy, born in rural Kentucky, joined what he called a "minstrel show" as a dancer after leaving the army at nineteen. He traveled from Maine to Mississippi with the show, making the trip a few times before getting into a fight with a white man in a gambling game in North Carolina in 1951. He moved up north to live with an aunt afterward and soon got involved with the numbers (policy) racket.

He said, "I could never stand that day job thing because I couldn't take orders from nobody, white or Black. The numbers game was very exciting to me. I could make $80 or $90 [per day] without even trying, and pretty soon, I was making a hundred, two hundred. And, for a kid, that was like being rich." Frenchy got involved with drugs through the numbers racket. Many of his customers would ask him for "reefer," and he started selling it. This was during the 1950s and 1960s. He's the brother of my sister's husband, and he allowed me to write about his life as a drug peddler and operator of the after-hours club.

A cocaine peddler's main line of work is to sell cocaine, though on occasion one may sell anything from marijuana and heroin to typewriters, stereos, tape recorders, and other gadgets they get from street hustlers. But the main business is dispensing cocaine. As a peddler, he must possess a certain knowledge of drugs, have acute street skills, and be able to determine, without the assistance of chemicals and equipment, a drug's quality and value. He must be able to tell whether it is synthetic, how pure it is, and how much it is worth on the street.

He must identify cocaine adulterants and have a working knowledge of the metric system (since sales are based on metric weight, much of the time). He must use critical judgment in acquiring the drug, in combination with sharp, "streetwise" bargaining skills. He must know how to measure, package, and cut the drug, which skills are learned through doing. Dealers are usually taught by someone who has "street-drug knowledge" already, but Frenchy didn't say whom he learned from. The actual selling of the cocaine also involves interpersonal skills, and the peddler must be able to "lay low" when necessary and be able to recognize "narcs" (undercover police). In other words, dealers must be sharp, cunning, and persuasive.

A dealer with a regular house clientele does not necessarily have to be an extrovert with a "sharp rap," but the street peddler and/or bar dealer must be articulate and a good salesperson. All kinds of dealers must be able to sell in a competitive market, that is, by making their product seem better than it actually is. In addition, the dealer must be "street tough": he must be able to use a gun or other forms of defense or coercion when necessary.

Street hustling involves a complicated network of interacting factors, and whether the hustle is three-card monte (a street card game also called three-card molly) or cocaine dealing, it involves some degree of risk. Cocaine hustling is no different in that it involves the ability to con, a degree of risk, and an awareness of socioecological conditions (such as selling cocaine in closed areas, like a bar or an apartment, as opposed to open areas like the street corner, or convincing buyers the drug is better than it really is, even selling part-bogus, part-real drugs). And finally, the dealer must have a certain business sense because he ideally should know how to invest his earnings once the sales are made. In our talk, some of these hustling elements are borne out:

> There are a coupla things you should know about this business; number one, anybody you meet you don't know is either on the pad [bribed] or wants to be [bribable], and I haven't met a stranger in this business who wasn't a cop. Number two, if you on the phone for longer than one minute the receiver is tapped; number three, if you dealing with the club, don't cut the product, keep it strong because everybody else is cutting it and that would make your end stand up; and four, keep your stash and the product separated; if you got a piece [gun] make sure you ain't carrying it in the spot, stash it unmarked.

NEW YORK CITY 3

Conchita was described by one of her girlfriends: "She's a trip, but she's smart. You should talk to her." I've been lucky to have met some teenagers who hang out in the nightclubs. I don't usually like to do field notes in such a scattered way, but I realize to document the lives of people in the after hours, especially the teens at night, I will have to step up and write notes every day, since things are starting to blend together. I ask myself what it means to have kids at this level of the hustling scene, buying and selling coke, doing coke, being players at such a young age. Otherwise, I would have a more trying situation on my hands. I usually write every two days after I've been in the field, and that has worked for me all this time, but lately with all the events I've been attending, all the things I've doing, the late nights and all, I've had problems keeping up.

NEW YORK CITY 4

Conchita is a sensitive, extroverted, and attractive girl who longs for self-realization or, to put it another way, longed to realize herself. Yet she was frustrated at her inability to cope with life, you could say even her inability to deal with her own immaturity or her inadequate (coping) abilities. But I may be wrong about this; perhaps I'm projecting these reasons onto her and playing the psychologist here, which I should not be doing, but it's only the way I feel. I do sense that for her, life is one great adventure, and her come-what-may-devil-may-care attitude gets her into most of the trouble she finds herself in, but I recall what her mother said, that she's a "survivor," so maybe she's right and, whatever happens, and though she has no idea what will come, she goes anyway just for the adventure.

And I should not say she is immature because that is not the right word to use. There are those very forces that, I felt, were beyond her control, forces she could not possibly control or for that matter wished to resist. I must say out of all the women I met in this little adventure, Conchita was by far the most interesting and, besides Frenchy, Cookie, Byron, Julio, Vital, and a few others I got to know outside of the club, the only one who revealed so much of herself. I should mention that when I began my study involving teenagers in the city and when I recruited Conchita to be part of that study, I had no idea that our acquaintance would last as long as it did. This is the third year since we first met.

As I thought about it, it was clear Conchita was on the edge, a marginal woman-child, in a liminal place, not quite part of society, though she wants to be, yet not quite the successful hustler type she admires and sees herself being. This ambivalence causes her to fabricate her relationships with those she believes will assist in conferring a privileged street status on her. She constantly makes reference to this or that person (he-say-she-say). It is a perfectly easy way to assume self-importance that would endear the subject to others in the hustling/drug world and as a way to get drugs without paying for them.

It is common in the street to say one knows an important person, be they real or imagined, to build up one's own reputation. She says she knew Frenchy and Alpo (a name unfamiliar to me) and saw Nicky Barnes (a known heroin dealer) at a party and hung out with him, this type of thing. I had no way of knowing if these stories were true or not, but to indicate that one knows a person is one of the oldest means of self-aggrandizement. I believe she fabricates relationships with others to raise her own status in the drug subculture.

Conchita's impression management uses material success symbols—M. Benz ("baby Benz," she calls it), gold chains, diamond rings—which allow her to maintain a street front to aid in perpetuating an image of wealth that will assist in making her "game" credible. This often leads to a trusting smokescreen, "fronting off" in the drug world, which gains her entry into that world. As a risk taker she has developed certain street values and ways of behaving so common to street life.

She epitomizes the street philosophy "I've got to get mine," which describes her own attitude toward life. It is because of these past experiences that she has opted to make money at any cost without regard to the consequences. Conchita has a northern background, uses street slang and phrases when she speaks, but masks a middle-class upbringing, though she never finished high school. She is without a doubt "street smart."

At the same time, she begrudgingly admires the success of those who make it "big," regardless of where they come from in the larger society. She plays with language by using hidden cultural wordplay as deceptive talk, often misunderstood by outsiders. At one point she insisted she was never told the talks we had would be tape recorded and acted surprised when I produced the recorder, even though I had told her at the beginning that some sessions with certain employees and certain patrons who specifically ask I tape their stories would be taped.

But from that point on, she acted as if she was offended by the recording and became short when answering some of my questions and more difficult to understand. She deliberately tried to confuse me with her wordplay, offering no clear meaning in much of her slang talk, particularly in reference to drugs, money, and specific events in her life, as these references were partially formulated plans of action open to many interpretations.

Conchita does not appear to be particularly worried about anything for very long, for example, her father's illness, or the possibility of arrest by the police at the bar she works in, or her boyfriend's delinquency. She has developed several skills distinctly related to everyday survival in the streets, but since she comes from a stable middle-class family it is unlikely she will need them. Contrary to the idea that she was a small-time street operator, it appears she was very much involved in some criminal activities. She referenced cocaine and cocaine buying and selling frequently; heroin was mentioned several times as well, along with her work in an illegal operation at another after-hours club.

She justifies her activities there, for example, by saying that the clubs' patrons needed stimulants, and cocaine, being the most popular stimulant around, is usually the drug of choice. I surmised that supplying cocaine at the high price it brings on the street, especially to a nightlife customer base of fifty or more people on a seven-day basis (or she says they are open only six days), is not a small-time affair. There are people who know others in the street, but it is just as common a phrase to say one knows a person when in fact they "know of" the person. This does not suggest real intimacy or real knowing. Here she waxes poetic on the meaning of the night, that part of the natural twenty-four-hour day during which the sun is below the horizon, the dark part of the day from sunset to sunrise.

"One might call me a nocturnal person," she says, raising her head between tastings:

> I love darkness, late-night hours, and the moon, its mellow warm glow. The night possesses a certain mysterious quality for me that I often have attempted to touch. I now realize that it is intangible and just there to wallow in and enjoy. I've heard night time described as dangerous, unhealthy, perverted, and often people of night hours considered negative. Yet all of this has seemed to have attracted me at a very early age and drawn me towards it more and more as I've grown older.

Conchita let me see her diary notes (and journal), and when I went to return them one day, she told me I could keep them, and I did.

FRENCHY

In the following account, Frenchy talks about getting drugs for the spot; he boasts about having cocaine 365 days of the year. Today he said he had run out. "Call me back later about six," he says to the caller. "Everything should be cool." This was a Friday afternoon, 1:45 to be exact. Fridays are days not many cocaine entrepreneurs are supposed to be without product because weekends mean big dollars. But by six, he was still out of coke. His phone rang constantly; he didn't answer because he knew it was not his connect, who has a special way of communicating.

He's confident the "material" will eventually arrive; cocaine is plentiful and its distribution organized so thoroughly that dealers like Frenchy never or rarely run out of the drug for long. And importers and other high-level traders know it is bad business to be without product when buyers call. And that's why it's preferable not to answer the phone, to let it appear busy even when you have call waiting, than to answer with "no, I don't have anything." Coke dealers hate to say no to a potential sale.

Frenchy: "It's better to let 'em [buyers] think you are home with material and busy than to know you are home without material because they will go looking for product with somebody else. You understand me? If they think you have coke and you have a good rep, they will more likely than not wait, at least, a minute, for you to get something." Frenchy mentions that when he got busted, the sudden loss of the power, money, and prestige that come with dealing hurt him badly. "You see, when you get busted you got nothing. So it's not the fall that kills you, it's the sudden stop of all the action; the money stops, the women stop, the clubbing stops, the scene stops, that's what kills you, you have nothing any more. All you have is what used to be. And we all know that a used-to-be is like a never-was." He shows what a typical Friday was like when he has "product."

Friday, 12:30 p.m.

The dealer is the connecting point between the workaday world of the daytime and the leisure world of the after-hours clubs and nighttime. His sense of work time is not altogether different from regular workers but is organized as if it were not work at all. Frenchy's regular day begins around noon, but that depends on his having product on time. He dresses, eats breakfast, packages his cocaine product, and gets ready to go over to the post office, where he makes his first sales to a changing shift of postal workers who know and expect him at this time. Some employees who work double shifts buy cocaine to help them get through the long workday. Frenchy cracked, "This is one of my best spots. It's a gold mine as long as I keep it up." What he means was he has not usually slept the night before.

Friday, 3:30 p.m. to 4:00 p.m.

Frenchy struggles daily to make the 4 p.m. break of some of the local workers (he likes to nap during this time), which is tough because of his late hours. "A few years ago, I wouldn't have bothered to go over there every day [to the Post Office] because I was making too much bread to bother. But now, well, it's tough, and it's too good to turn down." He sells small amounts to the workers but does not tell me how much.

Friday, 6:00 p.m. to 8:00 p.m.

After making his rounds, it is 6 p.m., and Frenchy is at a local bar called the Cozy on 125th Street between Morningside and St. Nicholas, relaxing, drinking Remy Martin, and making occasional sales but mostly sniffing with his friends. Every few minutes, they will saunter to the lavatory and emerge sniffing, loudly. The bar is a dealer's zone. Here, he waits for the "lames" and "squares," the nine-to-five crowd, to come in, drink, and buy cocaine from him. Freddy, a regular customer, works in a

Garment District factory packing buttons every day, and on Wednesdays, Thursdays, and Fridays, he stops by the bar religiously at 6:15, orders a beer, and buys two twenties from Frenchy. If Freddy isn't there, Frenchy has been known to leave a tiny package (with a red rubber band around it) for him with the barmaid.

Between 6:00 and 8:00, the lame crowd has disappeared, and Frenchy goes back home to change clothes. He eats quickly, sniffing as he eats. Cookie says, "He is the only man I know who can sniff cocaine and eat at the same time."

Friday, 10:00 p.m.

By 10:00, he dresses and goes back to the bar. Many sales are made. Monday through Wednesday at the bar are generally considered slow days, and his income from those three days amount to about fifty sales a day of $10, $20, and $50 foil "packages," worth about $1,000. On Thursday, Friday, and Saturday, sales pick up considerably. He makes mostly $50 and $100 sales during the weekends. I admit I can't truly determine his profit margin correctly and base some of this guesstimating on what Cookie tells me. He gives almost every buyer a taste, a "one-'n'-one," before or during the transaction. He enjoys this interaction and, as a result, gives away a lot of cocaine. It is also important to note that the amount he sniffs and gives away may yield more than the $300-to-$500 figure per day. But most cocaine dealers know they cannot sell all the cocaine they get because a certain amount of it is "business coke," "calling-card coke," or "personal coke." A percentage of cocaine is put aside for these purposes. Most buyers want to be given a sample, whether a small amount to "walk with" or at least a "blow," "a one-'n'-one," to test the potency of the cocaine before purchasing it. What Frenchy does is take the uncut coke (the rocklike pebbles he crushed into the foil) and let the buyer sniff before they taste the "cut" package he eventually sells them. However, there is little difference between the two packages, since he is known to sell good product unless he's "in a bind."

Dressed in overalls, loose fitting, with lots of pockets to hold both money and product, a .38-caliber revolver in his belt under his overalls, he's off to the next bar. This is not his first outfit of the night, and he will change his attire at least one more time before retiring. Cookie is told not to leave the apartment and to expect a call at eleven from a man named Jack. Frenchy whispers he will be back at about one o'clock. The next bar we go to is called the Sham, on 118th Street; it is an established "home base" for him. The operations from the Sham are mostly cocaine sales, while the bar on the "Avenue" (Eighth Avenue), Harry's Bar, is junkie turf, exclusively heroin sales.

We walk into the street and see three men standing around the garbage-can fireplace. One comes over to see him. "What's happening, French? What's good?" "Hey Snake, everything's on the money." Frenchy does not actually stop walking. He has a swift stride; Snake is walking between the two of us. Frenchy walks with him toward a local bar (Tom's Place) and sells him either cocaine or heroin. He continues up the street. As we walk, people either speak out loud to acknowledge his presence or whisper under their breath to one another and point, not so much at him but toward the ground. He never really slows his gait and walks about three blocks with only brief pauses here and there. The red streetlight on Edgecombe Avenue stops us.

Snake, whom I have seen around, asks me what I have been doing lately and inquires about Gator, a mutual friend. He motions for the cars to go ahead. It has gotten colder since we've come out, and Frenchy sees a man across the street he recognizes. He approaches him and yells, "Motherfucker, if you don't pay me what you owe me real soon, your heart ain't gonna be able to stand the pressure!"

The guy is frail boned with big eyes and a bandana around his head. "Don't worry, Frenchy." He nervously goes into his pocket. "I wouldn't shit you, man. I just ain't got nothing right now. This is all I got"—he pulls out a few dollars—"and I gotta eat. You know I gotta eat." Frenchy raises his hand as if to hit the guy. He screams, "I don't care if you never eat, motherfucker. You didn't say nothin' about eatin' when you took *my* shit and spent *my* money, did ya?" Frenchy makes part of his profit from "crediting," a practice of lending out heroin or cocaine to others who sell it for him; this is not the same as consignment because the amount is minuscule. Occasionally, the creditors become debtors who don't reciprocate quickly enough and often come back short or with what he calls "short stories": "All these motherfuckers come into my face with a story. Some long, mostly short. I get them all, though. They say like they got robbed or things were stolen from their apartment. They all stories, no matter how you shake it and, in the end, coming up short on my money. A day late and a dollar short."

They know Frenchy is volatile yet also in a precarious position, in the sense that he cannot go to the police for help. He has to take matters in his own hands and cannot do too much if they don't pay on time. They know he's not going to kill them because then he'll never get his money, and so on it goes. A few years back, Frenchy had several young men selling heroin for him. One of these individuals was continually delinquent in his accounts. After repeated warnings and protestations, Frenchy saw him sitting on a car near the Cozy Bar and struck him on the back of the head with a small lead pipe he picked up in the street. The man suffered a concussion, and Frenchy's "rep" grew.

Now, as the man retreats, Frenchy tells him one last time to get him his money or else. Frenchy, who had appeared visibly upset, gives a quick wry smile as we cross the street to the Sham and finally breaks out in a grin, saying, "I was just woofin', but the dude knows that if I don't get my money, I'll kill him. He'll have it the next time I see him." He offers some reassurance behind his attitude. He says, "You gotta be like that. I got to be tough with these cocksuckers because they will suck your blood. If you let 'em get away with a nickel, they will try a dime the next time, then a dollar the next." This is street accountability and all part of the hustle game.

4:00 a.m.: Heading to the Spot

I left Frenchy around eight in the evening, and he told me that heroin (pronounced "herr-ron") was in short supply. "The drought in skag is here, man. It ain't coming. It's here. If a man wanted to make a million really quick, let him come out with some good dope right now. No, some bad dope right now, and he'll make it. If, of course, he's got the nerve." While the drought in heroin exists, he says cocaine is the most logical substitute. Although the highs are opposite, he adds, "The [junkies] just wanna get high." I ask Frenchy why he doesn't use the new devices out on the market to communicate with his people, and he says he doesn't believe in all that "techno shit."

Conchita, Mavis, Jessica, and the other women had been talking about the new technology and several individuals in the club who have been involved—one way or another—with the drug scene. I had noticed that teen dealers had these devices for their drug businesses before anyone else did: beepers, pagers, cellular phones, radar systems, computers, and other devices were often mentioned. I found this interesting because many of these dealers are not educated in the strict sense of the word. Most never graduated high school, yet they are quite aware of new technologies on the market and how to operate them. All of which has relevance for their "business" practices.

Pagers, for instance, are very useful, as one person can communicate with another simply by plugging in a few code numbers. No words need be spoken. The quantity of drugs to be purchased, the location where the delivery is to be made, and the person who will make the delivery all could have codes, and these numbers can be plugged into the beeper without a word spoken over the phone. In this way, there is no way to trace the call; it could be risk free. Other technology includes police scanners, which can monitor the conversations of the police on patrol. Since these devices are legal, people can purchase them and monitor when the police are in the neighborhood and can even listen in on police conversations. Frenchy goes back home to change clothes and arrives at Le Boogie Woogie, which is open for business. Of course, since the Le Boogie Woogie days the technology has changed, and TV shows like *The Wire* have shown how it has developed.

NEW YORK CITY, 2016

This is another of my contacts speaking here, a friend of Buddy, young, nineteen. He spent time in the South American interior and introduced me to several people at Murphy's. He also made a few important points in conversations with me. First, the after-hours club is not what it used to be back in the 1980s and 1990s, and, second, the ownership is not what it used to be, either.

As a sociologist, I see a redefinition of the after-hours club, a modern version, transient, mobile, technological, a liquid city where what constitutes the city is still guided by a wired element of the fast cityscape. I notice a sharing behavior still present, where patrons pass cocaine to one another in a reciprocal fashion, and if a patron passes cocaine to another, the first person being offered would reciprocate by offering their own cocaine. But the person may still feel an obligation to reciprocate by offering to buy a drink or to share a joint at some point later.

This reminds me of a story by Nikolai Gogol about two Ivans:

> Ivan Ivanovich, when he treats you to snuff, always licks the lid of the snuff box with his tongue first, then flips it open and, offering it to you, says, if you're an acquaintance, "May I venture to ask you, my good sir, to help yourself?" and if you are not an acquaintance, "May I venture to ask you, my good sir, not having the honor of knowing your rank, name and patronymic, to help yourself?" Whereas Ivan Nikiforovich hands you his snuff bottle and only adds: "Help yourself?"[3]

In the next account, Buddy, another Murphy regular, describes how he came to the city for the first time when he was twenty-three and attending school. He is from an upper-class Boston family and got into cocaine as a teenager. He drifted to New York with a girlfriend and was getting money from "mom and dad." He's a tall, skinny man with a serious look about him, appears healthy, with a keen interest in books and technology. We hit it off talking about my latest book. We also both liked foodie talk and trading the names of places where great food could be found in the city. “I live on the Upper East Side more now,” he tells me, “but I hang out downtown because my girl introduced me to Murphy’s. I found the place kind of dull, but I come occasionally and hang.” Then we started talking about cocaine. “When I first got into the drug, I was interested in what you mentioned about the first hit. Do you remember that part?” I said I did but wanted to hear his recollection.

> Well, what the drug does is try to make you realize or at least try to make you grasp on that present moment. It is elusive, you know what I’m saying? It is elusive and unobtainable, except for this drug, which allows the taker, the user, to take hold of it for that split second. That’s why the user says, he is always chasing that first hit. Well, this takes me back to Bono.
>
> You know what I’m saying here right? What I’m talking about is that present moment is what she, I should say Bono, she was my first girl who I got high with on freebase. And what she made me feel while I was on that high was something extraordinary, and one day I’ll tell you why I had to leave that thing alone, and what it took for me to do that wasn’t no easy trip. But what that drug wanted me to do was stay a while longer because of its beauty, its power, its loveliness, its intimacy, its forgiveness—all the sadness of life disappears. In that nanosecond of that feeling, your senses become ecstatic, wowed, because sight, sound, scent, a circus of events, a cavalcade of emotions, sensations, stampede through the skull, each movement signifying a galaxy but somehow lost in a second.
>
> You know what I mean? That drug makes you stop and grasp hold onto that fleeting moment, that apogee, that apex of the high, and so you keep taking that drug to recapture that moment, though it’s impossible to capture that moment, to capture that fragment, but you want to attain those fragments or maybe you

> just want to obtain the elusiveness of those fragments, the mere possibility of recapturing the whole thing again and again creates the craving, the challenge, creates the chase, and this is the elusiveness of the chase, and this becomes the addiction.

I could see Buddy had spent a lot of time thinking and reflecting about these experiences, and I was extremely interested in hearing more of his thoughts about his encounters and his intelligent—brilliant—discussion. But it was months before I saw him again. He also mentioned something about Hazelden but stopped in midsentence and didn't say much more about it, until he mentioned the recently deceased singer Amy Winehouse, who had written a song about rehab. He said how much he liked the song. I tried to bring up the subject about rehab once more, but he didn't pursue the topic, and I didn't either. I assume part of his knowledge about "the first hit" and his problems with his girlfriend were related to this issue.

Hazelden is the name for the Betty Ford Clinic, a rehab center for upper-class clientele. He said he would tell me about Bitcoin and other cryptocurrencies. He also said Amazon might be going into the cryptocurrency business soon and that we should talk about Ethereum (another cryptocurrency) too. He told me about caviar, and that was another way we got to talking about other things we both liked. At any rate, I started going to a place uptown by the end of November, and I met him around midnight; much of what we talked about was again food and drugs. I had a beer and waited outside for him, but after an hour I left. Murphy's Bar includes a diverse group of people.

Appendix 3

WHERE ARE THEY NOW?

Conchita	married and lives in upstate New York
Frenchy	last seen working as a bathroom attendant at Tavern on the Green
Cookie	unknown
Vital	unknown
Julio	rumor has it he was murdered in Washington Heights
Mavis	unknown
Frank	died from overdose of ketamine
Sonny	attending graduate school
Buddy	lives in California
Alice	unknown
Jessica	unknown
Dana	unknown
Margo	unknown
Stevie	unknown
Dustin	unknown
White Mike	bartender in Las Vegas
Nellie	hanging out at Murphy's
Gabriella	unknown

Sonny	unknown
NB	unknown

Some members of the Murphy's crowd are still at the bar.

GLOSSARY

SLANG AT LE BOOGIE WOOGIE

AC/DC: bisexual person

AFTERS: after-hours scene

ALL-SHE-WROTE: the end; final; finished

BABY PRO: teenage prostitute

BAD: good; excellent

BLACK BUTT PLAYER: musician who can't read music (archaic)

BLAST: to get high on any drug or have a good time

BLOW, GIRL, WHITE, WHITE GIRL: cocaine

BLOW JOB: oral sex

BOO, "BAMBU": a brand of rolling paper or an affectionate expression

BOODY BANDIT: person who enjoys anal sex (prison slang)

BOOSTER: shoplifter

BOX: vagina

BOY, BROWN, BROWN BOY, DOOGIE, DOPE, SKAG: heroin

BREAD: money

BUCK-FIFTY: 150 dollars

BULLSHIT TIP: frivolous act, as in "I got busted on a bullshit tip."

BURN: to cheat or to be cheated

CAKE: money

CHICK: woman

CHICKEN HEAD: girl who enjoys oral sex

CHUMP: loser

CLEAN: to be dressed elegantly

COCKSUCKER: a woman or a man who engages in fellatio; also used in a derogatory way

CREAM: semen

CRIB JOINT: house of prostitution

CRYSTAL, SPEED, TINA, TWEAK: methamphetamine

DEAD AND STINKIN': have no money

DIME: ten dollars

DIPPER: pickpocket

DOG FOOD: heroin

DROP A DIME: to make a phone call in a phone booth to inform on someone

FAGGOT: homosexual person, usually male (derogatory)

FELONY SHOES: sneakers

FIRE: to terminate a relationship

FLIP: dead

FLOSSIN', FRONTIN', STRUTTIN': pretending to be what you are not

GEECHE: dressed nice

GET YO' JOLLIES OFF: to have fun

GIMME SOME: to ask for sex

GO DOWN: to engage in oral sex

GONE: a euphemism meaning to go somewhere in an exaggerated way; to be "gone" would not be simply to walk but to fly

HALF-A-"O": half an ounce of any drug

HEAD: to engage in oral sex

HEADHUNTER: a woman who enjoys giving oral sex exclusively

HIT ON: to approach a woman or man verbally in the hope of winning favor

HO: whore

HOG: Cadillac

HUH: to instruct the talker that what was said was not clear and bears repeating

I AIN'T MAD AT YOU: not angry

I'M OVER YOU: don't like the person

IT'S ALL GOOD: things are fine

JELLY ROLL: penis

JOHN: male customers of a prostitute

JOHNSON: penis

JOINT: marijuana cigarette; jail; an after-hours club; penis

THE JOINT: the quintessence of a "thing"; the highest quality

JOOK JOINT: bawdy street café

KICKIN IT': enjoying the situation

KEY: kilogram of any drug

KOIGI: busted

LAME GREEN: an outsider, newcomer, or virgin in experience in life

LAY [*sic*] LOW: to restrict one's activity

LIT: to be high

LOOSE JOINTS: sale of individual marijuana cigarettes

MARK: victim in a con game

METH: methamphetamine

MICKEY MOUSE: denotes amateurishness; a thing or situation on a low scale—"She had a Mickey Mouse game."

MY PEOPLE: loved ones (can be friends)

NICKEL AND DIME: small-time hustler; individual who has not reached a level of sophistication in the trade

NICKEL BAG: five dollars' worth of heroin, cocaine, or marijuana

OCTAGON HEAD: usually dense or feeble-minded person

OFAY: white person, man or woman (archaic)

ONE-'N'-ONE: two pinches of cocaine, one in each nostril

O-Z: an ounce

PIECE: eighth of an ounce of cocaine; a gun

PIMP STEAK: hot dog or frankfurter

PLAY: to seek approval from a man or woman by using various verbal and nonverbal cues

POPPED: to be arrested—"So-'n'-so got popped the other day coming out of Piggy's."

TO PULL: "She attracts the men and is considered the prize if a dude is able to pull her." This word implies motion, a form of play between men and women, as opposed to "getting play" or simply "hitting on" or "rapping to." To pull is actually to "cop," that is, to secure a relationship beyond the moment.

PURE: highest quality of any drug

PUSSY: vagina

RAPPING: random informal talk or conversation

ROACH: the small end of an almost-finished marijuana cigarette: its color and shape resemble that of a German cockroach.

SCOOP: matchbook cover folded diagonally used to lift cocaine into the nose; winning a woman in an encounter

SCRATCH: money

SET: place; an apartment or club where people gather

SHARDS: crystal (meth)

SHORT: car

SHORT HEIST: pornographic literature (prison slang)

SKAG CRAVERS: heroin buyers

SKIMMER: hat

SNORT: to inhale cocaine through the nose

SOLID: great, all right

SPEEDBALL: mixture of heroin and cocaine injected intravenously

SPOON: fifty dollars of cocaine; also may refer to heroin

SQUARE: an outsider; any newcomer who is not part of the subculture

STREET WORD: the street-culture communication network

STUFF PLAYER: a con artist

TAKE IT TO THE BRIDGE: to go to the maximum effort

TATER PIE: vagina

TELL ME SOMETHING SLICK: give a person new information; a form of greeting

"THINK WITH THE WISE, HANG WITH THE VULGAR": proverb

THOT: those ho's over there

THREE-CARD MONTE: street con game

THROUGH: to be finished; complete

TIGHTEN UP: to give or repay a favor; to give someone money, drugs, or sex

TRICK: customer of the prostitute

UH-HUH: to affirm, a guttural sound indicating agreement

VIBES: feelings between people

WEIGHT: larger-than-usual quantity of drugs

WEINER: penis

WHAT IT IS: form of greeting

WHAT'S POPPIN': what's happening

WIG: head or hair

YO: form of greeting or way of getting the other's attention

SLANG AT MURPHY'S BAR

AFTERS: after-hours scene

BOWL, BUBBLE, GLASS ROSE, OIL BURNER, SHILL, STEM, TWEAKER, VALENTINE: Glass tubes enclosing a fabric rose. The term is also used for crack pipes, as there are glass roses also used for smoking crack. These have openings on both sides and are straight, lacking the bulb on the end.

BREAKING OFF: to give a portion of a drug, food, or money

BUST DOWN: share a cigarette

CAPS: metal cap used to render a drug into an injectable liquid

CHRISTIAN, COFFEE, CRYSTAL, METH, SPEED, T, TWEAK: methamphetamine

COME DOWN: aftereffects of an upper, usually a form of lethargy and depression

COOKER: someone who makes methamphetamine

COOKING: act of making methamphetamine; act of rendering a drug into an injectable liquid

COTTONS: cotton balls used to filter liquid drugs; cigarette filters

DUCK OFF: to go to a more private place; to leave the actors involved

HARD: crack cocaine

HIT: successful injection of a drug

NARCAN+: opioid antagonist used to revive a person who is overdosing on heroin or other opiates. Originally offered as an aerosol spray that could revive a person overdosing on heroin, the spray is less successful with fentanyl and its analogs. However, the injectable kits carry a stigma.

PWUD: people who use drugs

REGISTER: see blood in the needle, indicating that one is in the vein and ready to inject a drug

RIGS, WORKS: the collection of instruments used to inject a drug, usually including an IV needle

SHAKE: tiny rocks or powder that equal the purchased weight/amount. Often seen as a sign of the drug being adulterated.

SHARD: solid piece of methamphetamine, similar to a slab of crack

SHOT: the amount of the drug injected. There is no dollar or weight amount associated.

SLAB: single solid amount of crack

SPOOKED: extremely high to the point of paranoid hallucinations, which often become threatening. A person may become actively dangerous. In the South, the term also describes someone who has used a lot of crack.

SPUN-GEEK: extremely high on methamphetamine. In the South, this is also used to mean being extremely high on crack or any other stimulant.

TRACK MARKS, TRACKS: physical marks from repeated intravenous use in the same area. It is a raised red mark that may scar over time.

WELL: normal state. After doing a certain amount a person is no longer feeling the mental and physical effects of withdrawal but are also not high.

WORKS: the collection of instruments used to inject a drug

DRUGS

COCAINE AND METH: the prices are based on whether the drug has been diluted and on who is selling the drug. An undiluted product costs more than a diluted one. A buyer purchasing directly from a high-level dealer may be able to purchase good-quality product without paying the highest prices.

MARIJUANA: the prices fluctuate according to the grade and quality of the plant. Marijuana from certain regions is higher priced than from others.

EIGHT BALL: 3.5 grams, an eighth of an ounce

DOLLAR: 100 dollars' worth of a drug

DIME: 10 dollars' worth of a drug

NICKEL: 5 dollars' worth of a drug. Other amounts, like "fifty cents," may be used, but rarely.

NOTES

PREFACE

1. Sarah Daynes and Terry Williams, *On Ethnography* (London: Polity, 2018), 170.
2. M. Kusenbach, "Street Phenomenology: The Go-Along as Ethnographic Research Tool," *Ethnography* 4, no. 3 (2003): 455–85.

INTRODUCTION

1. Kenneth Burke, *Perspectives by Incongruity* (Bloomington: University of Indiana Press, 1964), 106–7.
2. Howard S. Becker, *Outsiders: Studies in the Sociology of Deviance* (New York: Free Press, 1963), 12.
3. Mario Small, "De-exoticizing Ghetto Poverty: On the Ethics of Representation in Urban Ethnography," *City & Community* 14, no. 4 (December 2015): 355.
4. Sarah Daynes and Terry Williams, *On Ethnography* (London: Polity, 2018), 170.
5. Eduardo Kohn, *How Forests Think: Toward an Anthropology Beyond the Human* (Berkeley: University of California Press, 2013), 22.
6. Phil Brown, *Catskill Culture: A Mountain Rat's Memories of the Great Jewish Resort Area* (Philadelphia: Temple University Press, 1998).
7. Daynes and Williams, *On Ethnography*, 171.
8. Cornel West, *Prophetic Fragments* (London: Eerdmans, 1988).

I. THE SETTING

1. Jack Buerkle and Danny Barker, *Bourbon Street Black* (New York: Oxford University Press, 1973).
2. My contacts never talked about speedballing in the place. "Speedballers" often admit that cocaine overpowers the heroin, and this is why it is so often preferred. Patrons refer to it as "going fast slow."
3. These effects are well documented by the medical use of cocaine. Cocaine was first used as a local anesthetic in eye, ear, nose, and throat surgery because it constricted blood vessels and kept blood from entering the surgical field.
4. The sociologist Georg Simmel spoke of greetings as a form of pure exchange in which people are allowed to reveal themselves or conceal who they are. Georg Simmel, *On Individuality and Social Forms* (Chicago: University of Chicago Press, 1992). The sociologist Tilman Allert suggests greetings "can bring people together or keep them apart" because "they are often considered empty rituals that people perform unconsciously in order to get to what comes afterward—the ends to be achieved once the initial formalities have been dispensed with. But greetings are also signifying structures: they carry their own meanings, set their own preconditions, and entail to some extent their own outcomes." Tilman Allert, *The Hitler Salute: On the Meaning of a Gesture* (New York: Picador, 2009), 5.
5. The sociologist Thomas Gieryn argues: "A place is a unique spot in the universe. Place is the distinction between here and there, and it is what allows people to appreciate near and far. Places have finitude, but they nest logically because the boundaries are analytically and phenomenologically elastic." Thomas F. Gieryn, "A Space for Space in Sociology," *Annual Review of Sociology* 26 (2000): 464.
6. To receive money from a male or female for sex. A "trick" is usually a female prostitute's customer.
7. This is what the sociologist Sherri Cavan calls an "open region," referring specifically to drinking places, but the concept readily applies here and to any bar, club, or lounge setting. "In open regions, those who are present, acquainted or not, have the right to engage others in conversational interaction and the duty to accept the overtures of sociability

proffered to them." Sherri Cavan, *Liquor License: An Ethnography of Bar Behavior* (Chicago: Aldine, 1966), 49.

8. My friend Marlene, a social thinker and scholar of the night, saw this in the 1980s and said: "Cool became a subtle, spiritual guide, a 'correctness within their soul' and with the community (for today's young black males, community is translated into '*hood*'). The struggle to remain cool was very internal." Marlene Connor, *What Is Cool: Understanding Black Manhood in America* (New York: Crown, 1995), 19–20.
9. The 29 percent of central Harlem residents who live below the federal poverty level make up the second-poorest neighborhood in Manhattan. According to the 2010 U.S. census, 62 percent of the 117,943 residents in the area are Black, with 10 percent white, 23 percent Hispanic, and 3 percent Asian. The tourists number in the millions every year. Population by age is interesting: 34 percent are 25–44 years; a healthy, vibrant 21 percent are between 0–17 years; and another 10 percent are 18–24 years.
10. Dapper Dan is a Harlem impresario who incorporated Gucci, Louis Vuitton, and Fendi designs into his collagist ghetto-fabulous fashion; he is a Harlem legend.
11. Terry Williams, *The Cocaine Kids: The Inside Story of a Teenage Drug Ring*, new ed. (New York: Da Capo, 1990), 97–98.
12. The lack of walls is not only a reality but also a stand-in for the message of what a club is. The lack of walls is a metaphoric representation of a city with no walls. Jana Leo, *Rape New York* (New York: Feminist Press, 2009).
13. Those patrons who knew nothing about what I was doing still behaved the old way, and that was fine, but I also noticed there were times when I could see stark changes, for example, in a conversation with a man who didn't want his name discussed regarding Preacher. Before this conversation, he often told me stories without worrying about confidentiality. But with the mention of Preacher, mum was the word. Preacher was a notorious character also known in Harlem as the Undertaker. It was rumored he killed people on contract for big-time dealers and buried them in abandoned buildings. Some say he was more myth than reality; others say he was very real. See Clarence Preacher Heatly, interview, *F.E.D.S.* 2, no. 9.

14. Terry Williams, *Crack House: Notes from the End of the Line* (Boston: Addison-Wesley, 1992), 37.
15. Dave, a patron at a midtown club, expressed his concern this way: "I don't put nothing in my nose that my tongue don't try first. I have to watch out because they be putting Ajax, all kinds of shit in the coke."
16. Cavan's *Liquor License* (138–40) points out how the home-territory bar is patronized over an extended period of time. "Some public drinking places derive their special place from their use as centers of exchange for various goods and services, as well as clearing houses for certain kind of information, other than liquor. Perhaps the commodity most frequently handled in the public place is sex, on either a commercial or non-commercial basis. But there are also bars that deal with stimulant drugs, gambling, stolen merchandise and a variety of other illicit goods. Like the general category of market places, the bar itself is in most instances merely the physical setting where the transactions are carried out."
17. W. C. Alee et al., *Principles of Animal Ecology* (Philadelphia: W. B. Saunders, 1950).
18. In light of what Cavan referred to as centers of one kind of exchange, meaning public sex, the scholar Kimberly Kay Hoang in her enlightening account of global sex work in Vietnam reveals several issues, among them gender. She writes about one typical "girly bar" in Ho Chi Ming City: "The windows were heavily tinted to reveal only dim pink and yellow lighting. When the front door swung open, outsiders caught a view of women dressed in short, skintight Chinese-style dress or leather dresses. There was no exclusivity to the bar; any man could recognize the bar from the street and enter. But Secrets was clearly a male-dominated space; as witnessed on multiple occasions, when white foreign women opened the front door, they immediately turned away as if they had witnessed something private and quickly left the bar. Men generally went there to drink with the expectations that they would receive the exclusive company of an attractive Vietnamese hostess." Kimberly Kay Hoang, *Dealing in Desire: Asian Ascendancy, Western Decline, and the Hidden Currencies of Global Sex Work* (Berkeley: University of California Press, 2015), 46.
19. Hoang refers to women as "Mommies": "At the age of twenty-nine, Hanh, the top mommy of Khong Sao Bar, was highly sought after by

HCMC's [Ho Chi Ming City] most affluent men. Everyone referred to her as one of the most-well-networked women in the world of high-end commercial sex. She had established strong ties with some of the country's richest businessmen and most powerful political officials. She carried herself with poise and had clearly invested a considerable amount of money in plastic surgery, clothing, and accessories to maintain her image. One afternoon, while rummaging through her clothes for hand-me-down dresses to give to me, she told me how she had entered the sex industry." Although the Vietnamese Mommy could be seen as a player, she clearly was more than that, but while operating in "a liminal space connecting relationships established in the informal economy to those in the formal economy. Compared with the other niche markets in HCMC, in Khong Sao Bar the relationships between well-known clients and the mommies seemed to involve more reciprocity, as well as exchanges of equal status." This meant land-development projects and global economic-restructuring deals all linked to high-end hostess bars. In a word, social capital performed in an extraordinary manner. Hoang, *Dealing in Desire*, 80–82.

20. Arnold Van Gennep, *The Rites of Passage* (Chicago: University of Chicago Press, 1960).
21. According to Kimberly Hoang, there are explicit rules for the women, with respect to the hierarchy of male clients seated at the tables. "Implicit rules related to drinking also signified deference. First, when sitting at the table, a woman had to invite the men to take a drink before taking a sip from her own cup. It was considered rude to drink from one's glass without first toasting one's client and the other men at the table. Second, when refilling a client's drink, workers had to hand men their glasses with two hands, one placed to the side of the glass and the other placed underneath. Third, and most important, when clinking her glass against a man's glass, the worker had to cheer according to the man's status relative to other men at the table." Hoang states: "These gestures were critical to helping foreign investors understand who had the most money or political connections. Vietnamese clients rewarded hostess-workers for acting out these subtle gestures that not only buttressed their sense of superiority in relation to their business partners but also helped to establish interpersonal hierarchies among the men in the bar." Hoang, *Dealing in Desire*, 71.

While such deference is not the custom here as it is in Vietnamese and other East and Southeast Asian countries among sex workers, there are many other implicit drug-use rules.

22. "The use of the handkerchief—like that of the fork—first established itself in Italy and was diffused on account of its prestige value. The ladies hung the precious, highly embroidered cloth from their girdles. The young 'snobs' of the Renaissance offer it to others or carry it about in their mouths. And since it was precious and relatively expensive, at first there are not many of them even among the upper class." Norbert Elias, *The Civilizing Process: Sociogenetic and Psychogenetic Investigations*, rev. ed. (London: Blackwell, 2000), 126.

23. "From the 1920s to the 1950s, the juke box did what all popular-culture media must do to succeed: it continually registered desire in terms of economic choice. You put your money into this bizarre-looking creature with its blinking lights and eerie record-changing mechanism bathed in florescence, and you heard your song." James B. Twitchell, *Carnival Culture: The Trashing of Taste in America* (New York: Columbia University Press, 1992), 5. I might add that you reacted to the music with exuberance, and it sometimes made you jump, scream, and shout. The jukebox made the body move. What Twitchell refers to is not only the fact that the "juke box made one person's taste a group experience" but that the personal participation in the after-hours scene could be a lecherous and sexual activity as well. The jukebox, combined with the nasty blues of Dickie Williams's "Come Back Pussy," Chick Willis's "Nuts for Sale," Blues Boy Willie's "Let Me Funk with You," Clarence Carter's "Kiss You All Over," and Artie White's "Don't Pet My Dog" made the action in the club particularly inviting.

24. "The picture of the city that we carry in our minds is always slightly out of date. The cafe has degenerated into a bar; the vestibule that allowed us a glimpse of patio and grapevine is now a blurred hallway with an elevator down at the far end. Thus, for years I thought that a certain book store, the Libreria Buenos Aires, would be awaiting me at a certain point along Calle Talcahuano, but then one morning I discovered that an antique shop had taken the bookstore's place, and I was told don Santiago Fischbein, the owner of the bookstore had died." Jorge Luis Borges, "Unworthy," in *Collected Fictions* (London: Penguin, 1998), 352.

25. "The first introduction of the ticket-a-dance system, a requisite feature of the taxi dance hall, was an importation, not from the west coast, but from New York City. This ticket-a-dance plan was devised—as far as the available information indicates—by a former dance-hall proprietor of San Francisco who in his New York Ballroom combined the line-up system, common to dancing schools, with the ticket-a-dance plan of San Francisco with which he was familiar." Paul G. Cressey, *The Taxi-Dance Hall* (Chicago: University of Chicago Press, 1932), 183.

26. The mores and changes in values and attitudes toward sex in America since the 1960s have led many minority-group women to marginal occupations like strip teasing, go-go dancing, and other forms of nude or seminude dancing. While the internet has made live pornography less attractive to many, strip clubs are still going strong.

27. "In fact, the beach today is something like a dance floor: a space instituted by a juxtaposition of bodies, a space of contacts, sensations, excitement, and pleasure whose free expression is broadly authorized. Although codified and highly ritualized, the language of pleasure is relatively clear—although this had not always been the case." Jean-Didier Urbain, *At the Beach* (Minneapolis: University of Minnesota Press, 2003), 91. But whether the beach or the dance floor, the joint be jumping. Patrons usually dance in couples, but on occasion a member will be seen dancing alone. As I gaze at this scene, this night, the refulgence of the present time, no one has a past life, it is now. Life was right this minute, and everything about the past faded away as if no one ever lived it. Everyone was in the moment, the here and now. There was no used-to-be.

28. This is racial backstage, as Goffman would call it, but at the same time, for the people who hung out there it was front stage and center. Erving Goffman, *Interaction Ritual: Essays on Face-to-Face Behavior* (New York: Doubleday/Anchor, 1967).

29. Ethnographers in dangerous situations or at least very sensitive ones have to "ear hustle" when they cannot overtly take notes or use a tape recorder. I have spent a lot of time watching and writing about what I see, but I could argue I've spent even more time listening. And I also pay a great deal of attention to the ways people talk and sound. For instance, I heard the woman talking about the CeeLo gambling game say: "It's like putting a band-aid on a dead man." I didn't know what

that meant and wanted to find out, though I never did. I just like the phrase. The term "ear hustling" comes from prison slang: it means to listen in on another person's conversation. It is eavesdropping with a twist, because you are hoping to use the information heard to your advantage. This is a context in which deception is a strategy for survival. The club is a place where, when eavesdropping, you can overhear talk relating to homicides, evading a drug warrant, or other such situations. Ear hustling is a street technique with methodological implications because it is also a form of espionage and surveillance and is contingent on hearing *and not* hearing—which is to say a kind of visible invisibility. There are times when I must be like a ghost. I had to listen carefully without appearing to be listening at all. It was my primary way to pick up vital information. Other times my opinion was asked, and on occasions, patrons would take me into their confidence and tell me all kinds of things unsolicited.

2. THE SCENE

1. The rules were different, for example, at a gay after-hours club downtown called the Mineshaft. Here the dress code was opposite to the one uptown: it "expressly forbade designer clothes of any kind, suits and ties and dress shoes, 'drag,' and cologne. It also applauded clothes associated with American culture with working class masculinity: Levi's and leather, t-shirts, boots, lumber jackets and uniforms, and just plain sweat." Joel I. Brodsky, "The Mineshaft: Retrospective," *Journal of Homosexuality* 24, nos. 3–4 (1993).
2. I should point out that I believe there was a certain moral code at the club in which behavior was either condoned as proper or rejected as improper, and that it all began at the door. "The greeting is the first step in a triadic sequence of offer, acceptance, and response. The briefest of gestures within the infinitely variable choreography of human encounters, the greeting opens a door between the greeter and the person greeted and assigns them specific social roles; it creates a mutual present for them and gives them access to each other's past and to a possible common future. Every greeting, even if rejected, reflects how the participants see themselves and their relationship." Tilman Allert,

The Hitler Salute: On the Meaning of a Gesture (New York: Picador, 2009).

3. Loud talking is first cousin to what the linguist John McWhorter would call Ebonics as "he began to study the language-ness of Black English and other informal speech variants, such as Jamaican patois, Swiss German and Haitian creole." Vinson Cunningham, "The Case for Black English," *New Yorker*, May 15, 2017.
4. Talking shit is akin to bullshitting: "The bullshitter may not deceive us, or even intend to do so, either about the facts or about what he takes the facts to be. What he does necessarily attempt to deceive us about is his enterprises. His only indispensably distinctive characteristic is that in a certain way, he misrepresents what he is up to." Harry Frankfurt, *On Bullshit* (Princeton, NJ: Princeton University Press, 2005), 54.
5. "Different after-hours bars attracted different crowds, had different entrance requirements, and featured different atmospheres and activities. A common feature of after-hours bars was their 'backroom' function, that is, the sheltering of sexual activity. After the 'regular' bars closed, their remaining patrons would migrate to the after-hours bars where they could be assured of sexual activity. Employees of the regular bars would also go to the after-hours bars to relax after work. These bars were thus complementary in their market functioning to the regular bars, encouraging customers to stay until closing and reducing social pressures to meet and arrange sexual encounters. At the same time, they competed for customers with other late night or all-night establishments which sheltered sexual activity such as bath-houses and discos." Brodsky, "Mineshaft," 240–41.
6. There is a duet of sorts between club owner and patron: a great "dyadic" need in the social psychological sense, and perhaps the need here is not simply about money but about a desire to provide a location for people in the hustling world to come together free of the constraints in other places in the city. In my field notes I wrote: "Neither Frenchy or Cookie [wife] ever ask why he ran the club, perhaps these questions were in the 'none of-my-business-category,' but based on his conversation with others and hearing him more generally discuss 'the business,' the place could well have been a 'front,' that is, he was not really the owner but 'fronted' as the owner. I had my theories about that and

I sincerely believe 'Piggy' was the real owner, because he was the cop who supplied Frenchy with cocaine; the drugs Frenchy got from 'home base.'" "Home base" is a term used by Frenchy, meaning the local police precinct.

7. "Indeed, human odor was of no importance to him whatever. He could imitate human odor quite well enough with surrogates. What he coveted was the odor of certain human beings: that is, those rare humans who inspire love. These were his victims." Patrick Suskind, *Perfume* (New York: Knopf, 1986), 188.
8. See the story about Pacman Jones, a star professional football player for the Dallas Cowboys, in a Las Vegas strip-club brawl after a raining incident: *Las Vegas Sun*, July 17, 2007. At the time of the incident at Le Boogie Woogie, the term "raining" was not being used.
9. People tempered their displays of emotion, tried avoiding uncouth behavior (most of the time), and above all cultivated an attitude of detachment. A newcomer, for example, could get immediate status by entering the club and giving away large amounts of cocaine to everyone present. Even greater status was won by repeating the performance. As a member of an exclusive set, the patron was expected by all others to possess cocaine and share it to remain in good standing. Status implied respect, awe, envy, and sometimes jealousy.
10. N. Aldrich, *Old Money: The Mythology of America's Upper Class* (New York: Vintage, 1988), equates old money with several values, one of which was a disdain for new money, but in the after-hours world money mattered no matter where it came from—this was hustlers' money. The average patron has his or her cocaine, but if someone showed up with a full baggy, that signified wealth, and they got instant respect and envious looks. All this translates into worthiness, respectability, a higher social standing, if you will, in the place. What the patrons see is what they cannot acquire, cannot do, or cannot be at that time. In this way, the club's stratification system is not necessarily composed of high ranks, middle ranks, and lower ranks but instead made up of a "continuous spectrum of statuses" devoid of a clear-cut hierarchical pattern. W. S. Landecker, "Class Crystallization and Its Urban Pattern," *Social Research* 27 (Autumn 1960): 308–20.
11. Veblen argued that the rich or those who wanted to appear rich would purchase expensive goods not because they are better quality but

because they are expensive. Thorstein Veblen, *The Theory of the Leisure Class: An Economic Study in The Evolution of Institutions* (New York: Macmillan, 1899).

3. THE CHARACTERS

1. Cocaine, as one patron put it, "loosens the tongue." Because of its stimulant properties, the drug lowers inhibitions, and the regulars are bound to a setting where interaction is not only possible but expected. One expects to be sociable in the club and to meet others who are sociable in turn, and cocaine facilitates this sociability. Strangers meet other strangers in a setting where an obligation exists to engage in conversation. The sociologist Sherri Cavan calls this an "open region": those who are present, acquainted or not, have the right to engage others in conversation and other "overtures of sociability." Sherri Cavan, *Liquor License: An Ethnography of Bar Behavior* (Chicago: Aldine, 1966), 138–39. In the clubs, such overtures might include unauthorized touching, in some cases. I noticed the barmaid and the dancer allowed men to touch them, pinch them, or grab hold of their asses, though this was not all barmaids or dancers, only certain ones. I noticed this was not permitted all the time but was a ploy to get more tips and, in some cases, more cocaine. I did see a man grab a woman's ass and get slapped; another time a guy was warned not to touch a woman because if her man came around, he would probably kill him. Touching seemed to be unacceptable behavior under most circumstances, but I did notice it happening with some frequency.

The sociologist Beverly Yuen Thompson, writing about personal-space rules in her study of women with tattoos, notes: "Women already face sexual objectification and harassment in public; it is behavior that is familiar and usually evokes an already-programmed response, which is often to ignore the harassment and seethe on the inside, feeling insulted and disempowered." She goes on: "Women's bodies are also considered more public: open to critique, touch, and sexual objectification. Sierra Furtwangler expressed that people seem to forget rules of personal space and respectability when presented with the heavily tattooed woman." The goal of the ethnography is to move toward the intimacy of the insider's knowledge. As such I am slowly trying to move toward familiarity. Beverly Yuen Thompson, *Covered in Ink: Tattoos, Women, and the Politics of the Body* (New York: New York University Press, 2015), 160.

2. "At Jelly's, all the men of the extended primary group are 'regulars' in the sense that they come regularly to Jelly's and have a social stake in the establishment and in the group. But there has emerged a small group of men who consider themselves a distinct and identifiable category of the wider group. They refer to themselves and are referred to by others as 'regulars.'" Elijah Anderson, *A Place on the Corner* (Chicago: University of Chicago Press, 1976), 55. This passage suggests that any patron whose presence on the scene is regular constitutes a regular because they have a stake in the place.
3. Anderson, *A Place on the Corner*, 55, notes how this is one of those liminal moments where the private use of the space is about to be transformed into a public arena—when the place is not quite open for business but is technically open, yet things are still being set up, chairs being arranged, the jukebox coined so people will hear music as they enter, barmaids putting on makeup and setting the tables, a few customers drifting in and sitting at the bar.
4. A. R. Ratcliffe-Brown, *Structure and Function in Primitive Society* (New York: The Free Press, 1965), 91.
5. Marcus Hunter argues that urban Black nightclubs provide a "vital space for patrons to enhance social capital," by leading people to "better navigate poverty and segregation by setting up ties or establishing ties that provide a community of support and/or ways to amplify their social locations." Marcus Hunter, "The Nightly Round: Spaces, Social Capital, and Urban Black Social Life," *City & Community* 9, no. 2 (2010): 165–86.
6. Eva Van Zanten, Tjeerd Van der Ploeg, Joris J. Van Hoof, and Nicholaas Van der Lely, "Gender, Age, and Educational Level Attributed to Blood Alcohol Concentration in Hospitalized Intoxicated Adolescents; A Cohort Study," *Alcoholism: Clinical and Experimental Research* 37, no. 7 (July 2013): 1–1251.
7. This was a MacArthur Foundation study conducted with William Kornblum that later became a book, *Growing Up Poor* (Minneapolis: Lexington, 1985).

8. And similarly to Kimberly Hoang, who speaks of objectifying and sexualizing rituals in her research in Vietnam, in many situations I too had the uncanny experience of becoming the observed. In an urban world where relationships do not easily go beyond the agreed-upon fleetingness of interactions between strangers, I would find myself in those specific locations: urban "scenes" often designed (or used as such) because these were places and times where strangers meet and interact.

   Hoang appropriately points out how complicated the issue of participation becomes when sexuality is involved, both the way "the question" would always pop up in conferences and her own difficulties in answering it. In the end, she decided not to answer the question but instead to leave the modalities of her participation open, speaking of her fieldwork as "a deeply embodied ethnography." "In the end, I decided not to disclose whether I engaged in sex work. I have chosen to answer this question with another set of questions of my own: Why is it that when sex moves into the realm of pay that this intimate question suddenly becomes appropriate to ask? And why is this question, and others like it, used to scrutinize scholars, often scholars of color? To make myself useful in my field sites, I had to do what most ethnographers are afraid to speak of—I had to engage in my own dealings with desire. I engaged in a deeply embodied ethnography that transformed who I was." Hoang's research reveals to us how forms of capital, economic and otherwise, are gained or exchanged between Vietnamese sex workers and the different groups of male clients. She shows that within the sex industry, expressions of race, class, and gender change the meaning of sex work and determine what exactly is being desired by specific clients. Kimberly Kay Hoang, *Dealing in Desire: Asian Ascendancy, Western Decline, and the Hidden Currencies of Global Sex Work* (Berkeley: University of California Press, 2015), 22.
9. Randol Contreras provides a rather profound account of this particular way of life: "Drug robbers also have an elite. I call them the 'robber elite.' Gus is one. In drug robberies, he took charge—he was the first to confront the dealer, then beat and torture him. True, others got their kicks and punches in, and a few dabbled in torture. But this violence was supportive. Most listened for neighbors, searched for valuables,

and communicated with lookouts on the street. It was Gus, from the stories I heard, who purposely took the violent center stage." What Contreras refers to as center-stage violence was the use of hot irons, electric wires, chopping fingers, and earlobes, a kind of freak violence. "In fact, the torture resembled the workings of a southern White lynch mob. During race-based lynchings, White mobs castrated Black men, a cruel response to their freed status and alleged lust for white women. This masculine concern, then, raised their emotions—added the gender ingredients to their violence. In drug robberies, the social structural reasons differed, yet had the same aim: answering a perceived manhood challenge through brutal emasculation." Randol Contreras, *The Stickup Kids: Race, Drugs, Violence, and the American Dream* (Berkeley: University of California, 2013), 164.

10. But "teenager" is a broad category, and there is no evidence the teens who showed up at Le Boogie Woogie are responsible for those robberies, even though recent news articles were reporting kids being caught as stickup bandits. When one barmaid called teenage patrons "guttersnipes," I later asked her why the negative tone, and she remarked how she'd heard it was teenagers behind the robberies. This was during the end of the crack era in the city and of the gang violence related to it. This also meant that drug markets had reduced dealers and users to retail routines, and this is when crack dealers became vulnerable to robberies and when stickup boys began to rob dealers more blatantly. Personal self-esteem became the new mantra, along with a new generation of drug users who did not see crack as cool but as a true scourge. I should remind the reader that the recruitment of kids and especially teenagers dates back forty years and was a direct effect of the Rockefeller drug laws, which demanded a prison sentence for anyone over the age of eighteen in possession of an illegal drug. One *New York Times* writer noted: "The crack epidemic behaved much like a fever. It came on strong, appearing to rise without hesitation, and then broke, just as the direst warnings were being sounded." But I also noticed a new drug cycle following new ways to ingest familiar drugs like beer, tobacco, marijuana, and opioids. Kids and teenagers came to reject drugs like crack, which was seen as an old person's high,

and began using another cheap high I called "blunt work," which is a cigarillo or cigar stuffed with marijuana. I see evidence of this "blunt work" all over the street: telltale piles of discarded tobacco on the sidewalk, mixing with the 40-ounce cans kicked to the curb.

The 40-ounce and a blunt became the new way teenagers got high. The young dealers didn't use crack, only sold it to others. "Thug life" took on a new meaning as well. The term "thug" could be heard on the lips of everyone from hip-hop artists to the ghetto fabulous. "Thug" came to English from the Hindi term for "bandit," to reappropriate it as a term of empowerment. Thug life is the life of the infiltrator, the life of the revolutionary, the life of resistance. Thug life acknowledges the complex relationships between violence and gender, race, and power and traces paths out of violence through the retelling of the life stories of "thugs" who have come before us. The term is used to embrace the life of people like the radical Yuri Kochiyama, Tupac Shakur, Assata Shakur, and others.

11. A good example of this madness is mentioned in Spradley and Mann: "A third skill the girls must develop in order to be a good waitress and make work easier for bartenders involves rearranging orders. She must translate the customers' orders into a convenient language and a proper sequence for the bartenders. Once the order is taken from the table it may undergo a couple of alterations. Names of drinks are shortened or changed altogether. A customer may order 'Special Export Beer' and 'Screwdriver.' Also, drinks must be arranged so that the bartender did not have to run back and forth behind the bar just to fill one order and so that he could better remember what the waitress asked him to prepare." James P. Spradley and Brenda J. Mann, *The Cocktail Waitress: Women's Work in a Man's World* (New York: Wiley, 1975), 51.

12. "Although George and Stephanie work together to fulfill the necessary task, waitresses feel that the division of labor is far from equal. George performs the major task of mixing the drinks and ringing up the totals for the orders on the cash register. And Stephanie must do all she can to make this easy for George: translating the customer's order into language the bartender can immediately recognize; adding straws and fruit to drinks; stirring the drinks as the mix is added to

the alcohol; totaling the order for him; handing him the correct amount of money for the order; and finally, placing the drinks on the tray." Spradley and Mann, *The Cocktail Waitress*, 31–32.

13. Take, for example, the political scientist Cristina Dragomir, who explains her work with Indian Roma and Narrikurovar women. Reflecting on fieldwork she has been conducting in India and Romania for the past two years, she writes: "The first aspect reveals my almost automatic acceptance of 'essentialist notions of womanhood' I employed to gain access and acceptance. While in my work and daily life, I reflect and critically engage with essentializing notions of womanhood, in this instance I dived right into these gendered expectations, which I deemed necessary for me (and my interpreter) to proceed. For instance, I knew that refusing to hold the baby would have been a great offense, and probably an unforgettable one, for the mother and the others in the group." Cristina Dragomir, personal communication. In the Roma and Narrikurovar communities, women are the primary caregivers. As a result, whenever Dragomir interviewed women, there would often be children in the room, and she soon realized that she was expected to take on her gendered "motherly" role. She understood that this dynamic is part of the larger social fabric of Romania, which accepted and expected that if children are present, they would be a part of the interaction: "I would ask them questions about their name, age and give them my blessing with the hope that they reach an old age. If an infant was present, the mother or the caretaker would immediately hand the child to me to hold and caress." This proximity to children of folks she had never met before is part of her own Romanian heritage, and she could easily recognize it in India as well. She reflected upon these familiar encounters, in which she enjoyed taking part, and identified them as gendered social rituals that "sucked" her right into their vortex. "My case of conforming to gender norms is not unique. Many female researchers regardless of race are more 'pressured than men to conform to local gender norms, which may create difficulties and dilemmas for feminist researchers working in highly patriarchal settings.' In my case, while it was easy to slip into assumed gender roles, it was hard to negotiate certain aspects of identity that did not conform to these roles, such as being unmarried and

childless." Dragomir was keen to suggest that researchers entering as outsiders into communities might find gendered roles especially challenging and might resist inhabiting them, creating frictions and ill dispositions, but that being an insider also gives an air of familiarity, which makes critical reflection upon these dynamics difficult.

14. "When we greet someone, we turn our attention to that person and offer him or her access to ourselves in a particular way. Seen from this angle, a greeting is an initial and symbolic gift to the person to whom it is addressed. A gift in its most abstract form, it nevertheless imposes a predetermined series of concrete obligations on both parties—the greeter and the person being greeted. The greeting is the first step in a triadic sequence of offer, acceptance, and response." Tilman Allert, *The Hitler Salute: On the Meaning of a Gesture* (New York: Picador, 2009), 3.
15. This conversation was recorded in an interview with Sam while also taking copious notes.
16. They all needed time to think about and figure out how they could functionally and socially fit into a world of conformity and standardization. By seeing Le Boogie Woogie as a racial stage, I could conceptualize it as an ethnic outpost, in a sense, because it is a culture of refusal where Black culture happens and where most outsiders, including whites, are not present. The sociologist Shatima Jones sees after-hours clubs as analogous to the Black barbershop: "The black barbershop as a privileged site for conversation and community making— a kind of 'racial backstage' are where they [Black folk] can work on constructing respectable identities in the absence of white scrutiny. It demonstrates how this space encourages and sometimes even demands that people put on racial performances; in doing so, blackness is made moral in this setting." But Jones goes on to say, "In other words I conceptualize the barbershop" (and, I argue, the after-hours cocaine club as well) "as a racial backstage where blacks can discuss things that they might not do in front of whites, but it is also a front stage for blacks to perform racial authenticity." The values that are prized here and made prominent are street values, not middle-class or respectable Black collective values. Street values include violence; uncouth, raw, thuggish behavior; and a kind of chameleon effect. By that I mean the acting

out of a kind of Black cultural social world not monolithic but multilayered and adaptable, which shows that mainstream values and mainstream behaviors can be suspended and other values lived without stigma attached to certain pariah behaviors. Shatima Jones, "The Black Barbershop: Constructing Black Identity," PhD diss., Rutgers University, 2015.

17. Another type of patron is the lone woman, youngish, under thirty, who is characterized as a "vacuum cleaner sniffer," "coke ho," or "skank," who uses her youth and attractiveness to ingratiate herself into a scene. Most men will invite single women to sniff with them, so opportunities are almost always there. This attention to beauty and what Wacquant calls "bodily capital" is in play at the club. Loïc Wacquant, "Suffering Beings: Ethnography as Embedded and Embodied Social Inquiry," University of California–Berkeley, Centre de sociology europeenne–Paris. Take the point made by Ashley Mears in *Pricing Beauty: The Making of a Fashion Model* (Berkeley: University of California, 2011), 6, about the "look": "The 'look' seems to describe a fixed set of physical attributes such as how a person looks. It's true that models conform to basic Western standards of attractiveness, for instance, youthfulness, clear skin, healthy teeth, and symmetrical features. Within that frame, they adhere to narrow height and weight specification." But physical attractiveness becomes currency that can be bartered to advantage either socially in the spot or economically, if the "right hookup" can be made. By the same token, the drug cancels out unattractiveness because it stimulates the user sexually, and what may be unattractive before the drug takes effect becomes less an issue under the influence. Take, for example, a conversation I heard about lips. "I know she's ugly, but she's got them beautiful big lips and I know she can suck dick." This is not the first time I heard mention of lips as valued in the sex scene. During my crack-house studies, women often said they "sold their lips for cash," in reference to fellatio. Portable sex is preferred in the club, since that is the only option unless you can access the back room, which was usually off limits.

18. By the time of publication it had been changed to the Showman.

19. "Thus, members of socially and racially stigmatized groups have devised ways to earn respect and ways to project their value and knowledge,

including: facial expressions, gait, and verbal expressions, physical appearance, clothes, jewelry and grooming. These play an important role in how a person is viewed." Elaine Richardson, *Hip-Hop Literacies* (New York: Routledge, 2006), 44.

20. The following case is not typical, in the sense that he still wears work clothes.
21. Here I must explain she said something else to him, which I could not hear, and I was a bit unsure as to why he didn't do what the sociologist Vernon Boggs says pimps do, which is "charge a bitch" if she was all in his face like that.
22. I think the value of the player is similar to the hoodlum in Anderson's *A Place on the Corner*: "The values of the hoodlum are indicated by his presentation of self. Generally, hoodlums value 'big money' and 'being tough.' Accordingly, when money becomes a status issue hoodlums often attempt to present themselves as 'slick': adept at tricking unsuspecting strangers—or other group members—out of their money" (129). I believe Anderson's point would apply to the dancer whom the player is trying to "catch" but whose "game is weak."
23. Getting high from cocaine is a form of catharsis different from ingesting whiskey or marijuana. It encourages aggression but also fosters touching, a sentimental gesture. Under the influence of cocaine, the patron was more amplified, and the more cocaine ingested the more amplified the experience became in the desire to be touched.
24. I use "dealer," "peddler," and "pusher" interchangeably.

4. AFTER-HOURS NOW

1. "Retro" refers to a self-conscious fetish for period stylization in music, clothes, and design expressed creatively through pastiche and citation. Simon Reynolds, one of our most engaging music critics, sees retro "in its strict sense to be the preserve of aesthetes, connoisseurs and collectors, people who possess a near-scholarly depth of knowledge combined with a sharp sense of irony. But the word has come to be used in a much more vague way to describe pretty much anything that relates to the relatively recent past of popular culture." Simon Reynolds, *Retromania: Pop Culture's Addiction to Its Past* (New York: Faber and Faber, 2011).

2. NYC Community Health Profiles 2015, Manhattan Community District 10, Central Harlem.
3. "The person being greeted has had his options limited, but he can still choose to accept, reject or simply ignore the greeting—that is, to answer or not. Yet rules like these do not completely determine the range of possibilities. Rules of greeting also provide a space in which people can express their personal attitudes towards the rules themselves and the social order that dictates them." Tilman Allert, *The Hitler Salute: On the Meaning of a Gesture* (New York: Picador, 2009), 10.
4. By the early 1980s, the fashionable snorting culture that had made a home for itself in the after-hours clubs was dying out, and a new free-basing (inhalation) and synthetic culture emerged in its stead. "New drugs are being churned out at an extraordinary rate. The United Nations' Office on Drugs and Crime says that in 2013, it was alerted to ninety-seven new synthetic drugs. It now monitors 350 and counting of these 'new psychoactive substances' around the world. The agency, usually upbeat about progress in the war on drugs, admits that 'given the almost infinite scope to alter the chemical structure of new psychoactive substances, new formulations are outpacing efforts to impose international controls.' Meanwhile, coca leaf cultivation in Bolivia, Peru, and Colombia exploded from 220,000 acres in 1980 to over 520,000 acres in 1988. The price of a cocaine kilo dropped from $50,000 in 1980 to roughly $12,000 in 2017. Brazil is now the mecca for crack and the second largest market for cocaine." Tom Wainwright, *Narconomics: How to Run a Drug Cartel* (New York: Public Affairs, 2016), 155–56.
5. See Patrick A. Langan and Matthew R. Durose, "The Remarkable Drop in Crime in New York City," Bureau of Justice Statistics, U.S. Department of Justice, October 21, 2004. The highest peak for violent crimes was reached in 1990 (above 170,000, including more than 2,200 homicides); in 2007, by contrast, the number of homicides fell below five hundred for the first time since 1963.
6. Zoning laws were fought in court; more details can be found in Katherine Liepe-Levinson, *Strip Show: Performances of Gender and Desire* (London: Routledge, 2002).

7. M. Kusenbach, "Street Phenomenology: The Go-Along as Ethnographic Research Tool," *Ethnography* 4, no. 3 (2003): 455–85.
8. What follow are field notes made with my contacts at Murphy's in 2016. I avoid the term "informant," since it now has a law-enforcement connotation. I mostly use "contacts."
9. I also interviewed an economist, N. V. Filippova, who told me more about these currencies. She discussed features of cryptocurrencies and the role they play in facilitating the trade of illegal drugs. The use of Bitcoin instead of a real currency such as the U.S. dollar makes it possible to buy and sell drugs on the internet/darknet. Considered an illegal activity, this led to the closing by the federal government of an online black market called the Silk Road, an electronic platform for selling illegal drugs. Most monetary systems are based on fiat money, which usually represents the legal tender of a government. Fiat money performs a variety of functions: it serves as unit of accounting, means of payment, means of exchange, and a store of value. However, sometimes money can take a different form when it performs only one or two functions, for instance, as a means of payment and/or exchange. Economists call this kind of money "quasi-money" precisely because of its limited functions. Food stamps, school vouchers, and the Ukrainian Kupon (introduced into circulation as a transitional currency right after the collapse of the Soviet Union) are examples of quasi-money. Now we can add another form of money: virtual currency, or cryptocurrency. The emergence of blockchain technology facilitated the development of cryptocurrencies, pioneering with Bitcoin, which was invented as electronic currency that would function as means of payment between peers. Money and quasi-money play a role as a regulator of economic activity. For a cryptocurrency to play such a role, a few conditions must be met. First, a cryptocurrency cannot exist in a vacuum; thus the virtual monetary system (supported by an electronic trading platform) should be constructed in such a way that individuals have easy access to Bitcoins or other virtual-currency systems. Second, individuals must consider those cryptocurrencies (Bitcoin, Ethereum, and over eight hundred other cryptocurrencies) to be acceptable monetary assets. Third, the volume of those assets will determine the scale of economic activity. Cryptocurrencies are money forms of value

that are connected through usage to a particular organization of economic activity on the internet. Filippova argues that the use of cryptocurrencies as opposed to, for example, the U.S. dollar has many advantages for electronic platforms that sell illegal drugs. Since Bitcoin and other virtual currencies exist only on the internet, the transactions do not rely on paper records and are not required to be reported to a third party; they are anonymous.

In most cases, the dark web is accessed through "the Onion Router" (Tor) technology, which allows the users of the network to hide their identities, IP addresses, real-world locations, and frequency and volume of transactions. The Silk Road, a website launched in February 2011, was the first darknet marketplace for selling illegal drugs that used Bitcoins as electronic currency. The FBI closed the website down in October 2013. Its founder, Ross William Ulbricht, was convicted in the U.S. Federal Court in Manhattan and sentenced to life in prison.

10. The chemical name for MDMA is 3,4-methylenedioxymethamphetamine.
11. Le Boogie Woogie's patrons explore this dimension of building on the city "in ways that suit oneself." For instance, the novelist Teju Cole discusses this in what he calls the "open city," where the city is seen as a "site of power, desire and community." Teju Cole, *Open City* (New York: Random House, 2011).
12. Currently, the drug scene is changing in many South American countries. Bolivia has rewritten its constitution to recognize the right to use coca leaves for traditional and legal purposes; Uruguay became the first nation in the world to adopt a legal regulated marijuana market; Columbia, Mexico, Guatemala, and Ecuador are openly critiquing the prevailing international drug-control paradigm at the United Nations; and the United States, while relaxing or remaking its marijuana laws state by state, now finds itself regressing by starting the War on Drugs all over again, with the election of Donald Trump and the nationalist (that is, fascist) policies of Attorney General Jeff Sessions, whose policies are at odds with almost every country in the world.

The historian Alfred McCoy writes: "As leading American anthropologists Sidney Mintz and Eric Wolf have taught us, the modern commerce in commodities involves much more than economic exchange. Since the rise of the modern world economy, commodities have in a fundamental sense shaped the politics, culture and social structure of peoples around the globe." Alfred W. McCoy, "Can Anyone Pacify the World's Number One Narco-State?" *Mother Jones*, March 2010, https://www.motherjones.com/politics/2010/03/narco-state-opium-afghanistan/.

13. National Institute of Drug Abuse, "Current Statistics," 2017, http://www.drugabuse.gov/drugs-abuse/cocaine.
14. Since 2014, nearly fifty thousand people have died from drug overdoses, with 61 percent of those deaths involving OxyContin. In 2014, an estimated 914,000 people aged twelve years or older had used heroin in the past year, a 145 percent increase since 2007, and mortality related to heroin use since 2000 has increased fivefold. National Institute of Drug Abuse, https://archives.drugabuse.gov/trends-statistics/monitoring-future-survey-archive.
15. In 2014, an estimated 1.5 million current cocaine users aged twelve or older (0.6 percent of U.S. population) used cocaine. Adults aged eighteen to twenty-five have a higher rate of current cocaine use than any other age group, with 1.4 percent of young adults reporting past-month cocaine use. National Institute of Drug Abuse, http://www.drugabuse.gov/drugs-abuse/cocaine.
16. "Go at random into one of those seemingly ordinary bars in Montmartre, or into a dive in the Goutte-d'Or neighborhood. Nothing to show they are owned by clans of pimps, that they are often the scenes of bloody reckonings." Brassaï, *The Secret Paris of the 1930s* (New York: Pantheon, 1976).
17. If I had the time and did not wish to bore the reader, I would outline a social history of the center city from the 1960s to 1990s, in an effort to understand those social forces that provided support for the rapid and widespread adoption of crack cocaine after 1983–1984 and the decline of sniffing or intranasal use.
18. Margaret Talbot, "The Addicts Next Door," *New Yorker*, June 5, 12, 2017.
19. Talbot, "The Addicts Next Door."

CONCLUSION: A CULTURE OF REFUSAL

1. The recent case of Joaquin Guzman Loera, or "El Chapo," is a good example of this: his undoing was related to his desire to turn his life into a movie. Liam Stack, "Sean Penn and 'El Chapo': What We Know," *New York Times*, January 10, 2016.
2. See Dan Waldorf, Sheigla Murphy, Craig Reinarman, and Bridget Joyce, *Doing Coke: An Ethnography of Cocaine Users and Sellers* (Bethesda, MD: Drug Abuse Council, 1977).
3. Marek Kohn, *Dope Girls: The Birth of the British Underground* (London: Lawrence and Wishart, 1992), 8.
4. The "soft city" is the place of sex shops and bawdy houses, hotels of assignation, prostitute strolls, gay spots, after-hours clubs, burlesque joints, peepshows, and five-dollar sex emporiums.
5. Murray Melbin, "Night as Frontier," *American Sociological Review* 43 (February 1978): 3–22.
6. Kohn, *Dope Girls*, 1.
7. Kai Erikson, *Wayward Puritans: A Study in the Sociology of Deviance* (Boston: Allyn and Bacon, 1966), 6.
8. Howard Becker, *Outsiders: Studies in the Sociology of Deviance* (New York: Free Press, 1963), 163.
9. These locations morphed into "crack spots" (places where crack cocaine could be used and sold); they later transformed again and became the precursors to the crack house.
10. Michael Pollan, "The Trip Treatment," *New Yorker*, February 9, 2015.
11. Ta-Nehisi Coates, "The First White President," *Atlantic*, October 2017.
12. Benjamin Demott, "Rediscovering Complexity," *Atlantic*, September 1988.

APPENDIX 1. METHODOLOGICAL APPENDIX

1. UN Office on Drugs and Crime, Division for Policy Analysis and Public Affairs, *The World Drug Report* (2016).
2. UNODC, *The World Drug Report*.

APPENDIX 2. FIELD NOTE SAMPLES

1. Ralph Bolton, "Tricks, Friends, and Lovers: Erotic Encounters in the Field," in *Taboo: Sex, Identity and Erotic Subjectivity in Anthropological Fieldwork*, ed. D. Kulick, and M. Willson (New York: Routledge, 1995), 140–67.
2. Sarah Daynes and Terry Williams, *On Ethnography* (London: Polity, 2018), 77.
3. Nikolai Gogol, "The Tale of How Ivan Ivanovich Quarreled with Ivan Nikiforovich," in *The Collected Tales* (New York: Vintage, 1998), 198.

BIBLIOGRAPHY

Alee, W. C., et al. *Principles of Animal Ecology*. Philadelphia: W. B. Saunders, 1950.

Allert, Tilman. *The Hitler Salute: On the Meaning of a Gesture*. New York: Picador, 2009.

Anderson, Elijah. *A Place on the Corner*. Chicago: University of Chicago Press, 1976.

Ashley, Richard. *Cocaine: Its History, Uses and Effects*. New York: St. Martin's, 1975.

Atkinson, Paul. *The Sociological Readings and Re-Readings*. Burlington, VT: Ashgate, 1966.

Beals, Alan, George Spindler, and Louise Spindler. *Culture in Process*. New York: Holt, Rinehart and Winston, 1967.

Becker, Howard S. *Outsiders: Studies in the Sociology of Deviance*. New York: Free Press, 1963.

Bolton, Ralph. "Tricks, Friends, and Lovers: Erotic Encounters in the Field." In *Taboo: Sex, Identity, and Erotic Subjectivity in Anthropological Fieldwork*, ed. D. Kulick and M. Wilson. New York: Routledge, 1995.

Borges, Jorge Luis. *The Book of Sand*. New York: Dutton, 1977.

——. *Collected Fictions*. London: Penguin, 1998.

Brassaï. *The Secret Paris of the 1930s*. New York: Pantheon, 1976.

Brecht, Bertold. *Brecht on Theatre*. Trans. John Willett. New York: Hill and Wang, 1964.

Brodsky, Joel. "The Mineshaft: Retrospective." *Journal of Homosexuality* 24, no. 3–4 (1993).

Brown, Phil. *Catskill Culture: A Mountain Rat's Memories of the Great Jewish Resort Area.* Philadelphia: Temple University Press, 1998.

Brown, Richard H. *A Poetics for Sociology.* Cambridge: Cambridge University Press, 1977.

Buerkle, Jack V., and Danny Barker. *Bourbon Street Black.* New York: Oxford University Press, 1973.

Burke, Kenneth. *Perspectives by Incongruity.* Bloomington: University of Indiana Press, 1964.

Byck, Robert. *Cocaine Papers: Sigmund Freud.* London: Stillwell, 1974.

Byck, Robert, and Craig Van Dyke. "What Are the Effects of Cocaine in Man?" In *Cocaine 1977*, NIDA Research Monograph Series 13, ed. Robert Petersen and Richard Stillman. Washington, DC: U.S. Government Printing Office, 1977.

Calloway, Cab, and Bryant Rollins. *Of Minnie the Moocher and Me.* New York: Thomas Y. Crowell Co., 1967.

Campbell, E. Simms. "Early Jam." In *The Negro Caravan*, ed. Sterling A. Brown, Arthur Davis, and Ulysses Lee. New York: Arno, 1970.

Cavan, Sherri. *Liquor License: An Ethnography of Bar Behavior.* Chicago: Aldine, 1966.

Chagnon, Napoleon A. *Yanomamo: The Fierce People.* New York: Holt, Rinehart and Winston, 1968.

Clark, T., ed. *The City as an Entertainment Machine.* Oxford: Oxford University Press, 2004.

Coates, Ta-Nehisi. "The First White President." *Atlantic*, October 2017.

Cole, Teju. *Open City.* New York: Random House, 2011.

Connor, Marlene. *What Is Cool: Understanding Black Manhood in America.* New York: Crown, 1995.

Contreras, Randol. *The Stickup Kids: Race, Drugs, Violence, and the American Dream.* Berkeley: University of California, 2013.

Cressey, Paul. *The Taxi Dance Hall.* Chicago: University of Chicago Press, 1932.

Currie, E. "The Economics of a Good Party: Social Mechanics and the Legitimization of Art/Culture." *Journal of Economics and Finance* 31 (2007): 386–94.

Daynes, Sarah, and Terry Williams. *On Ethnography.* London: Polity, 2018.

Demott, Benjamin. "Rediscovering Complexity." *Atlantic*, September 1988.

Douglas, Jack D. *Research on Deviance*. New York: Random House, 1972.

Elias, Norbert. *The Civilizing Process: Sociogenetic and Psychogenetic Investigations*. Rev. ed. London: Blackwell, 2000.

Erikson. Kai. *Wayward Puritans: A Study of the Sociology of Deviance*. Boston: Allyn and Bacon, 1966.

Frankfurt, Harry. *On Bullshit*. Princeton, NJ: Princeton University Press, 2005.

Gieryn, Thomas F. "A Space for Space in Sociology." *Annual Reviews Sociology* 26 (2000): 463–96.

Glaser, Barney G., and Anselm L. Strauss. *The Discovery of Grounded Theory: Strategies for Qualitative Research*. Chicago: Aldine, 1967.

Goffman, Erving. *Interaction Ritual: Essays on Face-to-Face Behavior*. New York: Doubleday/Anchor, 1967.

Gogol, Nikolai. *The Collected Tales*. New York: Vintage, 1998.

——. *Dead Souls*. New Haven, CT: Yale University Press. 1996.

Grazian, David. *On the Make: The Hustle of Urban Night Life*. Chicago: University of Chicago Press, 2008.

Grinspoon, Lester, and James B. Bakalar. *Cocaine: A Drug and Its Social Evolution*. New York: Basic Books, 1976.

Hoang, Kimberly Kay. *Dealing in Desire: Asian Ascendancy, Western Decline, and the Hidden Currencies of Global Sex Work*. Berkeley: University of California Press, 2015.

Hughes, E. C. *Men and Their Work*. New York: Free Press, 1958.

Hunter, Marcus. "The Nightly Round: Spaces, Social Capital, and Urban Black Social Life." *City & Community* 9, no. 2 (2010): 165–86.

Hutchinson, J. "The Hip-Hop Generation: African American Male-Female Relationships in a Nightclub Setting." *Journal of Black Studies* 30, no. 1 (1999): 62–84.

Jackson, P. *Inside Clubbing: Sensual Experiments in the Art of Being Human*. Oxford: Oxford University Press, 2004.

Kohn, Eduardo. *How Forests Think: Toward an Anthropology Beyond the Human*. Berkeley: University of California Press, 2013.

Kohn, Marek. *Dope Girls: The Birth of the British Underground*. London: Lawrence and Wishart, 1992.

Kornblum, William. *Blue Collar Community*. Chicago: University of Chicago Press, 1974.

——. *Growing Up Poor.* Minneapolis, MN: Lexington, 1985.

Kusenbach, M. "Street Phenomenology: The Go-Along as Ethnographic Research Tool." *Ethnography* 4, no. 3 (2003): 455–85.

Landecker, W. S. "Class Crystallization and Its Urban Pattern." *Social Research* 27 (Autumn 1960): 308–20.

Langan, Patrick A., and Matthew R. Durose. "The Remarkable Drop in Crime in New York City." Bureau of Justice Statistics, U.S. Department of Justice, October 21, 2004.

Leo, Jana. *Rape New York.* New York: Feminist Press, 2009.

Liebow, Elliot. *Tally's Corner: A Study of Negro Street Corner Men.* Boston: Little, Brown, 1967.

Liepe-Levinson, Katherine. *Strip Show: Performances of Gender and Desire.* London: Routledge, 2002.

Lingeman, Richard. *Drugs from A to Z: A Dictionary.* New York: McGraw-Hill, 1969.

Mays, Reuben. *Talking at Trena's: Everyday Conversations at an African American Tavern.* New York: New York University Press, 2001.

McCall, George J., and J. L. Simmons. *Issues in Participant Observation.* Boston: Addison-Wesley, 1969.

McCoy, Alfred W. "Can Anyone Pacify the World's Number One Narco-State?" *Mother Jones*, March 2010.

Mears, Ashley. *Pricing Beauty: The Making of a Fashion Model.* Berkeley: University of California, 2011.

Melbin, Murray. "Night as Frontier." *American Sociological Review* 43 (February 1978): 3–22.

——. *Night as Frontier: Colonizing the World After Dark.* New York: Free Press, 1987.

Merton, Robert K. "Three Fragments from a Sociologist's Notebook: Establishing the Phenomenon, Specified Ignorance, and Strategic Research Materials." *Annual Review of Sociology* 13 (1987): 1–28.

Milner, Richard, and Christina Milner. *Black Players.* New York: Bantam, 1972.

Mortimer, William G. *History of Coca: The Divine Plant of the Incas.* San Francisco: And/Or, 1974.

Murray, Albert. *Stomping the Blues.* New York: McGraw-Hill, 1976.

Musto, David. *The American Disease: Origins of Narcotics Control.* New Haven, CT: Yale University Press, 1973.

Nero, C. "Why Are All the Gay Ghettos White?" In *Black Queer Studies: A Critical Anthology*, ed. E. P. Johnson and M. G. Henderson. Durham, NC: Duke University Press, 2005.

Park, Robert. *The City.* Chicago. 1930.

Patilla, M. *Black on the Block: The Politics of Race and Class in the City.* Chicago: University of Chicago. 2007.

Pollan, Michael. "The Trip Treatment." *New Yorker*, February 9, 2015.

Preble, Edward, and J. J. Casey. "Taking Care of Business: The Heroin User's Life on the Street." *International Journal of Addictions* 4:1–24.

Rainwater, Lee, ed. *Soul.* Chicago: Transaction, 1970.

Ratcliffe-Brown, A. R. *Structure and Function in Primitive Society.* New York: Free Press, 1965.

Report of the Mayor's Task Force on Social Clubs. New York, 1976.

Reynolds, Simon. *Retromania: Pop Culture's Addiction to Its Past.* New York: Faber and Faber, 2011.

Richardson, Elaine. *Hip-Hop Literacies.* New York: Routledge, 2006.

Sabbag, Robert. *Snow Blind: A Brief Career in the Cocaine Trade.* New York: Avon, 1976.

Sagarin, Edward. *Odd Man In.* Chicago: Quadrangle, 1969.

Sanders, B., ed. *Drugs, Clubs, and Young People.* London: Ashgate, 2006.

Scheppegrell, W. "The Abuse and Dangers of Cocaine." *Journal of Medical Science* 14 (October 1898).

Shibutani, Tamotsu. *Society and Personality.* Englewood Cliffs, NJ: Prentice Hall, 1961.

Simmel, Georg. *The Sociology of Georg Simmel.* Ed. Kurt Wolff. New York: Free Press, 1950.

Skipper, James K. Jr., and Charles H. McCaghy. "Strip-Teasers: The Anatomy and Career Contingencies of a Deviant Occupation." *Social Problems* 17 (1970): 391–405.

Small, Mario. "De-exoticizing Ghetto Poverty: On the Ethics of Representation in Urban Ethnography." *City & Community* 14, no. 4 (December 2015).

"Smoking Coke Encore." *Village Voice*, February 27, 1978.

Spradley James P., and Brenda J. Mann. *The Cocktail Waitress: Women's Work in a Man's World*. New York: Wiley, 1975.

Stearns, Marshall. *The Story of Jazz*. New York: Oxford University Press, 1956.

Suskind, Patrick. *Perfume*. New York: Knopf, 1986.

Suttles, Gerald D. *The Social Order of the Slums*. Chicago: University of Chicago Press, 1970.

Thompson, Beverly Yuen. *Covered in Ink: Tattoos, Women, and the Politics of the Body*. New York: New York University Press, 2015.

Twitchell, James B. *Carnival Culture: The Trashing of Taste in America*. New York: Columbia University Press, 1992.

Urbain, Jean-Didier. *At the Beach*. Minneapolis: University of Minnesota Press, 2003.

Valentine, Charles A. *Culture and Personality*. Chicago: University of Chicago Press, 1968.

Van Gennep, Arnold. *The Rites of Passage*. Chicago: University of Chicago Press, 1960.

Wainwright, Tom. *Narconomics: How to Run a Drug Cartel*. New York: Public Affairs, 2016.

Wald, Patricia M., and Peter Barton Hutt, Cochairmen of the Drug Abuse Survey Project. *Dealing with Drug Abuse: A Report to the Ford Foundation*. New York: Praeger, 1972.

Waldorf, Dan, Sheigla Murphy, Craig Reinarman, and Bridget Joyce. *Doing Coke: An Ethnography of Cocaine Users and Sellers*. Drug Abuse Council. Bethesda, Maryland,. 1977.

West, Cornel. *Prophetic Fragments*. London: Eerdmans, 1988.

Williams, Edward Huntington. "The Drug Menace in the South." *Medical Records* 85, no. 7 (February 1914): 247–49.

Williams, Colin, and Martin Weinberg. *Male Homosexuals: Their Problems and Adaptations*. New York: Oxford University Press, 1974.

Williams, Terry. *Cocaine Kids: The Inside Story of Teenager Drug Ring. London. Bloomsbury Publishing Limited. 1990.*

——. *Crack House: Notes from the End of the Line*. Boston: Addison-Wesley, 1992.

Winick, Charles. "Physician Narcotic Addicts." *Social Problems* 9 (1961): 174–86.

——. "Mass Communication and Drug Dependence." In *Sociological Aspects of Drug Dependence*, ed. Charles Winick. New York: CRP, 1974.

——. "Use of Drugs by Jazz Musicians." *Social Problems* 7 (1969): 240–54.

Winick, Charles, and Paul M. Kinsie. *The Lively Commerce: Prostitute in the United States*. Chicago: Quadrangle, 1971.

Woodley, R. *Dealer: A Portrait of a Cocaine Merchant*. New York: Holt, Rinehart and Winston, 1971.

INDEX